INTERPRETING
THE
MINOR
PROPHETS

INTERPRETING THE MINOR PROPHETS

Robert B. Chisholm, Jr.

Academie
Books Grand Rapids,
Michigan
Zondervan Publishing House

Interpreting The Minor Prophets
Copyright © 1990 by Robert B. Chisholm, Jr.

ACADEMIE BOOKS is an imprint of Zondervan Publishing House,
1415 Lake Drive, S.E., Grand Rapids, Michigan 49506.

Library of Congress Cataloging-in-Publication Data

Chisholm, Robert B.
    Interpreting the minor prophets / by Robert B. Chisholm, Jr.
        p.   cm.
    "Academie books."
    Includes bibliographical references.
    ISBN 0-310-30801-1
    1. Bible.   O.T.   Minor Prophets–Criticism, interpretation, etc.
    I. Title.
    BS1560.C47   1989
    224'.906–dc20   89-37728
                                                              CIP

Edited by Craig Noll and Leonard G. Goss

Printed in the United States of America

90 91 92 93 94 95 / AK / 10 9 8 7 6 5 4 3 2 1

To my father and mother, Robert and Ethel,
who taught me to fear, love, and serve
the God of the prophets

CONTENTS

PREFACE

After going through the looking glass, Alice discovered a nonsensical poem called "Jabberwocky." Having read it, she declared, "It seems very pretty, but it's rather hard to understand! Somehow it seems to fill my head with ideas—only I don't exactly know what they are!" Many have responded in a similar way to the strange and puzzling words of the Old Testament prophets. For example, Martin Luther said the prophets "have a queer way of talking, like people who instead of proceeding in an orderly manner, ramble off from one thing to the next so that you cannot make head or tail of them or see what they are getting at."[1]

Later on in the story Alice met a character by the name of Humpty Dumpty, who claimed he could interpret "Jabberwocky" for her. He boasted, "I can explain all the poems that ever were invented—and a good many that haven't been invented just yet." Despite his self-professed skills and confidence, even Humpty Dumpty would find the Old Testament prophets more than his match. Because of barriers of language, culture, time, and geography, the Old Testament prophetic literature continues to defy and frustrate interpreters. However, because it is the inspired Word of God, we must strive, with the aid of God's Spirit, to understand its message. To that end this volume is devoted. Despite its limitations, the author hopes that this book will give its readers greater appreciation for and insight into a major portion of this marvelous body of prophetic literature—the twelve books called the Minor Prophets.

Over the years God has used many individuals to broaden my understanding of the Minor Prophets. In direct and indirect ways many of my former students have contributed in a special way to my research and to the contents of this volume. Though space limitations prevent

---

[1] Quoted in Gerhard von Rad, *The Message of the Prophets*, trans. D. M. G. Stalker (New York: Harper & Row, 1968), p. 15 n. 1.

7

me from giving an exhaustive list, I would like to acknowledge Lee Adams, John Hilber, Gordon Johnston, Jon Owen, Steve Ozier, Alvin Thompson, Bill Uebbing, and Roger Wisdom for their kind encouragement and valuable insights.

I would like to thank the editorial staff at Zondervan for their expertise and efficiency. Stanley Gundry helped me formulate the idea for the book. Ed van der Maas guided me through the early stages of research and writing, and Len Goss has overseen the final editorial process with exceptional skill.

Last but certainly not least, I wish to thank my family. With her characteristic patience, love, and enthusiasm, my wife, Debra, has encouraged me throughout the writing process, while my children, Douglas and Stephanie, as always, have helped me keep life in proper perspective.

INTRODUCTION

TITLE AND ARRANGEMENT

"Minor Prophets," the title given to the last twelve books of the English Old Testament, is an unfortunate label. Though much shorter than Isaiah, Jeremiah, and Ezekiel, these twelve prophetic books proclaim significant messages, the theological import of which is by no means minor.

The Hebrew Bible is divided into Law, Prophets, and Writings, with the Minor Prophets included in the middle group. Taken as a unit and entitled "The Twelve," they combine with Isaiah, Jeremiah, and Ezekiel to form the so-called Latter Prophets. (The "Former Prophets" are Joshua, Judges, Samuel, and Kings.)

One Jewish tradition maintains that the Minor Prophets are arranged chronologically, the first six books coming from the eighth century B.C., the next three from the seventh century, and the final three from the postexilic period. The internal evidence of Joel and Obadiah, however, favors a date from the sixth or fifth century B.C. Joel and Obadiah flank the Book of Amos probably because of thematic and literary parallels, rather than for chronological reasons.[1] Nevertheless, with the exception of Joel and Obadiah, the arrangement is roughly chronological.

[1] See Hans W. Wolff, *Joel and Amos,* trans. Waldemar Janzen, S. Dean McBride, Jr., and Charles Muenchow (Philadelphia: Fortress Press, 1977), p. 3; Wolff, *Obadiah and Jonah,* trans. Margaret Kohl (Minneapolis: Augsburg, 1986), p. 17.

HISTORICAL BACKGROUND

The Minor Prophets span a period of over three hundred years, covering from the eighth to the fifth centuries B.C., in whole or in part. These were eventful times in the Near East, including Palestine. The following survey, which only touches upon the major events of the period, places each of the Minor Prophets in historical perspective.

The first half of the eighth century B.C. was a prosperous time for both Israel (the northern kingdom) and Judah (the southern kingdom). In the north Jeroboam II (ca. 793–753 B.C.) expanded Israel's borders (2 Kings 14:25, 28). Israel's success coincided with Syria's decline, the latter due in part to military defeat at the hands of the Assyrians.[2] However, Assyrian power gradually declined, and Syria was probably a subject state of Israel during the second quarter of the eighth century.[3] During this period Jonah made his journey to Nineveh, where the Assyrians, plagued by international and internal problems, were especially receptive to his message. Toward the end of the first half of the eighth century, Amos and Hosea appeared on the scene, denouncing the social injustice and idolatry that had swept over the economically prosperous, but morally and ethically bankrupt, northern kingdom.

With the rise of Tiglath-Pileser III to the Assyrian throne in approximately 745 B.C., that mighty empire again embarked on an imperialistic policy, which included Palestine within its scope of interest. Following the death of Jeroboam II, the northern kingdom entered into a period of political turmoil, epitomized by the regicide and wavering international policies mentioned by Hosea. Such a weak state was unable to resist the Assyrian war machine, and the northern kingdom was completely assimilated into the Assyrian empire in 722. In fulfillment of Amos's, Hosea's, and Micah's prophecies, the Assyrians destroyed Israel's capital, Samaria, and carried a large number of Israelites into exile.

The Assyrian presence in Palestine also threatened the existence of Judah. Micah, prophesying in the second half of the eighth century, warned the southern kingdom that it would be

---

[2]On Assyria's relations with Syria in the late ninth and early eighth centuries, see Wayne T. Pitard, *Ancient Damascus* (Winona Lake, Ind.: Eisenbrauns, 1987), pp. 160–67, 175.

[3]Ibid., p. 177.

destroyed if it followed in the moral footsteps of the north. Because of King Hezekiah's reforms the Lord miraculously spared Jerusalem, though the Assyrians overran most of the countryside of Judah. Though Micah foresaw a time when the nation would be freed from Assyrian imperialism, Judah remained an Assyrian vassal state on into the seventh century.

As the seventh century progressed, Assyrian power waxed and waned. Under Esarhaddon and Ashurbanipal the Assyrians extended their empire into Egypt. However, eventually this mighty empire, overextended as it was and plagued by internal problems, began to decline. Nahum, writing sometime between 663 and 612 B.C., announced that the Lord would totally destroy Nineveh, the capital of Assyria. This vivid prophecy was fulfilled in 612, when the combined forces of the Babylonians and Medes turned the city into a heap of ruins.

Assyria's decline and eventual demise allowed Judah some relief from foreign domination. Under Josiah (ca. 640–609 B.C.) the nation even experienced a spiritual renewal of sorts, though it was short-lived. Toward the end of the seventh century, Zephaniah warned of impending judgment on a worldwide scale that would include Judah and Jerusalem. The Lord informed Habakkuk that He would use the Babylonians as an instrument of judgment against His people.

With the defeat of the Egyptians at Carchemish in 605 B.C., the Babylonians established themselves as the dominant power in the Near East. As they turned their attention toward Palestine, Judah's weak and vacillating rulers were unable to appease or resist them. Within two decades the Babylonians had destroyed Jerusalem (586) and deported large segments of the population into exile.

Some of the surrounding nations (Edom in particular) took part in Judah's defeat by looting cities and capturing refugees, apparently for the purpose of selling them as slaves. Sometime after the Exile, Obadiah announced that the Lord would avenge His people by destroying the Edomites and others who had participated in Jerusalem's fall.

Like the preexilic prophets, Obadiah also foresaw a day when the Lord would restore His people to the Promised Land. The first stage in this restoration came in 538 B.C., when the Persian ruler Cyrus, who had conquered Babylon the year before, decreed that the Jews could return to their homeland. Led by Sheshbazzar, a group of exiles returned to Judah and began rebuilding the temple. Partly because of opposition from neighboring peoples, work on the temple was suspended until 520. Through the prophets Haggai and Zechariah the Lord encouraged the people and their leaders. With renewed strength, assurance, and vision they completed the temple in 515. Sometime later the Lord raised up Joel and Malachi to address specific problems encountered by the postexilic community and to remind the people of God's promises.

STRUCTURE AND STYLE

Structure

Individual Units

The prophetic books contain several distinct messages that were delivered on separate occasions, rather than at one time. Eventually these messages were collected and arranged into book form. These individual messages can sometimes be distinguished from one another by introductory and concluding formulas. Introductory formulas include the heading "This is what the LORD says" (e.g., Amos 1:3, 6, 9, 11, 13; 2:1, 4, 6) and the exhortation to "hear" the Lord's word (e.g., Hos. 4:1; 5:1; Joel 1:2; Amos 3:1; 4:1). A common concluding formula is the expression "declares/says the LORD" (e.g., Hos. 11:11; Amos 1:5, 8, 15; 2:3, 16; 3:15).

Sometimes the structural device of *inclusio,* where the conclusion to a message corresponds stylistically or thematically to its introduction, aids in delimiting the speech units. For example, the prophetic lament in Micah 1:8–16 begins and ends with mourning and with comparisons to animals. In Nahum 2:1–10 the fourfold description of Nineveh's terror (v.10b) corresponds to the fourfold exhortation that begins this call to alarm (v.1). The appearance of the word "loins" in both verses 1 and 10 also signals an inclusio ("brace yourselves" in v.1 is lit. "strengthen the loins," while "bodies tremble" in v.10 is lit. "anguish is in all the loins").

A more sophisticated and elaborate form of delimitation involves the use of *chiasmus,* where the themes or key words of the first half of a literary unit are mirrored in the second half. Often a pivotal element is highlighted by its central position in such a structure. Once the cycle of elements has come full circle, the reader (in the original context, the listener) senses the unit is complete. For example, the major themes of the salvation message of Joel 2:19–27 are arranged chiastically (see p. 58).

The prophets' individual messages also frequently follow established forms, some of the most common being the judgment speech, woe oracle, exhortation (or call to repentance), salvation announcement, and salvation portrayal.

The *judgment speech* contains two basic elements—the accusation (or reason for judgment) and the announcement of judgment. The latter often includes both a notice of the Lord's intervention and a description of its results. For example, each of Amos's oracles against the nations, following an introductory formula and summary statement, contains an accusation and announcement of judgment.

Judgment Speech	Introduction	Accusation	Announcement (Intervention/ Results)
1. Damascus	1:3a	1:3b	1:4–5 (1:4–5a/5b)
2. Philistia	1:6a	1:6b	1:7–8 (1:7–8a/8b)
3. Tyre	1:9a	1:9b	1:10 (1:10a/10b)
4. Edom	1:11a	1:11b	1:12 (1:12a/12b)
5. Ammon	1:13a	1:13b	1:14–15 (1:14a/14b–15)
6. Moab	2:1a	2:1b	2:2–3 (2:2a, 3a/2b, 3b)
7. Judah	2:4a	2:4b	2:5 (2:5a/5b)
8. Israel	2:6a	2:6b–12	2:13–16 (2:13/14–16)

The *woe oracle* is a type of judgment speech that begins with the word "woe" (Heb. *hôy*), followed by a direct address to the group that is guilty and will experience judgment. The address often carries an accusatory flavor. Elements of accusation and announcement, standard in judgment speeches, usually follow the address. Prime examples of the woe oracle are Amos 6:1–7 and Micah 2:1–5.

The introductory woe cry was an especially effective rhetorical device in that it was customarily heard at funerals as a cry of distress and mourning uttered over the corpse of the deceased. In 1 Kings 13:30, for example, *hôy* is translated "Oh," and in Jeremiah 22:18; 34:5, "Alas." By prefacing their judgment speeches with this word, the prophets were acting out in advance the funeral of the addressee. For an ancient Israelite this word would have conjured up the same emotions as an organ dirge and a black hearse do for twentieth-century Americans. Imagine the consternation of an audience when they heard themselves named after the woe cry!

The *exhortation,* or *call to repentance,* includes an appeal supported by motivation. The latter often takes the form of a promise or a threat. For example, the appeals of Amos 5:4–6 are supported by a promise (note "and live" in vv.4b, 6a) and two warnings (vv.5b, 6b). In Joel 2:12–14 the exhortation proper is supported by a reminder of the Lord's character (v.13b), as well as a reference to the possibility of forgiveness (v.14). An appeal to recent history strengthens the exhortations of Haggai 1.

The prophets were not exclusively messengers of doom and gloom. Messages of deliverance and restoration, or *salvation announcements* and *salvation portrayals,* are frequently juxtaposed with those of judgment. Often the prophets simply announced salvation, affirming that the Lord would intervene on behalf of His people with positive results. At other times, the prophets described the future blessings of God's people in idealized and, at times, hyperbolic terms.

For example, Amos 9:11–15 combines an announcement and a portrayal. In verses 11–12 the Lord announces He will intervene for His people and refers to the effects of this action. Verses 13–15, which also contain divine announcements of intervention, focus on the agricultural blessings this event will bring. Verse 13 in particular portrays this time of restoration in highly exaggerated, idealized language.

Overall Structure

A major problem faced by interpreters concerns the overall structure of the prophetic books. Some contend that there is little, if any, rhyme or reason to the arrangement of the individual units. According to this view, the prophetic books are, for the most part, disorganized collections of assorted speeches. Though a superficial reading of the prophets might suggest such a conclusion, careful literary analysis usually reveals artistry and purpose in the overall structure of the books and their major sections. In the introductions to the individual books that follow, I attempt to delineate these larger structures.

The prophets used several structural devices in arranging their material. One such device is a paneling technique whereby a formal or thematic pattern is repeated in cyclical fashion, yielding in its most basic form an AB//AB structure. For example, the structure of the Books of Hosea and Micah is based on the movement from judgment to salvation. Hosea contains five such panels (see p. 20), while Micah exhibits three (see p. 132). Paneled structures also occur on a smaller scale, within major sections of a book (cf. Zech. 9–14, p. 257).

Inclusio and chiasmus, which, as noted above, occur in individual units, also appear on a broader level. For example, in Nahum 2:1–3:17 literary forms are arranged chiastically. Nahum 1:12–15 and 3:18–19, which share several themes and key words, form an inclusio around this section (see p. 164). Further examples, among others, of chiastic structures based on formal or thematic correspondences occur in Amos 5:1–17; 18–27; Micah 4–5; 7; and Zechariah 7–8.

Stylistic Devices

The prophets employed a wide variety of stylistic devices in an effort to proclaim their messages with maximum vividness and power. Among the most common and effective of these are poetic imagery, wordplay, irony, and allusion.

The term *imagery* refers to the striking and vivid comparisons and descriptions used by the prophets. For example, Hosea compared God in His role of Judge to an assortment of things, including a jealous husband (chs. 1–3), a moth and bone decay (5:12), various predators (5:14; 13:7–8), a fowler (7:12), and a plowman (10:11). This same prophet compared God in His role of Israel's Benefactor and Deliverer to a passionate lover (2:14), a physician (6:1), the fructifying rains (6:3), a father (11:1), a kind farmer (11:4), and dew (14:5).

The prophets were masters at stirring their audiences' emotions through imagery. Nahum's graphic descriptions of the invasion of Nineveh (2:1–10; 3:2–3) are unsurpassed in intensity and emotion. One shudders when reading Habakkuk's theophanic description of the divine Judge and Warrior (3:3–15), Zephaniah's summary of the Lord's destructive day (1:14–18), and Joel's terrifying portrayal of the Lord leading His invincible army into battle (2:1–11). Amos's and Micah's poignant references to the injustice and insensitivity of the rich (Amos 2:6–8; 4:1; 6:1–6; 8:4–6; Mic. 2:1–2; 3:1–3) stir up one's anger and sense of justice to such a degree that their harsh judgment speeches bring the reader great relief and satisfaction.

The prophets also frequently used the poetic device of *wordplay*. The most basic form of wordplay is the simple repetition of a word. For example, the word "violence" occurs three times in Habakkuk 1:2–3, 9. In verses 2–3 it refers to the violence taking place in Judahite society during Habakkuk's time. In verse 9 it refers to the violent character of the Babylonians, whom the Lord would use to judge the violent evildoers of Judah. In this case the repetition draws attention to the appropriate nature of the punishment. The violent would be destroyed by the violent!

A brief scan of the English dictionary reveals that many words have multiple meanings. Their precise sense in any given case is thus determined by the context in which they appear. The same is true of many Hebrew words. Often wordplay involves the repetition of such a word in two or more of its meanings. For example, the Hebrew word *pāqad*, which carries the basic idea of "visit," appears in Zephaniah in both 1:8–9 and 2:7. In the former it refers to the Lord's visiting His people in judgment and is consequently translated "punish." In 2:7 it refers to the Lord's visiting His people for good and is translated "care for." The repetition in this case draws attention to the reversal from judgment to salvation in God's treatment of His people.

The most common type of wordplay involves words that sound alike in Hebrew. For example, Hosea 12:11 announces that the altars of Gilgal would become like *gallîm* ("piles of stones"), which sounds like the name Gilgal. This similarity in sound draws attention to the appropriate fate of idolatrous

Gilgal. One could even say its destiny was inherent in its very name.

One can see from these examples that observing wordplays is more than an exercise in aesthetic appreciation of the text. Through wordplay the prophets often drew correspondences and contrasts that were an important emphasis of their messages.[4]

Another poetic technique employed by the prophets is *irony,* which, according to Webster's, involves "an incongruity between the actual result of a sequence of events and the normal or expected result." For example, Amos warned that Gilgal would "surely go into exile" (5:5). This threat is exceedingly ironic in that Gilgal, Israel's first campsite in the Promised Land following their crossing of the Jordan under Joshua (Josh. 4:19– 5:12), had long symbolized the nation's possession of the land. Now, unexpectedly, even Gilgal's inhabitants would leave the land. One would have thought that at least Gilgal, of all places, would have been spared the humiliation of exile.

One sees in Amos's ironic reference to Gilgal's exile another device used by the prophets, namely, *allusion* to earlier literary traditions. Habakkuk's theophanic portrayal of the Lord (3:3–15) is a prime example of this technique. Throughout this poem Habakkuk described the Lord's future intervention for His people in terms of His past deeds on Israel's behalf. In this case, the prophet's use of allusion emphasizes that the God of Israel is the "everlasting" God (1:12) whose "ways are eternal" (3:6). Rather than being merely a God of the past, He controls the future of His people as well.

UNDERSTANDING THE PROPHETIC MESSAGE

Theological Background

Sin and Judgment

One need not read far in the Minor Prophets to realize that they had a great deal to say about the sin and judgment of God's people. To appreciate fully this aspect of the prophets' messages, one must view them against the background of the

---

[4]For a more detailed study of wordplay, see Robert B. Chisholm, Jr., "Wordplay in the Eighth-Century Prophets," *Bibliotheca Sacra* 144 (1987): 44–52.

Mosaic covenant. Through Moses the Lord instituted a covenant with Israel at Mount Sinai whereby He promised to be their God and they agreed to obey His commandments. If Israel obeyed the stipulations of God's covenant (i.e., the Mosaic Law), He promised to bless them with a land of their own, where they would experience peace and agricultural prosperity. However, it they rebelled against His authority, He would judge them, depriving them of their crops and allowing enemies to invade their land and carry them away into exile (Lev. 26; Deut. 28).

The preexilic prophets came as messengers of Israel's God to accuse the nation of breaking the covenant and to warn it of impending judgment as the consequence of this disobedience. A close examination of their accusations reveals several parallels with the Mosaic Law.[5] Likewise, many of the details of their announcements of judgment correspond to the covenant curses threatened in Leviticus 26 and Deuteronomy 28.[6] The postexilic prophets made it clear that God would deal with the restored community according to the same principles that had governed His relationship to their forefathers.

Salvation

Though the prophets warned that God would implement the covenant curses against His disobedient covenant partners, they also prophesied a future deliverance of the nation from exile. In so doing, they were simply following the lead of Moses, who had anticipated a time of restoration after judgment (Deut. 30:1–10).

Moses and his prophetic successors based this positive view of Israel's future on the unconditional covenant made by God with Abraham. In response to Abraham's faithfulness, God swore to give him a land (Gen. 15:18–21) and numerous offspring (22:15–17a), who would enjoy superiority over their enemies (v.17b) and ultimately impact the nations in a positive way (v.18). Abraham's descendents through Isaac (26:24) and Jacob (28:13–15; 50:24) inherited this promise. Several of the

[5] For example, see Richard V. Bergren, *The Prophets and the Law* (Cincinnati: Hebrew Union College Press, 1974), pp. 182–83.

[6] Douglas Stuart makes the same point and provides a convenient summary of Pentateuchal covenant curses in *Hosea–Jonah* (Waco: Word Books, 1987), pp. xxxi–xl.

Minor Prophets viewed Israel's future restoration as a fulfillment of God's promises to Abraham (e.g., Hos. 1:10; Amos 9:15; Mic. 7:18–20; Zech. 8:13). Eventually God chose David as the instrument whereby His promises to Abraham and his descendents might be fully realized (2 Sam. 7:8–16; Pss. 72, 89). In conjunction with God's covenant with David, Jerusalem, David's capital and God's dwelling place on earth, became the focal point of Israel's future hopes (cf. Pss. 46, 48, 76, 87). Many of the prophets anticipated the realization of God's promises to David (Hos. 3:5; Amos 9:11–12; Mic. 5:2–6; Hag. 2:20–23; Zech. 12:8) and the glorification of Jerusalem (Joel 3:17–21; Obad. 17; Mic. 4:1–3; Zeph. 3:11–19; Hag. 2:7–9; Zech. 1:14–17; 2:12; 8:3; 14:8–11, 16–19).

Eschatology and History

The early books of the Old Testament provide a history of Israel's salvation, the major events of which were the exodus from Egypt, the conquest of the Promised Land, and the triumphs of David. The preexilic prophets viewed God's future judgment of Israel as culminating in exile, which meant, for all intents and purposes, a reversal of this salvation history. Hosea even spoke of this exile as a return to Egypt, a symbol of slavery and oppression (8:13; 9:3; 11:5).

In similar fashion the restoration beyond judgment was sometimes viewed by the prophets as a repetition of salvation history. This new phase of salvation history would surpass the earlier events in magnitude and would culminate in the full and final realization of the Lord's purpose for Israel. For example, Hosea (11:11) and Micah (7:15) foresaw a second exodus from bondage. According to Hosea, Israel would repossess its land, once more entering it through Achor (2:15). However, this time Achor, the site of a sin that jeopardized the original conquest (Josh. 7), would be only a positive symbol of God's renewed relationship to His people. Several prophets also predicted the revival of the Davidic empire and the extension of Israel's suzerainty over the surrounding nations (e.g., Amos 9:11–12; Mic. 5:4–9). Israel's return to power would culminate in the willing worship and service of the Gentiles (Mic. 4:1–3; Zeph. 3:9), something never realized by prior Davidic rulers.

Prophetic Telescoping

The prophets' messages are filled with predictions about future events. From our perspective many of these prophecies have already been fulfilled, while others still await realization. What confuses many readers is the prophets' merging of these near (or fulfilled) and far (or yet to be fulfilled) events in one context. For example, Zephaniah's vision of the Lord's Day includes the destruction of Jerusalem by the Babylonians (1:4–13), judgment on surrounding nations of his time (2:4–15), judgment more cosmic and universal in scope (1:2–3, 18), the restoration of God's people (3:11–20), and the reclamation of the Gentiles (v.9). One must conclude that Zephaniah and his prophetic counterparts saw a unified picture of the future that, from our vantage point, tends to blur the chronological distinctions that eventually emerge with the progressive fulfillment of each element in their visions.[7]

In interpreting the prophets' predictions, one must carefully distinguish that which has been fulfilled from that which awaits fulfillment in the eschaton. One will thus be able to avoid two erroneous extremes. The first, common among skeptics, is to write off the prophets as wishful thinkers whose exaggerated hopes were never realized. Men and women of faith must reject this position, believing that the partial fulfillment of the prophets' visions guarantees the eventual realization of the whole. Earlier fulfilled events may even be viewed as prefiguring later ones. The second extreme overlooks the historical fulfillment and typological nature of many prophecies and projects the entire prophetic vision into the eschaton. Such an approach tends to view the prophets as crystal-ball gazers concerned only with cryptic predictions about distant events. In its more bizarre and naïve forms this approach can lead to some rather incredible and even preposterous interpretations of certain details in the prophetic books.

---

[7]For a helpful discussion of this subject, see Gordon D. Fee and Douglas Stuart, *How to Read the Bible for All Its Worth* (Grand Rapids: Zondervan, 1982), pp. 163–64.

1

HOSEA

INTRODUCTION

Date

According to the book's heading, Hosea prophesied during the reigns of the Israelite king Jeroboam II (ca. 793–753 B.C.) and the Judahite rulers Uzziah (ca. 792–740), Jotham (ca. 750–731), Ahaz (ca. 735–715), and Hezekiah (ca. 716–686).[1] The six Israelite rulers who followed Jeroboam II may have been omitted from this list because of their relative insignificance. Hosea's ministry probably began toward the end of Uzziah's and Jeroboam's reigns and may have concluded early in Hezekiah's rule.

Unity

Some scholars have questioned the unity of the book, attributing some of the material to later editors.[2] Since much of Hosea's message deals with judgment upon the northern kingdom, the book's references to salvation and to Judah have been treated with suspicion by some. However, the theme of

---

[1] The dates, which include periods of coregency, are Edwin R. Thiele's. See his *Mysterious Numbers of the Hebrew Kings,* rev.ed. (Grand Rapids: Zondervan, 1983), p. 217.

[2] For example, see William R. Harper, *Amos and Hosea* (Edinburgh: T. & T. Clark, 1905), pp. clviii–clxii; and Hans W. Wolff, *Hosea,* trans. Gary Stansell (Philadelphia: Fortress Press, 1974), pp. xxix–xxxii.

salvation through judgment is a prominent one in prophetic books,[3] deriving from Moses himself (cf. Deut. 30:1–10). The references to Judah need not be denied to Hosea. He easily could have anticipated the eventual reconciliation of north and south (cf. 1:11; 3:5) or have been concerned about Judah's following in the sinful footsteps of Israel (4:15).[4]

Structure

The Book of Hosea contains two major sections. The first (chs. 1–3) focuses on Hosea's marital experience, which pictured God's relationship with Israel. The second (chs. 4–14) includes several prophetic messages dealing with Israel's sin, judgment, and eventual restoration.

When viewed as a whole, the book displays five panels, each of which moves from judgment to salvation.

Panel	Judgment	Salvation
1	1:2–9	1:10–2:1
2	2:2–13	2:14–3:5
3	4:1–5:15a	5:15b–6:3
4	6.4–11:7	11:8–11
5	11:12–13:16	14:1–9

ANALYSIS

Hosea and Gomer (1:2–3:5)

Hosea's Wife and Children (1:2–2:1)

This biographical narrative tells how Hosea, in obedience to the Lord's command, married Gomer, "an adulterous wife," who bore him three children (1:2–9). The Lord instructed

---

[3]Cf. C. Hassell Bullock, *An Introduction to the Old Testament Prophetic Books* (Chicago: Moody Press, 1986), pp. 97–98. See also the remarks of Norman K. Gottwald, *The Hebrew Bible: A Socio-Literary Introduction* (Philadelphia: Fortress Press, 1985), pp. 362–63.

[4]For a more detailed discussion of the Judah passages, see R. K. Harrison, *Introduction to the Old Testament* (Grand Rapids: Eerdmans, 1969), pp. 868–70.

Hosea to give the children names symbolic of Israel's coming judgment. Yet He also promised to reverse the effects of this judgment and restore His people to a covenant relationship with Himself (1:10–2:1).

Troubled by the thought of God's commanding Hosea to marry a woman like Gomer, some have understood Hosea's marriage as visionary or allegorical in nature.[5] However, there is nothing in the narrative itself to suggest that the marriage was anything but literal. The Lord sometimes asked His prophets to perform difficult and seemingly unreasonable symbolic (but nevertheless literal) actions (cf. Isa. 20:1–4; Ezek. 4:1–5:4).

Gomer's status at the time of her marriage to Hosea is uncertain. Some understand the phrase "an adulterous wife" (1:2) to mean that at the time of the marriage she was already a prostitute or an initiate in the sexual rites of the Baal cult.[6] Others interpret the expression as anticipating what Gomer would become after marrying Hosea.[7] Since Gomer's activity symbolizes Israel's covenantal unfaithfulness (v.2b) and since the Hebrew word translated "adulterous" is used elsewhere in the book for the unfaithfulness of God's *wife* Israel (2:2, 4; 4:12; 5:4), it is probable that the phrase "adulterous wife" refers to Gomer's marital infidelity, rather than premarital experiences. In that case, knowledge of her status at the time of the marriage is precluded.

The "children of unfaithfulness" (1:2) are most naturally identified with those whose births are recorded in verses 3–9. Some have suggested one of Gomer's illicit lovers was the father of two of these children. In support of this proposal, they point out that verses 6 and 8, in contrast to verse 3, do not specify Hosea as the father. However, this conclusion is not necessary. Genesis 29:32–35 omits specific references to Jacob in the birth announcements of Leah's sons because he is already clearly identified as the father in the context.[8] The omission of

[5]For example, see Edward J. Young, *An Introduction to the Old Testament*, rev.ed. (Grand Rapids: Eerdmans, 1960), p. 253.

[6]For the latter view, see Wolff, *Hosea*, pp. 14–15.

[7]See Harper, *Amos and Hosea*, p. 207; as well as Francis I. Andersen and David N. Freedman, *Hosea* (Garden City, N.Y.: Doubleday, 1980), pp. 165–66.

[8]See Andersen and Freedman, *Hosea*, p. 168.

Hosea's name in verses 6 and 8 may be attributed to "economy of expression."[9]

"Unfaithfulness" describes the character of Gomer, not the children. They were children of unfaithfulness in that they were born in the context of Gomer's infidelity. Andersen and Freedman understand the phrase as elliptical, "children of (a wife of) promiscuity," comparing it to the phrases "sons of youth" (i.e., "sons born to a youthful parent," Ps. 127:4) and "son of old age" (i.e., "son born to an old man," Gen. 44:20).[10]

Hosea named his first child Jezreel to draw attention to coming events related to the place Jezreel (1:4–5). God would punish Jehu's dynasty because of the bloody deeds perpetrated by Jehu at Jezreel. The fall of Jehu's dynasty would be accompanied by the military demise of the northern kingdom in the Valley of Jezreel. This twofold prophecy was fulfilled in 752 B.C., when Shallum's assassination of Zechariah ended Jehu's dynasty (2 Kings 15:10), and in 733, when Tiglath-Pileser III conquered the Galilee region and made much of the northern kingdom an Assyrian province (2 Kings 15:29).[11] This was the beginning of the end for Israel. Eleven years later Samaria fell, and the northern kingdom was no more (2 Kings 17:3–6).

On the surface the Lord's condemnation of the "massacre at Jezreel" (v.4) is puzzling. After all, the Lord instigated, approved of, and rewarded Jehu's destruction of Jezebel and of Ahab's descendents (1 Kings 21:17–24; 2 Kings 9:6–10; 10:30). The execution of Baal's prophets and priests was also consistent with God's will (2 Kings 10:18–28; cf. 1 Kings 18:40). Hosea 1:4, then, cannot have these acts in view but rather refers to Jehu's needless slaughter of Ahaziah, king of Judah, and forty-two of his relatives (2 Kings 9:27–28; 10:12–14). Though Ahaziah's death was attributed to divine providence (2 Chron. 22:7), Jehu's attack upon the house of David was unauthorized by the Lord. Even though Ahaziah and his relatives did not actually die in Jezreel, their deaths occurred in connection with the blood purge that took place in that city and thus could be referred to as the massacre at Jezreel.

[9] So Wolff, Hosea, p. 20.

[10] Hosea, p. 168.

[11] See Yohanan Aharoni and Michael Avi-Yonah, The Macmillan Bible Atlas, rev.ed. (New York: Macmillan, 1977), pp. 94–95; and Yohanan Aharoni, The Land of the Bible, rev.ed., trans. A. F. Rainey (Philadelphia: Westminster Press, 1979), pp. 371–75.

Hosea named his second and third children Lo-Ruhamah ("Not Loved") and Lo-Ammi ("Not My People"), signifying that the Lord would no longer show Israel compassion or treat her as His covenant partner (vv.6, 8–9). By contrast, He would continue to show mercy to Judah, miraculously delivering it from the same enemy that would destroy Israel (v.7). The most vivid example of the fulfillment of this prophecy came in 701 B.C., when the Lord wiped out the Assyrian army in one night and preserved Jerusalem from destruction (2 Kings 19:32–36).

Even though Israel would be punished severely, the Lord would not abandon her forever. He promised to reverse the effects of judgment and to restore His people (1:10–2:1). This reversal is highlighted by wordplay involving the names of Hosea's three children. Whereas Israel was called Lo-Ruhamah and Lo-Ammi prior to her judgment, in the Day of Restoration she would be addressed as Ruhamah ("Loved") and Ammi ("My People"). The people whose national identity was seemingly lost in the Jezreel Valley (cf. vv.4–5) would sprout up like plants on "the day of Jezreel" (lit. "God plants"), when God would "plant" His people in the Promised Land (v.11; cf. 2:23).

God's promises to Abraham and David would then be fulfilled. As God promised Abraham, He would make Israel as innumerable as the sand on the seashore (v.10; cf. Gen. 22:17; 32:12). Once rejected, but now called "the sons of the living God" (v.10), the Israelites would be reunited with the people of Judah under a new David (v.11; cf. 3:5 and Ezek. 37:22, 24).

God and His Wife (2:2–23)

Comparing Himself to an offended husband, God described how He must harshly treat His unfaithful wife, Israel, in order to restore their marriage.

2:2–13. The Lord began by exhorting unfaithful Israel to abandon her adulterous ways (v.2). In an effort to prompt a positive response to this appeal, He threatened to remove her clothing and nourishment (v.3) and to disown her children (v.4). The threat "I will strip her naked" may reflect the practice of publicly shaming an adulteress (cf. Ezek. 16:35–42). The reality behind this figurative language included the loss of life's necessities, the destruction of the land's fertility, and the exile of Israel's population.

The Lord would punish His unresponsive wife in order to

pave the way for her restoration (vv.5–13). To bring Israel to her senses He would deprive her of her "lovers" (vv.5–7) and her blessings (vv. 8–13). Israel's lovers were the Baal idols (cf. vv.8, 13, 17), to whom she mistakenly attributed her agricultural prosperity. Through the Exile the Lord would effectively block the path to these lovers, making it geographically impossible for Israel to worship at the Canaanite cult centers (v.6). Finally in desperation Israel would be forced to look once more to her husband (v.7).

Because Baal, the Canaanite storm-god, was supposedly responsible for the land's fertility, it was understandable that idolatrous Israel would erroneously credit her prosperity to this false deity, rather than the Lord (v.8). To demonstrate His absolute sovereignty over the agricultural realm, the Lord would take away all of these blessings (vv.9, 11–13). The Baal idols would stand by helplessly, unable to rescue Israel from the Lord's mighty hand of judgment (v.10). As vivid proof of Israel's unfaithfulness ("lewdness," v.10), infertility would sweep over the land in fulfillment of the covenant curses (cf. Deut. 28:15–68).

2:14–23. After carrying out these drastic, but necessary, measures, the Lord would actively seek out His people. Comparing Himself to a romantic young lover, the Lord announced His intent to woo Israel with tender words of love (v.14). The word translated "allure" is used elsewhere of a man seducing a virgin (Exod. 22:16) and of a wife coaxing or enticing her husband into telling her a secret (Judg. 14:15; 16:5). The phrase translated "speak tenderly" is used on at least two other occasions of a young man speaking gently to his future bride (Gen. 34:3; Ruth 2:13). No wonder James Mays refers to the imagery of verse 14 as astonishing and daring.[12]

These romantic advances would take place during Israel's period of exile, which is likened to the wilderness wanderings following the Exodus (note "desert" in v.14). Compared with Israel's idolatrous stay in the land of Canaan, the wilderness period was one of devotion to the Lord (cf. Jer. 2:2), when Israel sang praises to her God (cf. Exod. 15:1–21). Poetic license permits this obvious idealization of the wilderness period.

As in Joshua's day, the Lord would again lead His people out of the wilderness and into the Promised Land. The Valley of

[12]James L. Mays, *Hosea* (Philadelphia: Westminster Press, 1969), pp. 44–45.

Achor, scene of Achan's sin, would be the gateway to the land (v.15). In the past this valley was a reminder of how Israel's possession of the land was tenuously connected to its absolute obedience to God's commandments. However, in the future it would become a symbol of hope because of its association with Israel's return to the land.

In the future the Lord would renew His covenant with Israel (vv.16–23). Comparing the covenant relationship to marriage, the Lord spoke in terms of betrothal, as if He and Israel would start their romance anew (vv.19–20). He would remove all traces of Israel's past unfaithfulness. She would address the Lord as "my husband" ('îšî) rather than "my master" (ba'lî) in order to avoid any recollection of her past adulterous activities with Baal (vv.16–17).

Total commitment would characterize this renewed relationship (vv.19–20). The Lord would never again allow the relationship to be severed. In "righteousness and justice" He would vindicate and deliver His people. Israel would experience His love, compassion, and faithfulness. In turn Israel would finally "acknowledge the LORD" as her husband and the source of her blessings (cf. vv. 8, 13).

Jeremiah later spoke of this new marriage as a new covenant (Jer. 31:31–34). God would write His law on the hearts of His people so that they might willingly obey Him. Like Hosea, Jeremiah foresaw a time when Israel would know the Lord ("know" in Jer. 31:34 translates the word rendered "acknowledge" in Hos. 2:20).

Having reestablished the covenant, the Lord would restore peace and agricultural prosperity to the land (vv.18, 21–22). Once again the Lord employed wordplay on the names of Hosea's children to highlight this reversal from judgment to salvation (vv.22–23). He called Israel Jezreel ("God plants"), for He would again "plant" her in the land. She who was called "Not Loved" and "Not My People" would be the special object of the Lord's compassionate love and would be addressed as "My People."

Hosea Reclaims Gomer (3:1–5)

As an object lesson of His love for Israel, the Lord commanded Hosea to reclaim his wayward wife, Gomer (v.1). To propose, as some do, that chapter 3 parallels chapter 1, or that a different woman is in view here, destroys the analogy between Hosea and the Lord. Like the Lord, Hosea was to marry a woman who would prove to be an unfaithful wife (cf. 1:2). He was also to follow the Lord's example of love by initiating the restoration of the relationship.

Though Gomer's exact status at the time of this reconciliation is uncertain, verse 2 makes it clear that she had become the legal property of someone other than Hosea. Perhaps she served as a slave or concubine. The wording "loved by another and is an adulteress" in verse 1 suggests she was living in an adulterous relationship with another man. However, the word translated "another" (lit. "friend") may refer to Hosea, not one of Gomer's lovers (cf. Jer. 3:20, where the same word is translated "husband"). NASB reflects this interpretation in translating Hosea 3:1, "Go again, love a woman who is loved by her husband, yet an adulteress." This interpretation is favored by the next statement, which contrasts the Lord's love for Israel with the nation's unfaithfulness.

Once Hosea purchased and took legal possession of Gomer, he placed her in isolation (v.3). She would no longer consort with other men but would reserve her love completely for him. This symbolized Israel's exile, when she was removed from Canaan and no longer allowed to worship Baal (v.4; cf. 2:6–7).

In exile Israel would be deprived of both political independence and her polluted, idolatrous worship system (v.4, "without king or prince, without sacrifice or sacred stones, without ephod or idol"; cf. 4:13, 19). Because of their pagan associations, Moses had prohibited the use of sacred stones (Lev.26:1; Deut. 16:22). Of course, Israel had blatantly violated this command (2 Kings 3:2; 10:26–27; 17:10; Hos. 10:1–2). The ephod and idol referred to here were divination devices, perhaps symbolizing the priesthood. (Both items are mentioned in Judg. 17:5; 18:14, 17–18, 20 as being part of the cultic equipment made by Micah the Ephraimite for his personal priest. The Danites abducted this priest, along with his ephod and idols, which they used in their unauthorized worship [cf. Judg. 18:27–31].) The idols mentioned here were especially abhorrent to the Lord (cf. 1 Sam. 15:23 and 2 Kings 23:24, where the word translated "idol" in Hos. 3:4 is rendered "idolatry" and "household gods," respectively).

Following this time of isolation in exile, Israel would finally come to her senses and seek the Lord, rather than false gods (v.5). In the past she had ardently pursued Baal (cf. 2:7), but now she would seek the Lord. "Look for" in 2:7 and "seek" in 3:5 translate the same Hebrew word. The repetition draws attention to the contrast between Israel's past unfaithfulness and her future devotion.

The rebellious spirit that led the northern kingdom to reject the Davidic monarchy would also be gone. Once-arrogant Israel would "seek . . . David their king" and tremble in humility before the Lord, no longer taking His blessings for granted (v.5; cf. Deut. 8:10–18; Hos. 13:6).

As in later prophets, the ideal Davidic ruler of the eschaton is called David in verse 5 as if David himself would return to rule over God's people (cf. Jer. 30:9; Ezek. 34:23–24; 37:24–25). Micah 5:2 also seems to view this ruler as the second coming of David (see p. 146). Other texts make it clear that this king is actually a descendent of David who would rule in the spirit and power of his illustrious ancestor (cf. Isa. 11:1–10; Jer. 23:5–6; 33:15–16). Of course, Jesus, "the son of David" *par excellence,* fulfills these prophecies (cf. Matt. 1:1; 21:9).

Israel's Sin, Judgment, and Restoration (4:1–14:9)

Israel's Spiritual Adultery (4:1–6:3)

This first panel of the book's second major section contains two extended judgment speeches (4:1–19 and 5:1–6:3), each of which is introduced by a call to attention (note "hear" in 4:1 and 5:1). The second speech ends on a positive note as it envisions the future repentance of God's people (5:15–6:3). The speeches may be outlined as follows:

I. First extended judgment speech (4:1–19)
  A. Lawsuit (vv.1–3)
    1. Accusation (vv.1–2)
    2. Announcement of judgment (v.3)
  B. Judgment speech against the people and their leaders (accusations and announcements interspersed; vv.4–9)
  C. Judgment speech against adulterers (vv.10–14)
    1. Announcement of judgment (v.10a)
    2. Accusation (vv.10b–14)
  D. Appeal to Judah (vv.15–19)
    1. Exhortation proper (v.15)

> 2. Motivation = judgment speech against Israel,
>   containing accusation (vv.16–18) and
>   announcement of judgment (v.19)

II. Second extended judgment speech (5:1–6:3)
   A. Judgment speech proper (accusations and
      announcements interspersed; 5:1–15)
   B. Exhortation (spoken by future repentant Israel;
      6:1–3)

4:1–19. The first of these judgment speeches begins with a formal charge of breach of covenant (vv.1–2) and a warning of judgment (v.3). Loyalty to the Lord had disappeared from the land. In its place was widespread and flagrant disregard for God's law. Verse 2 specifically mentions violation of five of the Ten Commandments ("cursing" refers to the misuse of the Lord's name in oaths and imprecations, as prohibited in the third commandment). Israel's sin would bring judgment upon the land in the form of drought, causing both people and animals to perish from lack of food (v.3).[13]

Even the religious leaders, supposedly the defenders of purity and orthodoxy, were guilty (vv.4–9). The Lord singled out the priests for special criticism. Like the people, the priests had rejected the law (v.6). Rather than guiding the people in righteousness, they encouraged them to multiply their hypocritical sacrifices (v.8). Ironically, as the number of priests increased, the moral climate of the land grew worse, not better (v.7).

The Lord's judgment upon the priesthood would strike at three generations, wiping out this sinful line of priests. He would "destroy" the mothers responsible for bearing these ungodly priests (v.5; cf. Jer. 22:26, which also views a mother as responsible for the sins perpetrated by her offspring). This punishment would be appropriate because God's people were "destroyed," in part because of lack of priestly direction (v.6). The Lord would also "reject" the priests themselves, because they had "rejected" knowledge (v.6). He would sweep them away with the rest of the rebellious people (v. 9), replacing

---

[13] The judgment-speech form, as well as parallel texts that *threaten* drought (cf. 2:9, 12), suggest that the verb tenses of v.3 be translated as future, rather than present. See Wolff, *Hosea,* pp. 65–66.

their priestly prestige with shame and disgrace (v. 7). (An alternate reading for v.7b appears in NASB, "I will change their glory into shame.") Finally, because the priests "ignored" His law, the Lord would "ignore" their children, meaning they would not inherit their fathers' office (v.6).

The Lord's people were participating in cult prostitution in order to promote agricultural and human fertility throughout the land (vv.10–14). These rites were associated with the worship of the Canaanite gods Baal and Asherah, who were responsible for fertility in Canaanite religion. The young women of Israel prostituted themselves at the idolatrous shrines scattered throughout the northern kingdom (v.13; cf. 2 Kings 17:10–11). However, the Lord would not single them out for punishment, since the men were just as guilty (v.14).

The Lord would frustrate the people's misplaced efforts to promote and ensure fertility. Ironically, they would experience a food shortage, and population growth would cease (v.10). The stubborn Israelites, who refused to allow their divine Shepherd to guide and protect them (v.16), would be swept away in their sin (vv.17–19).

Because Judah was susceptible to the same idolatrous sin as Israel (cf. 1 Kings 14:22–24; 2 Kings 16:3–4), Hosea exhorted the Judahites to reject the example of the north (v.15). He urged them to stay away from such Israelite cult sites as Gilgal (cf. 9:15; 12:11; Amos 4:4; 5:5) and Beth Aven (lit. "house of wickedness," a derogatory name for Bethel, "house of God"; see also 10:5) and to refrain from making hypocritical oaths in the Lord's name. Ironically, Gilgal and Bethel, associated in Israelite history with possession of the land (Gen. 28; 35; Josh. 4–5), are here referred to in conjunction with the sin that sweeps Israel away into exile (cf. v.19).

5:1–6:3. The second judgment speech is addressed to all Israel, although the priests and the king are singled out for special attention (5:1). Judah, which was earlier warned not to follow Israel's example (4:15), also comes within the scope of the accusation (5:5) and announcement of judgment (5:12–14).

As in chapter 4, the Lord's accusation focuses on Israel's spiritual adultery (5:1–7). The Israelites were rebels (v.2) who did not truly acknowledge the Lord (v.4), despite their hypocritical efforts to court His favor (vv.6–7). Israel was like an unfaithful wife whose promiscuous behavior results in the birth of "illegitimate children" (v.7). This may be an allusion to

Israelite children born as a result of the cult prostitution condemned in the previous chapter (cf. 4:13–14).

Israel's hypocrisy would prove to be her downfall (v.7). Even though the people observed the New Moon festivals prescribed in the Law (Num. 10:10; 28:11–15; Hos. 2:11), their lack of genuine devotion to the Lord rendered these rituals ineffectual. In fact, such sham merely heightened their guilt and would hasten their destruction.

The seeds of destruction had already been sown. The northern kingdom had suffered a degree of foreign oppression (v.11). The Lord was working behind the scenes, directing international affairs to bring about Israel's and Judah's demise. In this regard, He compared Himself to a moth devouring clothes and to decay eating away at bones (v.12; cf. Job 13:28; Prov. 12:4; 14:30; Isa. 50:9; 51:8; Hab. 3:16).

Although both Israel and Judah were aware of their precarious situation (compared here to sickness and sores), they turned to foreign alliances for security, rather than the Lord (v.13). (Though only Ephraim, not Judah, is specifically mentioned as turning to Assyria, the fact that Judah is mentioned in vv.13a and 14 strongly suggests that she is also in view in v.13b.) During the Syro-Ephraimite war (ca. 735–734 B.C.) Ahaz, king of Judah, bargained with Assyria (2 Kings 16:7–9). Hoshea, the last king of Israel, also formed a pact with Assyria (2 Kings 17:3), as had Menahem several years before (2 Kings 15:19–20).

The Assyrians were hardly a physician (v.13). Using the Assyrians as His instrument of punishment, the Lord would soon cause judgment to burst upon the land in full force. The sound of trumpets and battle cries would be heard, signaling an enemy invasion (v.8). The Assyrian invaders would sweep through Israel and even reach Gibeah and Ramah, located just a few miles north of Jerusalem. In fulfillment of a covenant curse, the Lord would devastate Israel (note v.9, where "laid waste" translates the word rendered "a thing of horror" in Deut. 28:37) and pour out His anger like water upon Judah (v.10). In His role of judge, the Lord compared Himself to a raging lion that rips its prey to shreds and carries it back to its lair (v.14).

This prophecy was fulfilled before the eighth century ended. In 725 B.C. the Assyrians invaded Israel, capturing Samaria in 722 (2 Kings 17:3–6). Twenty-one years later they devastated Judah, marching to the very gates of Jerusalem

(2 Kings 18–19). As prophesied by Hosea (1:7), Jerusalem miraculously averted disaster, thanks to Hezekiah's repentant attitude (cf. Jer. 26:18–19). Nevertheless, Jerusalem, like Samaria, would eventually fall (2 Kings 25).

God's ultimate purpose in judgment was to restore His people. In the misery of defeat and exile, they would genuinely seek His favor (v.15). The words of this repentant generation are recorded in 6:1–3, perhaps as a model for the exiles to follow (cf. 14:2b–3 for a similar model prayer).

Since 6:4 begins an exposure of Israel's insincerity, some regard 6:1–3 as the hypocritical, shallow words of Hosea's generation. However, verses 1–3 make excellent sense as the conclusion to the preceding chapter, if understood as an illustration of what true repentance (contrast 5:15 with 5:6) would entail. Several verbal links join 6:1–3 with chapter 5, including "return" (6:1; 5:4), "torn/tear" (6:1; 5:14), "heal/cure" (6:1; 5:13), and "acknowledge" (6:3; 5:4). The reference to God's *having* torn His people (6:1) indicates that those speaking in 6:1–3 are living after, not before, the judgment threatened in 5:14. Apparently, then, verses 1–3 envision a time, already alluded to in 5:15, when the genuine repentance of exiles replaces the hypocrisy of Hosea's day. As for the accusatory tone of 6:4 and following, such abrupt shifts from salvation to judgment (or vice versa) characterize the Book of Hosea (cf. 1:9–10; 2:1–2, 13–14; 11:7–8, 11–12; 13:16–14:1). Also, as discussed below, the direct-address style of 6:4 marks it out as the beginning of a new unit in the structure of the book.

Some argue that the reference to "two days" and a "third day" in 6:2 reveals how lightly Israel regarded God's discipline and thus proves the insincerity of the words in verses 1–3. However, the expressions need not be taken in a negative light. Verse 2 may be interpreted just as easily as an exuberant expression of confidence in God's grace that is firmly rooted in Israel's historical experience and hymnic tradition (cf. Psa. 30:5), as well as in God's promise (Deut. 30:1–10).

Verses 1–3 take the form of an exhortation to repentance, containing two exhortations (vv.1a, 3a) supported by motivational statements (vv.1b–2, 3b). God's people would repent, recognizing that their Judge is more than willing to heal them and quickly restore them to covenantal fellowship (vv.1–2). They would acknowledge His lordship, confident that He would emerge from His hiding place (v.3; cf. 5:6, 15). The comparison of the Lord to the winter rains and spring rains is apt, since God promised the regularity of these rains in exchange for Israel's devotion (Deut. 11:13–14).

Internal Corruption and Misplaced Alliances Bring Judgment (6:4–11:11).

Within this second judgment-salvation panel of chapters 4–14 (see p. 20) there are three main sections (6:4–8:14; 9:1–11:7; 11:8–11), each of which begins with a direct address to Ephraim/Israel (6:4; 9:1; 11:8). The first two sections focus upon Israel's impending judgment, while the third foresees a Day of Restoration. A reference to a return to or from Egypt signals the conclusion of each section (8:13; 11:5, 11).

6:4–8:14. This first section, like chapters 4–5, concerns Judah as well as Ephraim/Israel (cf. 6:4, 11; 8:14). Two subunits are discernible (6:4–7:16 and 8:1–14). Each refers to the broken covenant in its introduction (6:7; 8:1) and associates Egypt with Israel's judgment in its conclusion (7:16; 8:13). This section may be outlined as follows:

I. First extended message (6:4–7:16)
   A. Judgment speech (primarily accusation) against Ephraim and Judah (6:4–11a)
   B. Judgment speech against Israel/Ephraim (6:11b–7:16)
      1. General accusation (6:11b–7:2)
      2. Accusation against political rebels (7:3–7)
      3. Denunciation of foreign alliances (7:8–12)
      4. General accusation (7:13–16a) and announcement of judgment (7:16b)

II. Second extended message (accusations and announcements of judgment interspersed; 8:1–14)

6:4–7:16. An introductory rhetorical question reveals the Lord's frustration with His unfaithful people (6:4a). The Lord desired mercy (better, "genuine devotion") and acknowledgment (i.e., obedience), not empty ritual (v.6; cf. 1 Sam. 15:22; Isa. 1:10–17; Amos 5:21–24; Mic. 6:6–8). However, any devotion His people expressed was short-lived. Like the morning fog and dew, it evaporated quickly into thin air (v.4b).

Like an unfaithful wife, Israel was defiled by her adultery (v.10; cf. 5:3–4).

Verses 7–9 allude to specific examples of Israel's unfaithfulness to the covenant. While Hosea's contemporaries must have been familiar with the practices referred to here, the general and figurative nature of the description makes it difficult for modern scholarship to pinpoint the specific crimes in view.

Verse 7 simply speaks in general terms of covenant violations at the town of Adam, located near the Jordan River (cf. Josh. 3:16). The reading "as at Adam" (NIV margin, RSV) is preferable to "like Adam" (NIV) or "like men" (NIV margin, KJV). The presence of the word "there" in the next line indicates that Adam is a place-name. The appearance of place-names in verses 8–9 also supports this view.[14]

Verses 8–9 refer to violent crimes committed in Gilead and on the road to Shechem. Since Gilead was a region, not a city, Ramoth Gilead, located east of the Jordan River, must be in view in verse 8. In the case of Shechem, priests were involved in the violence (v.9). It is not clear whether literal acts of murder or oppressive acts of injustice (described in hyperbolic terms) are in view. The association of Ramoth Gilead and Shechem with murderous acts is ironic in that Joshua had designated both to be cities of refuge, where manslayers could find protection (Josh. 20:7–8). Even these cities, which should have been symbols of the Lord's concern for law and order in the land, were polluted by the blood of innocent victims.

Because of Israel's sin the Lord had brought upon her the judgments threatened by His prophets (v.5). The Lord would also punish Judah, which had followed in Israel's footsteps (v.11a). This judgment, like a harvest, was appointed for a specific and appropriate time (cf. Jer. 51:33; Joel 3:13).

Though the Lord desired to restore His people, their sins prevented any such reconciliation (6:11b–7:1a). Deceit and theft, both prohibited in the Ten Commandments ("deceit" in Hos. 7:1 and "false" in Exod. 20:16 translate the same Heb. word), were especially widespread (7:1b; cf. 4:2). No one stopped to consider that God would hold them accountable for

---

[14]The reading "at Adam" requires a change of kaph to beth. Confusion of these two similar-looking letters is attested elsewhere in the Hebrew scribal tradition. Cf. P. Kyle McCarter, *Textual Criticism* (Philadelphia: Fortress Press, 1986), p. 44.

their sins (v.2). Even the rulers, who were to oppose deceit and wickedness (cf. Ps. 101:4–5, 7–8), approved of such behavior (v.3). Because of the people's total disregard for the principles of the covenant, God called them adulterers (v.4a) and compared their passion for wrongdoing to a fire burning low in an oven, ever ready to burst into flames when stoked (v.4b).

This passion for sin found expression in the political revolts that characterized the northern kingdom during its final years. Between 752 and 732 B.C., four of Israel's kings died at the hands of conspirators (2 Kings 15:10, 14, 25, 30). This series of events provides the background for verses 5–7, which describe in highly figurative language how the assassins typically accomplished their deeds. On a festive occasion the conspirators would carouse with the naïve king, waiting for an advantageous time to spring into action. As in verse 4, the imagery of an oven is employed. Like a fire burning low in a baker's oven, the conspirators waited patiently so that their plot might not be discovered. When an opportune time arrived, they were like hot flames blazing forth and devouring the helpless king. To make matters worse, throughout this period of political instability none of Israel's kings looked to the Lord for help.

In addition to this internal corruption, Israel's self-destructive foreign policy also testified to her unfaithfulness. Instead of trusting in the Lord for security (7:10), Israel formed alliances with foreign nations (v.8a), particularly Egypt and Assyria (v.11b; cf. 2 Kings 15:19–20; 17:3–4). The Lord compared these alliances to the mixing of flour and oil to form cakes (v.8a). However, in an ironic twist of the baking imagery, the Lord observed that Israel was really like a burned cake that must be discarded (v. 8b). The heavy tribute payments demanded by Israel's overlords sapped her economic strength (v.9a). Yet, like a man who does not notice the signs of approaching old age, Israel failed to realize that such a policy would lead to her ruin (v.9b). As she went along like a naïve dove, attempting to court the favor of these nations, the Lord, like an accomplished fowler, prepared to bring inescapable judgment down upon her (v.12).

Israel's rebellious deeds made her destruction inevitable (7:13–16). Though the Lord had supported the nation in the past and desired to deliver her from the present distress, Israel responded with hostility (vv.13, 15). When drought robbed them of their harvest, they turned to the mourning rites of the

Baal cult, rather than to the Lord (v.14). Like the followers of Baal, they demonstrated their sorrow by wailing and lacerating their bodies (cf. 1 Kings 18:28), in direct violation of the Mosaic Law (Deut. 14:1).[15] Israel was as unreliable and useless as a faulty bow (v.16a; cf. Ps. 78:57). Appropriately, the rulers who had misled the nation would die by the sword, for the alliances of which they were so proud would prove to be futile. Ironically, Egypt, to whom they had looked for security, would ridicule them in their defeat (v.16b).

8:1–14. Chapter 8 reiterates many of the themes of 6:4–7:16. Once more the Lord opened His indictment with a charge of breach of covenant (v.1; cf. 6:7). Despite Israel's lip service and hypocritical gestures of worship, she had violated His commandments (vv.2–3a, 11–13). As in chapter 7, the Lord specifically condemned the nation's internal political upheaval (v.4a; cf. 7:3–6), as well as her self-destructive foreign alliances (vv.8–10a; cf. 7:8–11). He also denounced her idolatry (vv.4b–6), a theme only hinted at in the previous chapter (cf. 7:14).

The calf-idol of Samaria receives special attention in this regard (vv.5–6). The Old Testament makes no reference elsewhere to this idol. Perhaps Samaria here represents the entire northern kingdom, in which case the golden calves erected by Jeroboam I in Bethel and Dan may be in view (cf. 1 Kings 12:28–30; Hos. 10:5). Apparently these idols were incorporated into Israel's Baal worship (cf. Hos. 10:5; 13:1–2). If these golden calves are alluded to here, the words "it is not God" (v.6) may be a direct refutation of Jeroboam's claim, "Here are your gods" (1 Kings 12:28).

Israel had already sown the seeds of destruction (v.7). Her rejection of the Lord in favor of idols and foreign nations is compared to sowing the wind, here a symbol of worthless, futile activity. Israel would soon learn that one always reaps

---

[15] NIV "they gather together" (v.14) is based on the Masoretic text (MT). This reading, however, faces insurmountable difficulties and is clearly secondary. The Septuagint, as well as a few Hebrew manuscripts, preserves the original reading (Heb. *yitgôd⁽e⁾dû*, from *gādad*, "cut"), translated in the NIV margin "they slash themselves." This word appears in several other texts in conjunction with mourning rites (e.g., Deut. 14:1; 1 Kings 18:28; Jer. 16:6; 41:5; 47:5). The corruption in MT is the result of confusion of the almost identical letters daleth and resh. For other examples of textual corruption involving these letters, see McCarter, *Textual Criticism,* pp. 45–46.

what one sows (Gal. 6:7). The wind she planted would yield a whirlwind, here a symbol of violent and destructive judgment.

Israel's Maker would become her Destroyer (v.14). Ironically, the Lord would use Assyria, to whom Israel had looked for security (v.9), as His instrument of judgment (vv.1, 10). The sound of the trumpet would signal the approach of the mighty Assyrian army, likened here to an eagle (v.1), in an obvious allusion to the covenant curse of Deuteronomy 28:49. In that day the calf-idol would be destroyed (vv.5–6),[16] and the people would be carried off into exile (v.13). Though Mesopotamia would be the actual place of exile (cf. 2 Kings 17:6), Egypt is mentioned here because it had long symbolized bondage for God's people.

9:1–11:7. This next section, like the preceding one, begins with a direct address to the nation (9:1; cf. 6:4) and ends with a reference to Israel's return to Egypt (11:5; cf. 8:13). References to Israel's return to Egypt also appear at the beginning of this section (9:3, 6), thus forming an inclusio around 9:1–11:7. Within this section four judgment speeches appear, as outlined below. With the exception of the first, each of these begins with a figurative allusion to Israel's early days (9:10; 10:1; 11:1). Each then ends with a reference to Israel's impending judgment, the first speaking in general terms (9:7), the others with more specific predictions. The second threatens exile (9:17), the third violent military defeat (10:14–15), and the fourth both exile and defeat (11:5–6). The section may be outlined as follows:

I. First judgment speech (9:1–9)
   A. Announcement of judgment (vv.1b–6, 9b)
   B. Accusation (vv.1a, 7–9a)

II. Second judgment speech (9:10–17)
   A. Accusation (v.10)
   B. Announcement of judgment (vv.11–17, with accusatory elements in vv.15, 17)

---

[16]"Throw out" (v.5) and "rejected" (v.3) translate the same Hebrew word, signaling a wordplay. The significance of the wordplay depends on one's text-critical decisions. For fuller discussion, see Robert B. Chisholm, Jr., "Wordplay in the Eighth-Century Prophets," *Bibliotheca Sacra* 144 (1987): 45; and Patrick D. Miller, Jr., *Sin and Judgment in the Prophets* (Chico, Calif.: Scholars Press, 1982), pp. 17–18.

III. Third judgment speech (10:1–15)
    A. Accusation (vv.1–2a)
    B. Announcement of judgment (vv.2b–8)
        1. Intervention (v.2b)
        2. Results (introduced and concluded by quotations from the people; vv.3–8)
        3. Accusations and announcements of judgment interspersed (vv.9–15)

IV. Fourth judgment speech (11:1–7)
    A. Accusation (vv.1–4)
    B. Announcement of judgment (vv.5–7)

9:1–9. Moses taught that Israel's agricultural prosperity was dependent upon her loyalty to the Lord. He warned that idolatry would bring drought and eventually exile (Deut. 11:8–21). The Lord was about to make this threat a reality. Since the Israelites had worshiped Baal in an effort to promote agricultural prosperity, the Lord would deny them the joy of a successful harvest (v.1; cf. 2:5–13). Appropriately, the threshing floors, where Israel had attributed past harvests to Baal, would be empty (v.2). Israel would go into bondage (v.3), leaving briers and thorns to grow up over the deserted treasures and homes of the Promised Land (v.6).

Assyria, symbolically called Egypt (vv.3, 6; cf. 8:13), would be a land of death and uncleanness (vv.3–6). The force of the symbol is heightened by the reference to Memphis, a well-known burial place located in Egypt (v.6). Being in an unclean foreign land (v.3), the people would be unable to worship the Lord (vv.4–5). This punishment would be appropriate for those who had already defiled themselves (cf. 5:3; 6:10, where "corrupt" and "defiled," respectively, each translate the word rendered "unclean" in 9:3–4) and who offered the Lord only hypocritical lip service (cf. 6:6; 8:11–13).

In verses 7–9 the prophet again (cf. v.1) focused upon the reasons for the coming judgment. Israel's sins were both numerous (v.7) and vile (v.9). Her corruption is even compared to the "days of Gibeah" (v.9; cf. 10:9). The allusion here is to the brutal rape and murder of the Levite's concubine, about which the people of that day had said, "Such a thing has never been seen or done, not since the day the Israelites came up out of Egypt" (Judg. 19:30).

Israel's hostility to the Lord was epitomized by her rejection of His prophets, who were labeled fools and maniacs (v.7b). God sent them as His watchmen to warn the nation of the consequences of sin (cf. Jer. 6:17; Ezek. 3:17; 33:7–9). However, the people spurned their message and plotted their destruction (v.8; cf. Matt. 23:29–31).

9:10–17. God had not always found Israel so disgusting. In earlier days, when God led His people out of Egypt, they were a source of delight to Him, like grapes in the desert or the early fruit of the fig (v.10a; cf. 2:15). The latter is mentioned in several places as being particularly appealing and tasty (e.g., Isa. 28:4; Jer. 24:2; Mic. 7:1).

Unfortunately, it was not long before Israel turned to idols, establishing a pattern for the rest of her history (v.10b). At Baal Peor, Israelite men engaged in immoral fertility rites with Moabite women in conjunction with the worship of the Canaanite god Baal (Num. 25:1–3). Hosea's generation had done the same, prostituting themselves to this pagan deity and his cult.

Just as Israel's sin at Baal Peor prompted a violent outburst of God's anger and required drastic measures to appease His wrath (Num. 25:4–9), so this latest episode of spiritual adultery demanded harsh and extreme punishment. Appropriately, the Lord would deprive Israel of the very blessings they expected Baal to give them. He would close up the wombs of Israel's women (vv.11, 14). Those children who did happen to be born would be slaughtered by invading armies (vv.12–13, 16).

Throughout these verses Israel is ironically called Ephraim (vv.11, 13, 16). This name, which sounds like a Hebrew word meaning "fruitful," was traditionally associated with God's blessings of fertility (Gen. 41:52). Now God's judgment would deprive Ephraim of fruitfulness (v.16).

The Lord would drive the Israelites away into exile (v.15) and cause them to wander as fugitives among the nations (v.17). Perhaps Israel's fate is here compared to that of the world's first couple and their son Cain. The verb "drive out" (v.15) is also used of Adam and Eve's expulsion from the fruitful Garden of Eden (Gen. 3:24) and of Cain's punishment following his murder of Abel (Gen. 4:14). "Wanderers" (v.17) is the same word used of Cain in Genesis 4:12. A comparison with Cain, the world's first murderer, is especially appropriate in light of the reference to Israel's violent crimes in verse 9.

The appearance of the proper name Gilgal and the verb "drive out" in conjunction with an announcement of exile (v.15) is quite ironic. Gilgal, Israel's first campsite following the crossing of the Jordan (Josh. 4:19), symbolized the nation's entry into and possession of the Promised Land. The idolatrous practices now conducted there (cf. Hos. 4:15; 12:11), however, necessitated Israel's expulsion from that same land. When Israel entered the land under Joshua, the Lord promised to drive out the Canaanites from before them (Exod. 23:28, 31; Deut. 33:27). Now, because Israel had assimilated the religious practices of the Canaanites, the Lord was forced to drive His own people out of the land (here called "my house").

10:1–15. Once more Israel's promising beginning stands in contrast to her subsequent failure (vv.1–2; cf. 9:10). In the early days Israel was like a spreading vine as God blessed her with fruitfulness (cf. Ps. 80:8–11; Ezek. 19:10–11). However, as the people prospered, they began to flirt with pagan gods, compromising their relationship to the Lord.

The Lord's judgment would take dead aim on the symbols of Israel's false worship. He would destroy the altars and sacred stones (v.2; cf. 3:4). His instrument of judgment, the Assyrians, would haul away the calf-idol of Bethel, leaving its worshipers to mourn its departure (vv.5–6). Thorns and thistles would overrun the ruins of the high places, while those who had worshiped Baal there would beg to be destroyed quickly and thereby be spared the full horror of divine judgment (v.8). Perhaps the imagery of Genesis 3 is utilized again (cf. Hos. 9:15, 17), for the Hebrew expression translated "thorns and thistles" occurs only here and in Genesis 3:18, in both cases being used of punishment for sin.

The Lord would deprive Israel of her independence. Israel's king would be swept away, like a twig in a fast current (v.7; cf. vv.3, 15). The Assyrians would crush Israel's army and fortresses, of which she had been so proud (vv.13b–14). Israel's coming defeat is likened to Shalman's violent destruction of Beth Arbel, in which even women and children were ruthlessly slaughtered. Although this event must have been well known to Hosea's contemporaries, modern scholars have been unable to identify Shalman or Beth Arbel, let alone the battle to which reference is made.

The Lord employed agricultural imagery to picture Israel's coming judgment and exile. Like a heifer that freely eats as it performs the relatively undemanding task of threshing, Israel had been enjoying the Lord's benefits, while He asked little in return (v. 11a). However, because of Israel's sin (vv.9–10) the Lord would now place a yoke upon her neck and force her to perform the strenuous work of plowing (v.11b), which here represents the sufferings accompanying the nation's invasion and exile.

Continuing the farming imagery, the Lord graciously called Israel to repentance (v.12). When it came to social justice, Israel had been inactive ("unplowed ground"). The time had come to sow righteousness (i.e., justice) and reap unfailing love. In return the Lord would "shower righteousness" upon (i.e., deliver) His people, allowing their concern for justice to grow and bring prosperity to the land.

There was little chance that Israel would respond positively to the Lord's exhortation. Since the days of Gibeah (v.9; cf. 9:9) the nation had "planted wickedness," "reaped evil," and "eaten the fruit of deception" (v.13). The terms used here refer to the dishonesty and violence alluded to in verses 4 and 9.

11:1–7. For a third time the Lord recalled His early relationship with Israel, contrasting it with the disappointing developments that followed (vv.1–4; cf. 9:10; 10:1–2). The Lord compared this relationship to that of a father and son. The Lord loved His son, delivering him from bondage in Egypt (v.1).[17] He patiently taught His son how to walk, holding him steady when he stumbled and hurt himself (v.3a). Returning to the imagery of 10:11, the Lord also compared Himself to a kind farmer, who lifts the yoke from his animal's neck and feeds it (v.4) Despite these efforts, Israel failed to acknowledge the Lord's help (v. 3b). The more He called to them, the further away they drifted, eventually turning to other gods (v.2).

Israel's ingratitude and obstinacy made judgment inevitable (vv.5–7). Assyrian swords would flash in Israel's cities (v.6). Because Israel refused to repent (*šûb*, lit. "return"), salvation

---

[17] Matthew considered the infant Jesus' departure from Egypt as a fulfillment of Hos. 11:1 (see Matt. 2:15). On the surface this seems problematic, since Hos. 11 clearly has in mind the historical exodus of the nation, not a future event involving the Messiah. Apparently Matthew saw a typological relationship between the experiences of the nation Israel and those of Jesus. By providentially causing Jesus to repeat the nation's experience, God identified him as the new Israel. On Jesus as the new Israel, see R. T. France, *Jesus and the Old Testament,* paperback ed. (Grand Rapids: Baker, 1982), pp. 50–60.

history would be reversed as Israel returned (*šûb*) to a land of bondage (v.5; cf. v.1). Once again Egypt as the symbol of bondage stands parallel to the actual place of exile, Assyria (cf. 9:3).

The Lord used wordplay to contrast His past benevolence with His coming punishment. "Feed" (v.4) and "put an end" (v.6) both translate *'ākal* (lit. "eat"). In the past the Lord had fed His people. Now He would send a sword to devour them and their proud plans. Likewise "I lifted" (v.4) and "exalt" (v.7) are both from the root *rûm* (lit. "lift up"). Though the Lord had "lifted the yoke" in the past, He would display no such kindness in the Day of Judgment.

11:8–11. The section from 6:4 to 11:11 concludes with a sudden shift from the lengthy judgment message of the preceding chapters to a brief, but stirring, promise of salvation. This abrupt literary transition mirrors a profound emotional change within God's own being.

As the Lord considered the plight of His people and even contemplated their total destruction, His compassion was suddenly aroused (vv.8–9). He could never treat His covenant people like Admah and Zeboiim, which He completely destroyed along with Sodom and Gomorrah (Deut. 29:23; cf. Gen. 10:19; 14:2, 8). In other biblical references to this well-known event, the judgment is called an overthrow or overturning. (The verb, *hāpak*, appears in Gen. 19:21, 25, 29; Deut. 29:23; Jer. 20:16; Lam. 4:6. Gen. 19:29 uses the related noun *hᵃpēkâ*; another related noun, *mahpēkâ*, appears in Deut. 29:23; Isa. 13:19; Jer. 49:18; 50:40; Amos 4:11.) According to verse 8, however, the Lord would not overthrow Israel. Rather, His own heart was changed (*hāpak*, lit. "overturned"), causing His anger to relent.

Although He must harshly discipline Israel for her disobedience, the Lord would preserve a remnant, which He would eventually deliver from exile and lead back to the Promised Land (vv.10–11). In the coming judgment the Lord would tear Israel like a lion does its prey (cf. 5:14–15), but in the Day of Restoration His lionlike roar would be a summons to escape from bondage. Whereas Israel once flitted about from nation to nation like a silly dove (cf. 7:11), they would someday fly back to their land as swiftly as a dove.

Concluding Messages of Judgment and
Restoration (11:12–14:9)

This final panel of the book includes a lengthy judgment speech (11:12–13:16) and a concluding salvation message (14:1–9).

11:12–13:16. This judgment speech may be outlined as follows:

I. First message (11:12–12:14)
   A. Introductory accusation (11:12–12:1)
   B. Lawsuit (12:2–14)
      1. Announcement of judgment (note "repay"; v.2)
      2. Historical lesson (vv.3–5)
      3. Exhortation (v.6)
      4. Accusation (vv.7–8)
      5. Divine announcement of judgment (note "I"; vv.9–11)
      6. Historical lesson (vv.12–13)
      7. Announcement of judgment (note "repay" again [cf. v.2]; v.14)

II. Second message (13:1–16)
   A. Accusation (vv.1–2)
   B. Announcements of judgment (vv.3–16)
      1. Introductory announcement (note chaff imagery; v.3)
      2. Divine announcement (note "I"; vv.4–14)
      3. Concluding announcement (note east wind imagery; vv.15–16)

The Lord condemned His people's deceitful character (11:12), pointing specifically to their foreign alliances (12:1) and dishonest economic practices (v.7). This same kind of deceit had been present in Jacob, the father of the nation. From the time of his birth, when he grabbed his brother Esau's heel, his greed was apparent (v.3a). He later used deception to rob his brother of Isaac's blessing (in Gen. 27:35, "deceitfully" translates the word rendered "deceit" in Hos. 11:12 and "dishonest" in 12:7).

Of course, Jacob's life turned around when he wrestled with the Lord's angel at Peniel (vv.3b–4a; cf. Gen. 32:22–32). Afraid that Esau might kill him, Jacob demanded and received a blessing. God later met with Jacob at Bethel, changing his name to Israel and reiterating the promises of the Abrahamic covenant (v.4b; cf. Gen. 35:1–15). In the same way, Jacob's deceitful descendents must turn to God in repentance, which must take the form of a renewed commitment to love and justice and humble reliance upon the Lord (v.6).

The Lord reminded arrogant, self-confident Israel (v.8) that her very existence depended upon His providential care and mighty acts. He watched over Israel's father Jacob when he was a fugitive and servant in a foreign land (v.12). He raised up Moses to lead Israel out of Egypt (vv.9a, 13) and continued to give them direction through Moses' prophetic successors (v.10). As their sovereign Lord, He controlled their destiny. He could reverse their history by sending them into exile, where, as in the days of the wilderness wanderings, they would move about without a home (v.9b).

Israel's violent acts of bloodshed, such as those perpetrated in Gilead (v.11a; cf. 6:8), and her idolatrous practices, like those conducted at Gilgal (v.11b; cf. 4:15; 9:15), had provoked the Lord's anger (v.14). He would judge their deeds appropriately, as seen in the fate of Gilgal, whose altars would be turned into "piles of stones." This phrase translates Hebrew *gallîm*, which sounds like Gilgal and therefore draws attention to God's poetic justice.

Idolatry is the focal point of the judgment speech in 13:1–3. Though once a leader among the northern tribes, Ephraim turned to Baal worship (v.1). They multiplied their images and even kissed the calf-idols (cf. 8:4; 10:5) as a sign of their devotion to Baal (v.2; cf. 1 Kings 19:18). Like its short-lived devotion to the Lord (cf. 6:4), idolatrous Ephraim would disappear as quickly as morning fog and dew, chaff, and smoke (v.3).

"They offer human sacrifice" (v.2) is a questionable translation. The Hebrew of verse 2b literally reads, "Sacrificers of men kiss calf-idols." NIV understands "of men" as the object of verbal "sacrificers," interpreting this as a reference to human sacrifice. Though some Israelites apparently sacrificed children to pagan gods, the word used here (*'ā dām*, "men") does not refer exclusively to children. NASB translates, "Let the men who sacrifice kiss the calves," taking "of men" as appositional to "sacrificers." Other examples of *'ādām* used in this way include *pere' 'ādām* (lit. "wild donkey of a man," i.e., a man who resembles a wild donkey in character; Gen. 16:12), *'ebyônê 'ādām* (lit. "the poor of men," i.e., men who are poor; Isa. 29:19), and *nᵉsîkê 'ādām* (lit. "princes of men," i.e., men who are princes; Mic. 5:5). According to this line of interpretation, Hosea 13:2b does not refer to human sacrifice but, rather, points out the absurdity of *men* worshiping *calf*-idols.

Ephraim's ingratitude heightened its sin (vv.4–6) and aroused the Lord's anger (vv. 7–9). Having delivered His people from Egypt, the Lord in return asked only for their undivided loyalty (v.4). He provided for all their needs, even when they were traveling through the hot, dry wilderness (v.5). Failing to heed Moses' warning (cf. Deut. 8), Israel took the Lord's blessings for granted and became self-reliant (v.6). Like a hungry beast of prey or a "bear robbed of her cubs," the Lord would viciously attack His people and tear them to bits (vv.7–8). Israel had placed herself in the role of God's enemy, turning her Helper into her Destroyer (v.9).

Israel's punishment was certain. Her leaders, whom the Lord had reluctantly provided in the first place (v.11; cf. 1 Kings 12:16), would be unable to rescue the nation (v.10). The Lord had kept an accurate record of her sins so that nothing would be overlooked when the time of retribution arrived (v.12). Like birth pangs before delivery, the signs of impending judgment were already observable (v.13a); Israel should have responded to the signs of judgment by repenting. However, unwise Israel failed to do so, making her death inevitable (vv.13b).

Verses 14–16 describe this death. Rather than delivering Israel from the grave, the Lord would beckon death to come with its plagues and destroy His people. The Lord's judgment would come like a hot desert wind that dries up everything in its path. The Assyrian invaders would rob Israel's treasures and slaughter her people, committing atrocities against even helpless children and pregnant women.

Traditionally verse 14a has been interpreted as a promise of deliverance, with verse 14b then being taken as a defiant challenge to death (NIV, NASB). However, this interpretation is problematic. Though abrupt shifts in mood do appear in this book, a change from judgment to salvation at this point is premature. The last line of verse 14 states that God would have no compassion upon His people. Not until chapter 14, however, does the transition to a message of salvation occur.

Consequently the statements of verse 14a are better translated as rhetorical questions implying a negative answer, "Shall I ransom them from the power of Sheol? Shall I redeem them from Death?" (RSV).[18] In this case, verse 14b is an invitation to personified death to attack Israel. In quoting verse 14b as a defiant challenge to death, the apostle Paul in 1 Corinthians 15:55 was apparently drawing on the language of Scripture as traditionally understood, not commenting on the meaning of verse 14b in its original context. Paul may have purposely given the passage an ironic twist as he considered God's ultimate triumph over the "last enemy."

14:1–9. In this final chapter an exhortation to repentance (vv.1–3) precedes a promise of restoration (vv.4–8) and a concluding wisdom saying (v.9). The call to repentance, though certain to be rejected by Hosea's contemporaries, held out the hope of restored blessing to a future generation. Included within the exhortation is a model prayer for a penitent generation to offer to the Lord. In this prayer the repentant nation asks for forgiveness so that they might offer praise (v.2b). They confess the Lord to be their only source of protection and disavow false gods (v.3).

The Lord promised repentant Israel full restoration (vv.4–8). His love would replace His anger, bringing healing to the nation (v.4; cf. 6:1). In contrast to 13:15, where the Lord sends a destructive east wind, the Lord promised to come as "dew to Israel," causing her to grow luxuriantly (v.5a). In this regard, Israel is compared to a lily, a cedar of Lebanon, an olive tree, and a grape vine (vv.5–7). These images of fertility vividly picture the renewal of divine blessings. As Ephraim's attitude changes from rebellion to loyalty, the Lord would restore the fruitfulness He had earlier removed (v.8; cf. 9:11–16).

A wordplay draws attention to the Lord's changed attitude toward His people. The word translated "care for" in verse 8 is the same verb used in 13:7 (there "lurk") to describe the Lord crouching by the path like a leopard. In anticipation of judgment the Lord carefully watched disobedient Israel in the way a predator does its prey. However, in the Day of Restoration He would carefully watch over His people in order to bless and protect them.

In conclusion the prophet drew a lesson for his audience

[18] See also Wolff, *Hosea,* p. 221.

(v.9). The one who possesses true wisdom will acknowledge that the Lord's commandments (called here His ways) are right and will obey ("walk in") them. However, the rebellious find them to be a stumbling block that leads to their downfall.

THEOLOGY

Summary

Hosea's message revolves around the theme of God's covenant with Israel, which is likened to a marriage. The Lord initiated this covenant, delivering His people from Egypt and blessing them abundantly in a land of their own. Despite these acts of kindness, Israel quickly spurned the Lord, turning to another lover—the Canaanite fertility god, Baal. In addition to this spiritual adultery, Israel's breach of covenant also took the form of foreign alliances and social injustice. In order to purify His defiled people, the Lord would judge them severely. He would deprive the nation of the fertility that it erroneously attributed to Baal. Enemy armies would invade the land and carry the people away into exile, reversing the nation's salvation history. However, because of His great love for Israel, the Lord could never totally abandon her. He would recover His wayward wife and renew the covenantal bond. To illustrate this the Lord instructed Hosea to recover his own adulterous wife, Gomer. In the Day of Restoration the effects of judgment would be reversed, Israel's salvation history repeated, and the Abrahamic and Davidic promises fulfilled.

Analysis

Sin

Hosea highlighted Israel's sin by placing it against the backdrop of God's gracious deeds on the nation's behalf. The Lord delivered His people from Egypt (11:1; 12:9; 13:4) and led them safely through the wilderness (13:5). He abundantly blessed Israel (2:8), the object of His delight (9:10) and protection (11:3–4).

Israel responded to God's grace with ingratitude and disobedience. Hosea pictured Israel's rejection of her covenant God in a number of ways, the most prominent being the comparison of Israel's unfaithfulness to marital infidelity (2:2–

13). This unfaithfulness was primarily evident in Israel's idolatry. She blatantly violated the first and second commandments by worshiping Baal. By then hypocritically trying to maintain a semblance of devotion to the Lord, she only heightened her guilt (4:15; 5:6; 8:2, 11, 13). The Lord desired genuine loyalty, not empty ritual (6:6).

The Lord also condemned Israel for her foreign alliances (5:13; 7:8–11; 8:9–10; 12:1) and for her failure to follow His commands governing the socioeconomic sphere of life. Hosea 4:2 alone mentions violations of five of the Ten Commandments. The nation was defiled by bloodshed (6:8–9), political assassinations (7:3–7), and dishonest economic practices (12:7).

Judgment

Israel's disobedience demanded harsh and appropriate judgment. As symbolized by the names of Hosea's children (1:4–9), the Lord would reject His unfaithful wife. Because Israel looked to Baal for the fertility of her fields and people, the Lord would strike the land with infertility, depriving once-fruitful Ephraim of its agricultural abundance and its children (2:9, 12; 9:11–17). The Lord would actualize the covenant curses of drought (4:3; 13:15) and death (13:14–16) against Israel. Once Israel's Maker (8:14) and Helper (13:9), the Lord would now be the nation's Destroyer and Enemy. In this new role the Lord compared Himself to a moth (5:12), bone disease (5:12), a fowler (7:12), mighty predators (5:14; 13:7), and an enraged she-bear (13:8). Assyria, the very nation to whom Israel foolishly looked for security, would invade the land, slaughter its people, and sweep the survivors away into exile (8:14; 9:3; 10:6, 14–15; 11:5–6; 13:14–16). Israel's history of salvation would be reversed as the nation returned to another Egypt, a land of bondage (8:13; 9:3, 6; 11:5).

Salvation

Even in judgment the Lord's ultimate purpose was to restore His people. As He considered their terrible plight, His anger changed to compassion (11:8–9). Through the Exile, which is compared to the wilderness wanderings of Moses' time, the Lord would separate His people from their false gods (2:6–7; 3:4) and draw them back to Himself (2:14). He would eventually renew His covenant (2:19–20) with His repentant people (6:1–3; 11:10; 14:1–3), just as Hosea reclaimed his wayward wife, Gomer (3:1–3).

The Lord would completely reverse the effects of judgment. In a repetition of salvation history He would deliver exiled Israel from bondage (11:10–11) and lead her into the Promised Land (2:23; 11:11). Once again Israel would pass through the Valley of Achor, which would be transformed from a symbol of disobedience to a door of hope (2:15). The Lord would renew His blessings, giving the people agricultural prosperity and numerous children (1:10; 2:21–22; 3:5; 14:5–8). In so doing, He would fulfill His promises to Abraham, whereby He guaranteed the patriarch numerous offspring and eternal possession of the Promised Land. The Lord would also restore Israel's political independence and stability, reuniting the northern and southern kingdoms under a Davidic ruler in fulfillment of His promise to David (1:11; 3:5). In the progress of revelation this king, viewed by Hosea as David redivivus, is none other than Jesus the Messiah.

2

JOEL

INTRODUCTION

Author and Date

The heading of this book identifies the author as Joel son of Pethuel but does not indicate the date when it was written. Consequently one must rely on details within the prophecy itself to determine its date. The presence of the temple (1:14, 16; 2:17) indicates a date either before 586 B.C. (when the Babylonians destroyed Solomon's temple) or after 515 (when the returning exiles completed rebuilding the temple). The latter is favored by 3:2–3, which seems to refer to the exile of God's people (primarily Judah, cf. v.1) as an event that had already taken place. Within this judgment speech the verbs of verses 2b–3 ("for they scattered . . . divided . . . cast lots . . . traded . . . sold") most naturally refer to accomplished events that serve as a basis for the judgment threatened in verse 2a. Other features of the book, such as the absence of any reference to a king and the mention of Greek slave trade (3:6), are consistent with a postexilic date.[1]

Some scholars, however, have proposed a preexilic date of

[1] Among those favoring a postexilic date are Leslie C. Allen, *Joel, Obadiah, Jonah, and Micah* (Grand Rapids: Eerdmans, 1976), pp. 19–25; and R. K. Harrison, *Introduction to the Old Testament* (Grand Rapids: Eerdmans, 1969), pp. 876–79.

the ninth century B.C. for Joel.[2] In this view the book was written early in the reign of Joash (ca. 835–796). Since Joash was crowned at the age of seven, he was incapable of actually leading the nation until he was older, which would explain the book's omission of references to the king and its emphasis upon elders and priests (cf. 1:2, 9, 13; 2:16–17) as the nation's leaders. According to this view, the events referred to in 3:2–3 can be associated with those recorded in 2 Chronicles 21:16–17.

Supporters of this early date have pointed out that the book fails to mention Assyria, Babylon, or Persia, the world powers in the Near East from the eighth to the sixth centuries B.C. Instead it refers to Tyre, Sidon, Philistia, Egypt, and Edom, which were Judah's enemies in the tenth and ninth centuries. Second, they have argued that the canonical position of the book (between the eighth-century prophets Hosea and Amos) points to a preexilic date. Third, they note that Joel contains several verbal parallels with other prophets, which can be explained by assuming Joel's priority.[3]

Several objections may be raised against these arguments. First, later prophets, including those of the Babylonian period, also pronounced judgment upon Tyre, Sidon, Philistia, Egypt, and Edom (e.g., Jer. 46–47; 49:7–22; Ezek. 27–30; Zeph. 2:4–7; Obadiah; Mal. 1:2–4). As for the omission of any direct reference to a superpower between the eighth and sixth centuries, one contending for a late preexilic date (ca. 600–586 B.C.) could argue that Joel pictured the Babylonians vividly enough (in 2:1–11) to make formal identification unnecessary to an audience that was all too aware of their military presence and power. If the prophecy comes from after 515, then one would not expect any reference to Assyria or Babylon. The omission of a reference to Persia is not determinative for dating, since Malachi, a postexilic prophet, makes no mention of this kingdom either.

Second, the canonical position of Joel is inconclusive.

[2]See, for example, Hobart E. Freeman, *An Introduction to the Old Testament Prophets* (Chicago: Moody Press, 1968), pp. 147–49; and Gleason L. Archer, Jr., *A Survey of Old Testament Introduction* (Chicago: Moody Press, 1974), pp. 304–5.

[3]Some, using these and other arguments, date the book in the early eighth century B.C. See, for example, Richard D. Patterson, "Joel," in *The Expositor's Bible Commentary*, ed. Frank E. Gaebelein (Grand Rapids: Zondervan, 1985), 7:231–33.

Wolff suggests that Joel was originally placed before Amos because of literary parallels, not chronology.[4]

Third, arguments based on verbal parallels are notoriously subjective and inconclusive. The parallels may point to Joel's dependence on earlier prophetic materials, rather than his priority.

Perhaps the most telling argument against an early date (either late ninth or early eighth century) for Joel is its failure to account adequately for the statements of 3:2–3. The captivity of the royal sons and wives recorded in 2 Chronicles 21:16–17 hardly satisfies the language of the passage, which refers to a national catastrophe of the first magnitude.[5] Some proponents of an early date understand Joel 3:2b–3 as anticipating what the nations would eventually do.[6] However, this interpretation is improbable on formal and grammatical grounds.[7]

Some scholars date the book to the late preexilic period.[8] If Joel wrote after 597 B.C., the language of 3:2 would be satisfied, for the Babylonians deported thousands of Judah's finest men in that year (2 Kings 24:10–16). If the book also predates 586, we could easily account for Joel's references to the temple, which was not destroyed until that date (2 Kings 25:1–21). Several other features of the book harmonize well with a late preexilic date, including Joel's emphasis on the Day of the Lord (a prominent theme in seventh- and sixth-century prophetic literature) and the reference to Greek slave trade (cf. Ezek. 27:13).

The major problem with this dating scheme is its inability to harmonize 2:18–27 with the events of 586 B.C. According to this passage, the Lord took pity on Joel's generation and promised to protect them from the destructive elements of the Lord's Day (see analysis below). This was hardly the case in the final decade before the fall of Jerusalem. Even Josiah's revival in

[4]Hans W. Wolff, *Joel and Amos*, trans. Waldemar Janzen, S. Dean McBride, Jr., and Charles Muenchow (Philadelphia: Fortress Press, 1977), pp. 3–4.

[5]S. R. Driver, *Joel and Amos*, 2d ed. (Cambridge: Cambridge University Press, 1915), p. 15.

[6]See Carl F. Keil, *The Twelve Minor Prophets*, trans. James Martin, 2 vols. (Grand Rapids: Eerdmans, 1949), 1:221; and Patterson, "Joel," p. 260.

[7]Driver, *Joel and Amos*, p. 15.

[8]See Arvid S. Kapelrud, *Joel Studies* (Uppsala: A. B. Lundequistska Bokhandeln, 1948), p. 191; and Klaus Koch, *The Prophets*, trans. Margaret Kohl, 2 vols. (Philadelphia: Fortress Press, 1983), 1:160–61.

the late seventh century failed to move the Lord to spare His people (cf. 2 Kings 23:25–27).

Structure

The Book of Joel may be divided into two major sections—1:2–2:17 and 2:18–3:21. The first contains several appeals to Joel's generation (1:2, 5–14; 2:1, 12–17) prompted by a recent locust invasion (1:2–20) that was a harbinger of the Day of the Lord (2:1–11). The second section describes the Lord's merciful response to Joel's generation (2:18), His promise of deliverance for His people (2:19–32; 3:16b–18), and His announcement of judgment upon their enemies (3:1–16a, 19–21).

ANALYSIS

A Locust Invasion Signals the Day of the Lord (1:2–2:17)

This first major section of the book contains several individual formal units:

I. Call to attention (1:2–4)

II. Call to lament and repent (1:5–14)

III. Lamentation (1:15–20)

IV. Call to alarm (2:1–11)

V. Call to repent (2:12–17)

A Unique Event (1:2–4)

Joel urged the elders and all the people of the land to consider carefully the significance of a recent locust plague that had devastated the land. With a touch of hyperbole the prophet suggested that nothing of this magnitude had ever overtaken the nation (v.2). For generations to come this disaster would be remembered (v.3). Wave after wave of locusts had completely denuded the land of its vegetation.[9]

Some have associated the four Hebrew terms used for the locusts in verse 4 ("locust swarm," "great locusts," "young locusts," and "locusts") with the locust's consecutive phases of physical development. However, Wolff raises several objections to this view.[10] It is better to see the terms as roughly synonymous. The heaping up of synonyms probably points to a series of locust invasions. The threefold reference to one wave devouring what the previous wave had left draws attention to the scope of the disaster.

The Destruction of the Land's Vegetation (1:5–14)

Though the locust invasion would adversely affect the entire nation, certain groups of people would be more directly and severely hurt by it. Joel urged these groups, as well as the entire nation, to mourn the calamity that had overtaken them. He began with the drunkards (v.5), for the destruction of the vineyards (vv.6–7) meant they would be unable to satisfy their incessant craving for wine. He next urged the entire nation, likened to a young widow (v.8),[11] to mourn bitterly because the destruction of the crops (v.10) would paralyze the religious system, based as it was on sacrificial routine (v.9). Joel also appealed to the farmers and vinedressers, who would be deprived of the joy of the harvest (vv.11–12). Finally, the prophet addressed the priests (v.13), whose reason for lamentation he had mentioned in verse 9. In addition to mourning, the priests were to lead the entire nation in a ceremony of repentance, characterized by fasting and petitions for mercy (v.14; cf. 2:12–17).

In verses 11b–12a the detailed account of the effects of the locust invasion, which goes beyond the descriptions in verses 7

---

[9]For eyewitness accounts of locust plagues, see Driver, *Joel and Amos,* pp. 40, 89–93; George A. Smith, *The Book of the Twelve Prophets,* rev.ed., 2 vols. (New York: Harper & Brothers, n.d.), 2:391–95; and John D. Whiting, "Jerusalem's Locust Plague," *National Geographic Magazine* 28 (December 1915): 511–50.

[10]Wolff, *Joel and Amos,* pp. 27–28.

[11]The Heb. form translated "mourn" is feminine singular, suggesting that the land (standing figuratively for its inhabitants) is personified here (cf. 2:18). The meaning of the Heb. word translated "virgin" is debated (cf. NIV margin, "young woman"). If the translation "virgin" is retained, then reference is made to a betrothed woman who had not yet consummated the marriage. Cf. Deut. 22:23–24, which refers to a betrothed woman as both a virgin and a wife.

and 10, heightens the emotional intensity of this section. Verse 7 refers to the destruction of only the vines and fig trees, and verse 10 mentions fields, ground, grain, new wine, and oil. In verses 11 and 12 the list grows to nine (wheat, barley, harvest of the field, vine, fig tree, pomegranate, palm, apple tree, and the trees of the field) and then culminates with the withering away of joy.

The Approaching Day of the Lord (1:15–20)

Speaking on behalf of the nation, the prophet mourned the devastation caused by the locusts because he realized its full import (vv.16, 19)—it signaled the approaching Day of the Lord (v.15). Just as the locusts had ruined and destroyed (both translate the verb *šāḏaḏ*) the crops, so the Day of the Lord would bring "destruction [*šōḏ*] from the Almighty [*šadday*]." The wordplay in Hebrew draws attention to this fact and correlates the immediate past with the immediate future.

That the prophet would draw the connection between the locust plague and a greater judgment to follow should come as no surprise. When the Lord judged the Egyptians prior to the Exodus, a locust plague preceded the final plagues of darkness and death (Exod. 10–11; 12:29–30). The curse list in Deuteronomy 28 associates locust plagues with death and exile (cf. vv.38, 42).

Widespread drought, likened to destructive fire (vv.19–20), accompanied the locust plague, bringing famine in its wake (vv.16–17). Empty storehouses grew dilapidated (v.17b), while herds and flocks looked desperately for sustenance (v.18). Even the wild animals were unable to find food and water in the parched land and dried-up streams (vv.19–20).

The Lord's Army Marches (2:1–11)

Certain that the Lord's Day was around the corner, Joel issued a call to alarm (v.1). The Lord was marching against the land with an invincible army, before which even nature shook in fear (vv.2–11).

This section contains four units, with the introductory expressions "before them" (vv. 3, 10) and "at the sight of them" (v.6) marking divisions. Verses 1–2 correspond to verses 10–11, the two units forming an inclusio for the whole section. Both of these units refer specifically to the Day of the Lord (vv.1, 11), the darkness that accompanies it (vv.2, 10), the fear that it causes (vv. 1, 10), and the extraordinary size of the Lord's army (vv.2, 11). Two of these themes appear at the center of the section as well (cf. the references to the size of the army in v.5b and to the fearful response it elicits in v.6). Verses 3–9 emphasize the destructive nature of the army (vv.3, 5b) and its relentless charge toward its objective (vv.4–5a, 7–9).

What is the relationship of the army described in 2:1–11 to the locusts mentioned in chapter 1? Some equate the two, based on parallel imagery (cf. 1:19–20 with 2:3–5) and the statement in 2:25, which identifies the locusts as the Lord's great army (cf. this with 2:11). However, a closer examination of the text indicates otherwise. The locust invasion of chapter 1 had already occurred (cf. esp. 1:4, 6–7, 10–12, 16–20, as well as 2:25), while the army of chapter 2, like the Day of the Lord with which it is associated, had not yet arrived (cf. esp. 1:15; 2:1).[12] Nevertheless, though the locusts of chapter 1 and the army of chapter 2 should not be equated, neither should the distinction between the two be overdrawn. The locusts were the advanced troops in the Lord's campaign, which would culminate with the invasion described in chapter 2.

Does the army of 2:1–11 comprise locusts or men/nations? Several factors seem to indicate literal locusts. First, 2:25 identifies the Lord's army (referred to in 2:11 as well) as locusts.

Second, the army is compared to a human army in 2:4 (note "the appearance of horses" and "like cavalry"), 5 ("like that of chariots" and "like a mighty army"), and 7 ("like warriors" and "like soldiers"). If an actual army is used as an object of comparison, how can it be the reality in view?[13]

Third, several descriptive details correspond to the features of a locust invasion, including the great numerical size of the invader (2:2, 5), its destruction of the land (v.3), the leaping and scaling ability of the invaders (vv.5, 7), the loud sound they make (v.5), their horselike appearance (v.4), and the darkening of the sky (v.10).[14] At the same time, no mention is made of the army killing or stealing.[15] The destruction of the army,

[12] See Wolff, *Joel and Amos,* pp. 41–42.
[13] Cf. Driver, *Joel and Amos,* p. 28.
[14] Cf. 2:1–11 with the accounts of locust invasions recorded in ibid., pp. 50–53.
[15] Ibid., p. 28.

described in 2:20, also has parallels with eyewitness accounts of the destruction of locusts in the Mediterranean.[16]

Finally, literary parallels suggest a close connection between the armies of chapters 1 and 2 (cf. 1:2 with 2:2; 1:6 with 2:2, 11; and 1:19 with 2:3).

Nevertheless, other factors militate against this view. The army is associated with the Lord's Day. Elsewhere the Lord uses armies of nations as His instruments of judgment in connection with His Day (e.g., Isa. 13 and Jer. 46). And then, in 2:20 the army is called the northern army. Locusts usually invade Palestine from the south or southeast, rather than the north (though invasions from the north or northeast are not unknown). On the other hand, literal armies are often viewed as invading Israel from the north (e.g., Jer. 1:14–15; 4:6; 6:1, 22; 10:22; 15:12; Ezek. 26:7; 38:15).

In response to the arguments favoring an army of locusts, the following points may be made. First, though at first glance 2:11 and 2:25 appear to refer to the same army, such an interpretation cannot be sustained. The army of 2:11 was near but never arrived (cf. v.20). The army mentioned in 2:25 must be the locusts of chapter 1, for its effects could be reversed, but not averted.

Second, a Hebrew simile sometimes goes beyond mere comparison and points directly to the reality in view. This use of the preposition translated "like, as" is well attested.[17] For example, in Joel 1:15 the prophet laments that the Lord's Day would come "like destruction from Almighty" (i.e., it would indeed entail destruction sent by the Lord Almighty Himself). Perhaps the comparisons in Joel 2:4–5, 7 can be explained in this way, especially if the locust imagery of chapter 1 has been carried over to 2:1–11 and provides the basis for the enemy's description.[18] This close association between locusts and armies was natural, since both had similar effects on a land's agricultural produce (cf. Deut. 28:33; Isa. 1:7; Jer. 5:15–17). Another

---

[16]Ibid., pp. 62–63; Smith, *Twelve Prophets*, 2:411.

[17]For examples of this use of a simile, see E. W. Bullinger, *Figures of Speech Used in the Bible* (1898; reprint, Grand Rapids: Baker, 1968), pp. 728–29. On the grammatical point, see E. Kautzsch, ed., *Gesenius' Hebrew Grammar*, trans. A. E. Cowley, 2d Eng. ed. (Oxford: Clarendon Press, 1910), p. 376 (sec. 118x); and Ronald J. Williams, *Hebrew Syntax: An Outline*, 2d ed. (Toronto: University of Toronto Press, 1976), p. 47 (sec. 261).

[18]On the latter point, see Freeman, *Prophets*, pp. 152–53.

possibility is that neither locusts nor men are described in 2:1–11 but, as Wolff suggests, "locustlike apocalyptic creatures" along the lines of those described in Revelation 9:2–11.[19] This would explain both their locustlike qualities as well as the comparisons to human armies.

Third, there is no doubt that the army of 2:1–11 is described in locustlike terms, probably to stress the continuity between the locust invasion of chapter 1 and the Day of the Lord to which it pointed. Locusts had come; more "locusts" were on the way.

Finally, the literary parallels between chapters 1 and 2 also draw attention to this continuity without requiring 2:1–11 to describe literal locusts.

If 2:1–11 does not refer to literal locusts, what specific army does it have in view? Proponents of a preexilic date for the book sometimes identify it with one of the superpowers of the Near East—Assyria or Babylon. However, if the book is dated after 515 B.C., a specific historical referent is difficult to pin down. Perhaps none is intended, the figurative description simply pointing to an unidentified army that the Lord *would have* raised up as an instrument of judgment had Judah not responded to Joel's call for repentance. This would explain the apocalyptic character of the army and its somewhat cryptic identification with the north (cf. 2:20). In this case, the promise of the army's destruction, rather than having a literal historical fulfillment, reflects the Lord's decision not to raise up such an army. However, since the threat was portrayed in terms of locustlike creatures (2:1–11), the elimination of the threat is poetically likened to the destruction of locusts in the sea.

The Need for Genuine Repentance (2:12–17)

The proper response to the approaching Day of the Lord was repentance. Building on the prophet's earlier appeal (cf. 1:14), the Lord urged the people to return wholeheartedly to Him (v.12). Joel seconded this, exhorting them to repent with sincerity (v.13).

As motivation for a positive response, Joel reminded the people of their covenantal relationship to the Lord (note "the LORD *your* God," v.13) and of His gracious disposition (v.13b). This description of the Lord's character recalls the words of

[19]Wolff, *Joel and Amos,* p. 42.

Exodus 34:6, which were uttered shortly after the golden calf incident. On that occasion, in response to Moses' prayer (Exod. 32:12), the Lord "relented and did not bring on his people the disaster he had threatened" (Exod. 32:14). Joel offered this same possibility to his generation (v.14), though he was careful not to presume upon God's sovereign authority to dispose mercy to whom He wills (note v.14, "Who knows? He may turn . . .").

Joel called the entire nation to participate in a formal ceremony of repentance (vv.15–17). Even newlyweds, who were normally allowed freedom from all distractions, were to join with the assembly. The priests were to intercede for the nation, asking the Lord to spare His people so that they (and, by implication, His reputation) might not be ridiculed among the Gentiles.

God Delivers and Vindicates His People (2:18–3:21)

The phrase "and afterward" (2:28) divides this part of the book into two major units, 2:18–27 and 2:28–3:21. The first unit includes the Lord's promises to spare Joel's generation and restore to them the produce that the locusts had eaten. The second unit looks beyond the immediate future to the final vindication of Jerusalem. The Day of the Lord, threatened in 2:1–11, would indeed come. For God's people it would be a day of spiritual renewal and divine protection, rather than judgment. However, the nations would experience His vengeance because they had mistreated His people.

A chiastic structure is discernible in the message of 2:19–27.

A) Restoration of crops (v.19a) and cessation of shame (v.19b)

    B) Invasion (threatened in 2:1–11) averted (v.20a)

        C) Praise and exhortation (vv.20b–24)

    B) Effects of locust invasion (cf. ch. 1) reversed (v.25)

A) Restoration of crops (v.26a) and cessation of shame (vv.26b–27)

Within the central unit (C), each of the statements in 2:20b–21b is expanded in 2:21c–24 in consecutive order, producing a paneled structure.

A) Praise: "Surely he has done great things" (v.20b)
B) Exhortation 1: "Be not afraid, O land" (v.21a)
C) Exhortation 2: "Be glad and rejoice" (v.21b)
A) Praise: "Surely the LORD has done great things" (v.21c)
B) Exhortation 1: "Be not afraid, O wild animals . . ." (v.22)
C) Exhortation 2: "Be glad . . . rejoice . . ." (vv.23–24)

God's Pity upon His People (2:18–27)

The verbs of verses 18–19a are better translated in the past tense: "Then the Lord *was* jealous for His land and *took* pity on His people. The Lord *replied* to them . . ." (NIV margin). Apparently the people took heed to Joel's exhortation (2:12–17). In response the Lord took pity on them and promised restoration.

More specifically, the Lord's promises fall into three categories. First, He promised to restore the agricultural produce that the locusts had destroyed (vv.19a, 22–26a). Second, He assured His people that they would not again be an object of scorn among the nations (vv.19b, 26b–27). Third, He announced that the locustlike invaders depicted in 2:1–11 would not invade the land (v.20).

The fulfillment of the Lord's promises would elicit praise from His people (v.26). As in Israel's past, the Lord would work wonders (cf. Exod. 3:20; 15:11; 34:10; Josh. 3:5; Judg. 6:13; Ps. 77:14), demonstrating His powerful presence among His covenant people and His superiority to all other gods (v.27).

Two interpretive problems within verses 18–27 require attention. The first concerns the promise, directed to Joel's generation, that God's people would never again be put to shame (cf. vv.19b, 26–27). No matter when one dates the book, God's people subsequently suffered great shame at the hands of the Gentiles. How, then, can this divine promise be harmonized with later historical developments?

Perhaps the best solution is to understand the promise as implicitly conditional. Because of its repentant spirit Joel's generation would not experience humiliation at the hands of the Gentiles. Each successive generation would also be kept from such shame *if* it sustained the same kind of loyalty. Thus, as Allen observes, the Lord's words express "divine desire" and are "an implicit wish that the people for their part may ever be mindful of their obligations in return."[20] Of course, apart from the transformation promised in conjunction with the new covenant (cf. Deut. 30:6; Jer. 31:33–34; Ezek. 36:24–30), no such loyalty is possible. Only when Israel experiences this transformation (cf. Rom. 11:25–27) will the promise of verses 19b, 26–27 be fully and permanently realized.

A second problem concerns the translation of verse 23. Some suggest that the phrase "the autumn rains in righteousness" be translated "the teacher for righteousness" (NIV margin, NASB margin). Many proponents of this view then understand this as a promise of an eschatological teacher, identified by some with the Messiah. However, others understand this as a promise of the renewal of God's blessing in the form of rain (NIV). Support for this view comes from the last line of the verse, where the debated word *môreh* appears again, here with the clear meaning "autumn rains" (cf. also its use in Ps. 84:6).[21] The phrase "in righteousness" would then mean "according to what is just/proper," that is, in harmony with the covenantal principle that God rewards obedience with agricultural blessing. A mediating view translates the phrase "that which gives instruction in righteousness."[22] In this case, the renewal of rain (and agricultural blessing generally), being an outward sign of God's restored relationship to His people, is that which instructs in righteousness.

God's Vindication of His People (2:28–3:21)

For the most part, this section continues the divine speech recorded in 2:19–27, as the first-person pronouns in 2:28–30; 3:1–8, 12–13, 17–21 indicate. Observations by the prophet (2:31–32; 3:14–16) and a call to war (3:9–11) are interspersed

---

[20]See Allen, *Joel, Obadiah, Jonah, Micah,* p. 96, who cites Deut. 5:29 as an instructive parallel text.

[21]Proponents of the first view point out that *môreh* has the article in the first instance but not the second, perhaps indicating a distinction in referents. Some explain this apparent repetition of *môreh* as wordplay based on homonyms. Others eliminate the wordplay altogether by emending the second *môreh* to *yôreh,* which also means "autumn rains" and is found elsewhere in combination with "spring rains." This emendation has some Heb. manuscript support.

[22]Cf. Patterson, "Joel," p. 254.

with the divine speeches. In this section the Lord promised His people spiritual renewal (2:28–29) and deliverance from their enemies (2:30–32). The Day of the Lord would bring judgment upon the nations and vindication for God's people (3:1–21).

2:28–32. In conjunction with the Day of the Lord (cf. v.31), the Lord would pour His Spirit upon all people (v.28). Verses 28b–29 limit "all people" to all classes of people within Judah. The threefold use of "your" (referring to the people of Judah; cf. 2:18–19a) indicates this restriction, as well as parallel passages that prophesy the same event (Ezek. 39:29; Zech. 12:10). All inhabitants of Judah, regardless of gender, age, or social status, would experience this outpouring. The recipients of the Spirit would exercise prophetic gifts, fulfilling Moses' desire that "all the LORD's people" might prophesy under the control of God's Spirit (Num. 11:29).

Signs of judgment would also accompany the Lord's Day (vv.30–31). Blood, fire, and smoke all suggest warfare, while darkness symbolizes judgment. The reference to the moon turning to blood (v.31a) is a poetic description of its being darkened (cf. the parallel line, "The sun will be turned to darkness").

While the Lord's Day would mean judgment for some, those calling upon Him would be spared (v.32). In this context "everyone who calls" refers to the Spirit-energized people (cf. vv.28–29) with whom He chooses to establish a renewed covenantal relationship (v.32b). In Romans 10:13 Paul applies this text, which foresees the physical deliverance of the inhabitants of Judah, to the spiritual salvation of both Jews and Gentiles as they respond to the gospel.

On the Day of Pentecost Peter identified the outpouring of the Spirit with the prophecy of verses 28–32 (Acts 2:16, "*this is what* was spoken by the prophet Joel"). However, Peter's application of the Joel passage to the events of that day raises questions. The outpouring of the Spirit on Pentecost was not nearly as all-inclusive as that envisioned by Joel. Furthermore, nothing even remotely similar to the cosmic signs of verses 30–31 took place. In what sense, then, did the events of Pentecost fulfill Joel's prophecy? In answering this question, one must remember that Peter was anticipating the soon return of Christ in response to national repentance on the part of the Jews (cf. Acts 3:19–21). Only later did Peter become fully aware that the Jewish nation, represented by its leaders, would remain unresponsive to the gospel (Acts 4:1–21) and that the Gentiles would be incorporated into God's program (Acts 10). When Peter saw the outpouring of the Spirit, he reasoned correctly that the eschatological program prophesied by Joel was being set in motion. However, Jewish unbelief resulted in the suspension of the prophecy's complete fulfillment. The full realization of Joel's vision awaits a future day when, following the salvation of God's chosen ones among the Gentiles, Israel turns back to the Lord (Rom. 11:25–28).

3:1–21. Chapter 3 develops in detail the judgment theme introduced in 2:30–31. In the Day of the Lord the relative positions of God's people and the nations would be reversed. In the past the nations had mistreated God's people, even selling many of them into slavery (vv.2b–3). Although the language is general enough (note "my people Israel" in v.3) to include the deportations of both Israel and Judah by the Assyrians (in 722 and 701 B.C., respectively), these verses refer primarily to the exile of Judah in 605–586 (cf. vv.1, 6, 17 and 20–21, where allusion is made to Jerusalem's fall). A day of reckoning would come. The Lord would gather these nations into the Valley of Jehoshaphat and judge them for the way in which they had abused His people (v.2a). The location of this valley, which is mentioned only here and in verse 12, is unknown. Its importance lies not so much in its location as in the meaning of its name ("the Lord judges").

Having announced His intent to judge the enemies of His people, the Lord addressed two of these nations, Phoenicia (i.e., Tyre and Sidon, v.4a) and Philistia (vv.4–8). He challenged the motives behind their hostile actions, suggesting through two rhetorical questions that their cruel deeds were unjustified (v.4a). He announced He would repay them (v.4b) for their greed, exhibited by their robbery of Judah's wealth (v.5) and their sale of God's people to Greek slave traders (v.6). In the future the tables would be turned (vv.7–8). God would restore His exiled people, and they in turn would sell the children of the Phoenicians and Philistines as slaves.

This prophecy may have been fulfilled to some extent in the fourth century B.C. in conjunction with the conquests of Antiochus III and Alexander.[23] However, in the eschatological context of chapter 3, the Phoenicians and Philistines (cf. also

---

[23] Allen, *Joel, Obadiah, Jonah, Micah,* p. 114.

Egypt and Edom in v.19) may be representative of all nations who have opposed God's people. In this case, any literal historical fulfillment of the prophecy merely prefigures the eschatological reality it envisions, namely, Israel's eventual vindication before its enemies and its rise to a position of superiority among the nations.

The judgment announced in verse 2 becomes the focal point of verses 9–16. Unidentified heralds issue a call to war, urging the nations to forge weapons from their agricultural implements and to gather for battle (vv.9–11a). In dramatic fashion the Lord is also summoned to lead His warriors to the battle site (v.11b). The Lord Himself challenges the nations to meet Him for judgment (v. 12), and He then exhorts His warriors to annihilate the wicked nations (v.13). The destruction is compared to harvesting grain with a sickle and to treading grapes in a winepress. Both images suggest the realities of the battlefield, where soldiers are cut down by the sword and corpses are trampled by men, horses, and chariots until the ground is saturated with blood.

Verses 14–16 describe the battle scene in further detail. As a multitude of soldiers assemble in the "valley of decision" (i.e., the Valley of Jehoshaphat), the sky darkens (cf. 2:31) and the Lord emerges from His dwelling place in Jerusalem. His powerful battle cry causes the physical world to shake. As He destroys His enemies, He demonstrates once more that He is the Protector of His people.

For Judah and its capital, Jerusalem, this would mean the dawning of a new era. God's people would know that He dwells in their midst. His presence on Mount Zion would make it inviolable, never again to be desecrated by foreign invaders (v.17). The land of Judah would experience rich agricultural blessings and prosperity (v.18). Wine would be so plentiful that it would seemingly flow down the hills. The seasonal streams would no longer run dry. This abundance of wine, milk (implying the existence of large herds), and water stands in stark contrast to the famine and drought depicted in chapter 1 (cf. 1:5, 10, 18–20). As a symbol of the nation's prosperity and a reminder of its divine source, a stream originating in the Lord's temple would water "the valley of acacias," the location of which is not certain (cf. Ezek. 47:1–12; Zech. 14:8).

By contrast, Egypt and Edom, which here represent all of those nations who mistreated and exploited God's people, would be desolate (v.19). While Judah and Jerusalem would be inhabited forever (v.20), their enemies would pay the consequences for shedding the blood of God's people (v.21).

The NIV translation of verse 21 suggests the Lord would forgive Judah/Jerusalem for its bloodshed. However, such sins on the part of Judah/Jerusalem are not mentioned elsewhere in the book. Moreover, verse 19 foresees God's judgment upon those who have shed the innocent blood of His people. Therefore, verse 21 is better translated, "I will avenge their blood [i.e., the blood of His people shed by the nations] which I have not avenged" (NASB) or "Shall I allow their bloodshed [i.e., the bloody deeds of the nations perpetrated against God's people] to go unpunished? No I will not."[24]

THEOLOGY

Summary

The Lord disciplined His people severely by sending a locust plague that destroyed the land's agricultural produce. This locust invasion was a warning that the nation would soon experience the judgment of the Lord's Day. Only national repentance could stem the tide. In response to the repentant nation, the Lord announced He would spare His people, restore the crops eaten by the locusts, and never again make them an object of scorn. Looking beyond the immediate future, the Lord promised to renew His people spiritually and judge the nations for their mistreatment of Israel. The Lord would dwell in Jerusalem forever, protecting it from enemies and assuring the surrounding land of blessing and prosperity.

Analysis

The Day of the Lord

The theme of the Day of the Lord plays a prominent role in Joel's vision of the future. He portrayed this day, first and foremost, as one of divine judgment through battle (cf. 1:15; 2:1–11, 31; 3:14). Judah's relationship to this day depends on its spiritual condition. In the first half of the book the approaching Day of the Lord threatens the very existence of disobedient Judah (1:15; 2:1–11). However, through repentance Judah

---

[24] On the latter, see ibid., p. 117.

escaped this judgment. For God's people the Day of the Lord becomes one of spiritual renewal and deliverance, while the hostile and guilty nations take their place as objects of the Lord's wrath.

God's Position and Roles

God's sovereignty is readily apparent in the Book of Joel. He controls locusts (2:25), fearsome locustlike military forces (2:1–11), and the fate of nations (3:1–21). The entire cosmos reacts to His angry presence (3:15–16). According to Joel, the Lord is a mighty warrior who leads armies (2:11), issues terrifying battle cries (3:16), and annihilates His enemies (3:13). As a warrior-judge, He metes out appropriate justice (3:7–8, 21) to those who are guilty.

God and His People

Though God disciplined His people (1:2–20) and even threatened them with severe judgment (2:1–11), He still held out the possibility of restoration through repentance (1:14; 2:12–17). The grace, compassion, devotion, and mercy that He had shown Moses' generation were still available to the postexilic community (2:13).

Unlike most of the prophets, Joel never specified the nature of the people's sins. Again, unlike other prophets, he emphasized the cultic aspects of repentance rather than its socioeconomic forms of expression (cf. 1:14; 2:13b, 15–17). Nevertheless, for Joel repentance was not mere religious hocus-pocus but, rather, involved a genuine change of attitude (2:12a, 13a).

God's zeal for and devotion to His people are especially prominent in the second half of the book (cf. 2:18). The Lord would reverse the effects of His disciplinary judgment, transforming curse into abundant and lasting blessing (2:19, 22–26). His powerful deeds, like those of the Exodus period (2:26), would be revelatory, giving His people a fuller understanding of His nature and of their relationship to Him (2:27).

The future would be bright for God's people. The Lord would someday pour His Spirit out upon the whole nation (2:28–29). He would also vindicate them before their enemies and avenge the atrocities that they had endured (3:1–16). The Zion ideal would be finally and fully realized, as God's presence within the Jerusalem temple (3:17, 21b) would assure protection for the city (2:32; 3:16b, 17b) and blessing for the entire nation (3:18).

3

AMOS

INTRODUCTION

Date

According to the book's heading, Amos was a contemporary of Kings Uzziah of Judah (ca. 792–740 B.C.) and Jeroboam II of Israel (ca. 793–753). By mentioning only Uzziah and Jeroboam and omitting any reference to their predecessors, the heading may point to the period of their independent reigns. If so, then one may date Amos's prophecy to the period 767–753, when the independent reigns of these two kings overlapped.[1] Unfortunately, it is impossible to be more specific about the book's date. Even though the heading states that Amos prophesied "two years before the earthquake," the precise date of this event is not known.[2]

Unity

Many deny the authenticity of portions of the book. In particular, the oracles against Tyre (1:9–10), Edom (1:11–12),

[1] Jeroboam was a coregent with Jehoash from 793 to 782 B.C. and ruled independently from 782 to 753. Uzziah was coregent with Amaziah from 792 to 767 and ruled independently from 767 to 740. See Edwin R. Thiele, *The Mysterious Numbers of the Hebrew Kings*, rev.ed. (Grand Rapids: Zondervan, 1983), p. 217.

[2] At Hazor there is archaeological evidence for an earthquake in the eighth century B.C., although precise dating is impossible. See Philip J. King, *Amos, Hosea, Micah: An Archaeological Commentary* (Philadelphia: Westminster Press, 1988), p. 21.

and Judah (2:4–5); other references to Judah (see, e.g., 6:1); the so-called doxologies (4:13; 5:8–9; 9:5–6); the biographical narrative of Amos's encounter with Amaziah (7:10–17); and the messages of salvation (9:8b, 11–15) have been regarded as later editorial insertions.

Scholars have questioned the originality of the Tyre and Edom oracles on historical and form-critical or literary grounds. For example, Wolff points to structural differences between these oracles and the others in chapters 1–2.[3] He also contends that both oracles reflect the exilic period.[4] However, Shalom Paul demonstrates the literary unity and artistry of Amos 1–2 in its canonical form, in the process exposing the methodological weaknesses of the form-critical approach that denies this unity.[5] The historical allusions in the oracles are too vague to be used for dating purposes. Keith Schoville has even proposed that the events in question are best explained against the background of Jehu's reign in the ninth century B.C.[6]

The oracle against Judah has been denied to Amos on literary grounds. For example, Wolff draws attention to its formal variations from the other oracles and to its so-called Deuteronomic style, which he associates with a supposed Deuteronomic school that worked much later than the time of Amos.[7] However, Paul shows that such arguments have been pressed too far, even if one assumes the existence of a distinct Deuteronomic style characteristic of a Deuteronomic school.[8] The structure and language of the oracle are not determinative for dating. In fact, the oracle contributes in a powerful way to the rhetorical purpose of its context.[9]

Since Amos was commissioned to prophesy to Israel, not Judah (cf. 7:15), some scholars regard the book's other references to Judah as later insertions as well.[10] Admittedly, it is

[3]Hans W. Wolff, *Joel and Amos,* trans. Waldemar Janzen, S. Dean McBride, Jr., and Charles Muenchow (Philadelphia: Fortress Press, 1977), pp. 139–40.
[4]Ibid., pp. 158–60.
[5]Shalom M. Paul, "A Literary Reinvestigation of the Authenticity of the Oracles Against the Nations of Amos," in *De la Tôrah au Messie,* ed. J. Dore, P. Grelot, and M. Carrez (Paris: Descleé, 1981), pp. 189–204.
[6]Keith N. Schoville, "A Note on the Oracles of Amos Against Gaza, Tyre, and Edom,"*Supplements to Vetus Testamentum* 26 (1974): 55–63.
[7]Wolff, *Joel and Amos,* pp. 139–40, 163–64.
[8]Paul, "Authenticity," pp. 194–96.
[9]Ibid., pp. 196–97.
[10]Wolff, *Joel and Amos,* p. 112.

unlikely that Amos would have addressed northerners as "the *whole* family . . . brought up out of Egypt" (3:1) or as those "who are complacent in *Zion*" (6:1). Indeed, these words do appear to be later adaptations of Amos's original message to a southern setting. However, why must such adaptations be attributed to an editor? Is it not possible that Amos himself made adjustments when he returned to his homeland? Like other eighth-century prophets, he may have wanted to warn Judah that judgment would fall on them as well if they insisted on following in Israel's sinful footsteps (cf. Hos. 4:15; Mic. 1:5–16; 6:16).

Some consider the doxologies to be later additions because they supposedly fit awkwardly in their contexts and exhibit advanced theological concepts characteristic of a later period. However, Thomas McComiskey exposes the methodological weaknesses that lead to this conclusion and shows that the doxologies can be harmonized stylistically and thematically with Amos's message as a whole.[11]

Because it seemingly interrupts the series of visions and speaks of Amos in the third person, the biographical account of 7:10–17 has been labeled an addition by some. While its function within its context can be readily explained (see analysis below), the third-person references do seem to point to an author other than the prophet. Elsewhere in the book, including accounts of personal experiences (cf. 7:1–9; 8:1–3; 9:1–4), the prophet speaks of himself in the first person. Perhaps this account was included in the book by the same individual who gave the book its heading. Possibly he was a disciple of the prophet and an eyewitness of the events at Bethel.[12]

Many have rejected the originality of the concluding salvation message, arguing that it is inconsistent with the book's heavy emphasis on unconditional judgment and that it reflects an exilic or postexilic viewpoint. However, this juxtaposition of certain judgment and just-as-certain salvation has numerous parallels in prophetic literature, is consistent with Moses' view

[11]Thomas E. McComiskey, "The Hymnic Elements of the Prophecy of Amos: A Study of Form-Critical Methodology," in *A Tribute to Gleason Archer*, ed. Walter C. Kaiser, Jr., and Ronald F. Youngblood (Chicago: Moody Press, 1986), pp. 105–23. See also McComiskey, "Amos" in *The Expositor's Bible Commentary*, ed. Frank E. Gaebelein (Grand Rapids: Zondervan, 1985), 7:272–74.

[12]McComiskey recognizes this possibility as well. See "Amos," p. 271.

of Israel's future (cf. Deut. 30:1–10), and has ancient Near Eastern parallels.[13] This future hope of restoration finds its theological basis in God's unconditional promises to Abraham and David, to which Amos alludes (9:11, 15). The references to David's "fallen tent" need not presuppose the cessation of the Davidic dynasty, only its relative weakness in Amos's day when compared to the glory of the Davidic-Solomonic period. In the context of the book, the promise of verses 11–12 served as a rebuke to those northerners who had placed their hope in Jeroboam and other leaders in Samaria (cf. 6:1–2; 7:9–17). Though verses 14–15 anticipate a return from exile, the language does not necessarily imply that the people were already in exile. Amos prophesied Israel's exile (4:3; 5:5, 27; 7:11, 17; 9:4, 9–10) and, by also applying one such prophecy to Zion (cf. 6:1, 7), foresaw the same fate for Judah. If the prophet foresaw the Exile, then he could also have anticipated a release of God's people from it.

Structure

The book contains three major sections (chs. 1–2, 3–6, 7–9). Chapters 1–2 include a series of oracles against various nations, culminating in splendid rhetorical fashion with a judgment speech against Israel. The central section includes seven distinct judgment messages (five judgment speeches and two woe oracles). Chapters 3 and 6 correspond in several ways and form a bracket around the section. Though they focus on the destruction of the northern kingdom (3:9, 12, 14; 6:6, 14), both chapters begin with applications of the message to Judah as well as Israel (3:1; 6:1). In conjunction with their judgment announcements both chapters employ the remnant motif in a negative sense (3:12; 6:9–10). In denouncing the sinful people, both emphasize arrogant complacency (3:11; 6:1–3, 8, 13), social injustice and oppression (3:9–10; 6:3, 12), and luxurious living (3:12, 15; 6:4–6). The section begins with a reference to the Exodus, the event that set Israel's salvation history in motion (3:1), and ends with the reversal of the most recent event in that history (6:14; cf. 2 Kings 14:25).

[13] See John B. White, "Universalization of History in Deutero-Isaiah," in *Scripture in Context*, ed. C. D. Evans, W. W. Hallo, and J. B. White (Pittsburgh: Pickwick Press, 1980), pp. 182–86.

A series of visions (7:1–9) marks the beginning of the third major section. These visions are supplemented by other visions (8:1–3; 9:1–6) and additional material (7:10–17; 8:4–14). With its reference to God's discriminating judgment, the speech of 9:7–10 provides the transition to the concluding salvation message (9:11–15). Literarily this concluding message corresponds in several respects to key verses in chapter 7. Chapter 7 ends with Israel exiled from its land (7:17), while chapter 9 ends with them permanently restored to it (9:15). Terms used to describe Israel's judgment in 7:9 reappear in 9:11–15. Though the high places of Isaac would be "destroyed" (*šāmēm*, 7:9), the "ruined" (*šāmēm* again) cities would eventually be rebuilt (9:14). Though the Lord would "rise" (*qûm*) against Jeroboam with a sword (7:9), He would "restore" (again *qûm*) David's dynasty (9:11). These contrasts provide a thematic framework for this last section of the book.

ANALYSIS

The Heading to the Prophecy (1:1)

In addition to identifying the author and date of the prophecy, the book's heading testifies to the genuine character of Amos's call and message. Amos had been a sheep breeder by profession, not a prophet (cf. also 7:14–15). That such an individual would suddenly leave his occupation and homeland in Judah and embark on a prophetic ministry in hostile territory (cf. 7:10–17) demonstrated the reality of his divine call. The earthquake that occurred two years after Amos's prophecy legitimized his message as well. Since earthquakes were frequently associated with the Lord's theophanic appearance as a warrior (e.g., Judg. 5:4; 2 Sam. 22:8; Ps. 77:18; Isa. 13:13; 24:18; 29:6), the earthquake mentioned in the heading could be taken as a sign of the Lord's approach and as verification of Amos's warning of imminent judgment (cf. 4:12–13; 8:8; 9:1, 5).

Judgment Oracles Against Various Nations (1:2–2:16)

Introductory Matters

Structure and style. Following an introductory heading (1:2), the opening section of Amos's prophecy contains a series of eight judgment speeches against individual nations: Syria (vv.3–5), Philistia (vv.6–8), Tyre (vv.9–10), Edom (vv.11–12), Ammon (vv.13–15), Moab (2:1–3), Judah (vv.4–5), and Israel (vv.6–16). For an outline of these speeches, see the Introduction, p. 11. The arrangement shows careful design, moving from outright foreigners (Syria, Philistia, Tyre) to blood relatives (Edom, Ammon, Moab) to Judah and then culminating with the northern kingdom, Amos's primary target group. By delaying his message against the north, Amos would have gained the Israelites' attention. They would have listened with delight to his message of doom for the surrounding nations, not realizing the prophet would quickly lower the boom upon them.

Each of the eight oracles is introduced with a set formula, " 'This is what the LORD says: 'For three sins of [name of city/nation], even for four, I will not turn back (my wrath).' '" The numerical formula x/x + 1 (here 3/4), a fairly common literary technique in Old Testament lists, recurs in the oracles. Usually such graduated numerical sayings are followed by a list of items corresponding to the second number. In this way the final item in the list can be emphasized (cf. Prov. 30:18–19, 29–31). However, with the exception of the oracle against Israel, Amos's numerical sayings are followed by no such lists. In each of the first seven oracles the list of specific crimes never exceeds two. Only in the case of Israel are four crimes specified, namely, the social/judicial oppression of the poor, sexual promiscuity, drunken carousing at the expense of debtors (in combination with cultic violations), and ingratitude for the Lord's gracious provision of spiritual leaders. By enumerating only Israel's sins in the expected fourfold manner, Amos emphasized the extent of the nation's guilt vis-à-vis her neighbors. When filling out fourfold lists of national sins, one could complete Israel's list before the second or third sin of her various neighbors could be identified. Thus Amos's use of truncated or abbreviated lists in the first seven oracles, which initially seems inexplicable, proves to be an effective rhetorical device that highlights the relative corruption of the northern kingdom.

The oracle against Israel is unique in other respects as well. The basic accusation (2:6–8) is expanded by a recital of the Lord's gracious acts on Israel's behalf (vv.9–11), which stands in stark contrast to Israel's ingratitude (v.12). The description of judgment also differs in Israel's case. Rather than sending fire (the form of judgment in the first seven oracles), the Lord would crush Israel, just as the wheels of a wagon weighted down with grain crush everything over which they roll (v.13). The variation from the stereotypical pattern of the earlier oracles emphasizes the degree of Israel's guilt. Israel's uniquely excessive sin demanded a unique punishment.

The nations' crimes. Each of the oracles uses the word *peša'* (translated "sins") to describe the crime(s) of the nation with which it is concerned. This suggests that the sins of the various nations shared the same basic character. The essential idea of *peša'* is rebellion against authority (see, e.g., 1 Kings 12:19; 2 Kings 1:1; 3:5, 7; 8:22). Thus Amos viewed the nations' sins as acts of rebellion against the sovereign Lord. For Judah and Israel this rebellion found expression in their refusal to live by the requirements of the Mosaic covenant (cf. 2:4, 6–8). The precise nature of the other nations' rebellion is uncertain and has been debated among scholars.

Some propose that, in attacking Israel, the nations defied God. Israel is in view in the oracles against Syria and Ammon (note "Gilead" in 1:3, 13), but none of the other oracles clearly refers to God's people. In fact, the oracle against Moab in no way concerns Israel. Here the Moabite king is denounced for an atrocity committed against Edom (2:1). Something wider in scope than crimes against Israel must be in view in these oracles.

It is best to set the crimes of the nations against the background of God's mandate to Noah, recorded in Genesis 9. In verses 5–7 God prohibits shedding the blood of another person because such an assault is an attack upon the image of God Himself. It also violates God's mandate to be fruitful and multiply. Most, if not all, of the crimes mentioned in Amos 1:3–2:3 can be placed under the heading of disrespect for human life or the image of God in human beings. They include cruel, relentless slaughter (of even helpless women and unborn children), slave trade for economic profit, and desecration of a human corpse. In principle, these acts violate on a national level the Noahic mandate.

Isaiah, Amos's eighth-century contemporary, made a similar extension and application of the mandate to Noah. In the introduction to his prediction of universal judgment in chapters 24–27, he announced that God's curse would come upon the earth's inhabitants because they had broken the everlasting covenant (24:4–6), probably a reference to the arrangements established by God in Genesis 9 to govern His relationship with people. In Isaiah 26:21 God specified that the human crime involved bloodshed.

It is likely that both Amos and Isaiah viewed the universal covenant with Noah (and humankind) against the background of ancient Near Eastern treaties. These treaties carried with them curses, which would be actualized against a disobedient party. Both Amos and Isaiah described the Lord's judgment against the nations as the actualization of a curse. Isaiah specifically identified judgment with "curse" (Isa. 24:6). Amos, though not as direct, pictured the coming judgment as bringing widespread drought (1:2; cf. Isa. 24:4, 7), which is a common element in ancient Near Eastern curse lists, including those recorded in the Bible (e.g., Deut. 28:23–24), and in secular treaties. For example, a curse in the Aramaic Sefire treaty, dating to the eighth century B.C., states, "Seven years shall blight come upon the face of its land, and no grass shall sprout, so that nothing green can be seen and its vegetation does not appear."[14] In the vassal treaties of the Assyrian king Esarhaddon, who lived in the seventh century B.C., a curse reads: "Just as rain does not fall from a copper sky, so may there come neither rain nor dew upon your fields and meadows, but let it rain burning coals in your land instead of dew."[15] Against this background it is likely that Amos's audience would have associated the language of Amos 1:2 with an accursed condition resulting from breach of covenant.

To summarize, in the oracles of 1:3–2:16, Amos accused the nations of rebelling against the covenant demands of their sovereign Lord. Judah and Israel had violated the Mosaic Law. The other nations had violated, at least in principle, the ideal expressed in the Noahic mandate, which Amos (and Isaiah) viewed against the background of the ancient Near Eastern treaty model. In the coming judgment the covenant curses, epitomized in 1:2 by drought, would be actualized against the disobedient parties.

[14]James Pritchard, ed., *Ancient Near Eastern Texts Relating to the Old Testament*, 3d ed. (Princeton: Princeton University Press, 1969), p. 660.
[15]Ibid., p. 539.

Commentary

1:2. Amos's message begins with a bang, startling the reader with its vividness and intensity. Roaring like a fierce lion, the Lord emerges from His earthly residence in Jerusalem to take vengeance upon the nations. In its ancient Near Eastern context this word picture depicts the Lord as a mighty warrior-king who is capable of annihilating His enemies. Ancient rulers would often compare themselves to raging lions in order to emphasize their courage and prowess on the battlefield.

Before the Lord's thunderous, lionlike roar all nature, including even the most fertile regions (epitomized by pasture lands and the luxuriant Carmel region), withers in fright. As noted above, the full import of this imagery can be appreciated only against the background of ancient Near Eastern culture, where drought frequently appears in formal curse lists as a punishment for violating legal agreements.

1:3–5. Syria was guilty of extreme cruelty in warfare. Their treatment of the Gileadites is likened to threshing with sharp iron instruments (v.3). The Old Testament (e.g., 2 Kings 13:7; Isa. 41:15; Mic. 4:13; Hab. 3:12) and ancient Near Eastern literature use threshing as a figure for thorough and harsh military conquest. Gilead, the victim of Syria's militarism, was inhabited by Israelites. Many believe that the conquests of Hazael in the last third of the ninth century are in view (cf. 2 Kings 8:12; 10:32–33; 13:3–7), especially since the biblical account uses the threshing figure to describe his victories (2 Kings 13:7). Others contend that the invasion referred to in Amos 1:3–5 occurred later, during the reign of Jeroboam II, Amos's contemporary.

As in all the oracles but the last, fire appears as the instrument of the Lord's judgment (v.4a). In the Bible and the ancient Near East, fire often symbolizes the destructive power of a royal military leader. For example, Numbers 21:27–30 records an ancient poem that compares the Amorite ruler Sihon and his forces to a destructive fire. The Assyrian king Sennacherib, a contemporary of Isaiah's, referred to himself as the "flame that consumes the insubmissive."[16] According to an

---

[16]Daniel D. Luckenbill, *Ancient Records of Assyria and Babylonia,* 2 vols. (Chicago: University of Chicago Press, 1926–27), 2:115, par. 233.

Egyptian text, Ramses III (ca. 1198–1166 B.C.) was like a "consuming fire when it has found thick brush."[17]

The oracle mentions various details of the coming judgment. First, the Lord would burn down the royal palaces and fortresses (v.4b). The names Hazael and Ben-Hadad stand for the Syrian dynasty in general. Hazael founded the ruling dynasty in the ninth century B.C. (2 Kings 8:7–15) and was succeeded by his son, Ben-Hadad (2 Kings 13:3, 24).

Second, the Lord would break down the Syrian capital city's defenses, represented here by the gate (lit. "the bar of the gate"), and destroy the king (v.5). The "Valley of Aven" (lit. "valley of wickedness") is a derogatory reference to Syria. It stands parallel to "Beth Eden" (lit. "house of pleasure/luxuriance"), which carries an ironic, sarcastic tone here. The luxuriant house, perhaps referring to the royal palace, was about to be destroyed by fire (v.4).

Finally, the Lord would send the Syrians into exile (v.5). Kir, according to 9:7, was the Syrians' place of origin. By resolving to send them back to Kir, the Lord threatened to reverse their entire history. This punishment would be comparable to sending Israel back to Egypt (cf. Deut. 28:68). This message of judgment was fulfilled in ca. 732 B.C., when the Assyrians conquered Damascus, killed its king Rezin, and deported its people to Kir (2 Kings 16:9).[18]

1:6–8. The Lord addressed the Philistines next, mentioning all five of their major cities except Gath (cf. 1 Sam. 6:17; but see 6:2). The Lord accused the Philistines of exploiting human life for commercial purposes and profit (v.6). They had engaged in slave trade, selling to Edom whole communities of men, women, and children, whom they had captured in raids or warfare. Philistia's judgment, like that of Syria, would involve destruction of her fortified cities and rulers (vv.7–8). According to verse 8, the Lord's judgment would be as thorough as the Philistines' slave sales had been, destroying the very last of the Philistines.

1:9–10. Tyre, a major Phoenician trading center, had also

[17] William F. Edgerton and John A. Wilson, *Historical Records of Ramses III: The Texts in Medinet Habu,* vols. 1–2 (Chicago: University of Chicago Press, 1936), p. 47.

[18] For the very limited extrabiblical references to this event, see Wayne T. Pitard, *Ancient Damascus* (Winona Lake, Ind.: Eisenbrauns, 1987), pp. 187–88.

engaged in slave trade. Like the Philistines, the Tyrians had sold entire communities to the Edomites. Tyre's violation of prior treaty agreements with its victims made its crimes even worse.

The text refers to "a treaty of brotherhood" (v.9). In the ancient Near East and the Old Testament, family terminology (father, son, brother) was employed in treaties. Partners in a parity treaty were referred to as "brothers." For example, an agreement between Ramses II of Egypt and Hattusilis of the Hittites states that the two parties were in treaty relation "in order to bring about good peace and good brotherhood." It adds, "While he is in brotherhood with me, he is in peace with me; and I am in brotherhood with him, and I am in peace with him, forever."[19] Biblical examples include 1 Kings 9:13, where the Tyrian king Hiram calls Solomon his "brother," and 1 Kings 20:32–33, where Ahab regards the Syrian king Ben-Hadad as his partner (lit. "brother"), not his "servant."

If Israel was Tyre's victim, verses 9–10 may allude to either the treaty between Ahab and Tyre, which was solidified by marriage (1 Kings 16:31) or the earlier agreement between Hiram and Solomon (1 Kings 5:1–12). However, it is likely that events surrounding Jehu's rise to the throne ended close Israelite-Tyrian relations (cf. 2 Kings 9–10). If so, it is impossible to know the exact historical background of this oracle.

1:11–12. The Lord next moved to blood relatives of Israel, beginning with the Edomites, the descendents of Jacob's brother, Esau. Like Tyre, Edom had violated the trust of its treaty partners and mercilessly attacked them. Many identify Israel or Judah as the victim here because of the phrase "his brother" in verse 11. However, it is probably better to understand the brotherhood terminology in a political, not familial, sense. Support for this view comes from the immediate context, where "brotherhood" is used of treaty relations (cf. v.9). Also the term translated "compassion" in verse 11 is better rendered in this context "his allies" (NIV margin). Of course, if Israel is in view, the use of "brother" would be an effective double entendre. In this case, Edom would be guilty of attacking not only its treaty "brother" but its own flesh and blood as well.

1:13–15. The Ammonites, descendents of Abraham's

---

[19]Pritchard, *Ancient Near Eastern Texts,* p. 199.

nephew Lot (Gen. 19:38), had ruthlessly slaughtered Israelites living in Gilead, refusing to spare even pregnant women. Such brutality in warfare is mentioned elsewhere in the Old Testament (e.g., 2 Kings 8:12; 15:16; Hos. 13:16). The Ammonites hoped to expand their territory through these raids.

The Lord described in detail Ammon's punishment. Ammon's major city, Rabbah, would fall to an invading army. The Lord likened His judgment to a powerful storm. Elsewhere in the prophets windstorms portray figuratively the Lord's destructive attack on His enemies (e.g., Isa. 29:6; Jer. 23:19; Nah. 1:3). Like the lion and fire motifs used in this chapter, the storm imagery, when examined in its cultural context, depicts the Lord as a mighty warrior. Assyrian kings frequently applied similar imagery to themselves. Adadnirari II (ca. 1018–1013 B.C.), for example, boasted, "I blow like the onslaught of the wind, I rage like the gale."[20]

Ammon's defeat would culminate in the exile of its king and other leading officials (v.15). Some have suggested reading "her king" (*malkām*) as "Molech" (NIV margin) or "Milcom," the name of the chief god of the Ammonites (1 Kings 11:5). However, the parallelism with "his officials" militates against this change, as do the references in the immediate context to kings being punished (cf. 1:5, 8; 2:3).

2:1–3. The Lord next accused Moab, another of Lot's descendents, because it had desecrated the tomb of an Edomite king. The Moabites had burned his bones to ashes, the white appearance of which resembled lime (or plaster; note the use of the same Heb. word in Deut. 27:2, 4). Desecration of royal tombs was frowned upon in ancient Palestine and often carried with it a curse. For example, the tomb inscription of the Sidonian king Eshmunazar (fifth century B.C.) states:

> Whoever you are, be you ruler or commoner, let none such open up this resting-place or seek anything in it, for they did not lay anything in it; and let none such lift up the box in which I lie or carry me away. . . . For should any ruler or commoner open up what is over this resting-place, or lift up the box in which I lie or carry me away from this resting-place, may they have no resting-place, may they have no resting-place with the shades, and may they not be

[20]Albert K. Grayson, *Assyrian Royal Inscriptions*, 2 vols. (Wiesbaden: Otto Harrassowitz, 1972, 1976), 2:86, par. 418.

buried in a grave, and may they have no son nor seed to succeed them, but may the holy gods deliver them up to a mighty ruler who shall have dominion over them, so that they may perish. . . .[21]

2:4–5. In this oracle against Judah, Israel's sister nation to the south, the Lord moved one step closer to His ultimate target. He condemned Judah for breaking the Mosaic Law and specifically denounced the worship of "false gods" (lit. "lies"; cf. NIV margin).

2:6–16. Finally the cup of judgment comes around to Israel. As noted above, only here does a fourfold list of sins actually appear (vv.6–8, 12). First, many were guilty of selling the innocent and poor for financial profit (v.6; cf. 8:6). This probably refers to the practice of creditors' selling into servitude those unable to repay loans (cf. 2 Kings 4:1). "A pair of sandals," if taken as a literal bargaining price, indicates that these unfortunate debtors were regarded rather lightly. However, it is possible that land transfer is actually in view (cf. the practice outlined in Ruth 4:7–8). In accomplishing their sales, these creditors abused the judicial system, depriving the poor of the justice due them (v.7a; cf. 5:10, 12). A better translation of verse 7a would be, "They trample upon the dust of the earth that is on the heads of the poor and deny justice to the oppressed." The dust on the heads of the poor either points to their abject condition or suggests a posture of mourning (cf. 2 Sam. 1:2; 15:32). This disregard for the poor blatantly violated the principles laid down in the Mosaic Law, which commanded, "Do not deny justice to your poor people in their lawsuits" (Exod. 23:6; cf. Deut. 15:7–11).

Many Israelite men were guilty of profaning the Lord's name by using "the same girl," the second sin specified here by the Lord (v.7b). The precise meaning of this accusation is unclear. The "girl" has been variously identified as the son's lover or wife, a servant girl, a cult prostitute, or the hostess at a pagan religious meal.[22] If the crime is that of a man's having relations with his daughter-in-law (cf. Lev.18:15; 20:12), the son would be innocent. However, the tone of verse 7 seems to

---

[21]J. C. L. Gibson, *Syrian Semitic Inscriptions,* 3 vols. (Edinburgh: T. & T. Clark, 1971–82), 3:107.

[22]For the final view listed, see Hans M. Barstad, *The Religious Polemics of Amos* (Leiden: E. J. Brill, 1984), pp. 33–36.

implicate both father and son. Though fitting nicely with verse 8, the view that the girl is a cult prostitute is unlikely, since the Hebrew word here translated "girl" never refers elsewhere to a prostitute. Perhaps the exploitation of the lower servant class is in view. Such a crime would fit well in the context of verses 6–8, which emphasize social oppression. However, the term in question need not refer to a low-ranking servant or slave. Also, the reference to profaning the Lord's name favors some type of religious violation such as idolatry.[23] Finally, the hostess view finds support from verse 8, where some type of religious ritual is in view, and especially from 6:1–7, where a pagan religious banquet known as the *marzēaḥ* may be described.[24]

The third sin mentioned here (2:8) involved the exploitation of debtors and the misuse of their property. The sinners stretched out on garments taken as collateral. The language suggests that they slept on, and thus kept overnight, these garments. To keep a pledged garment overnight was expressly forbidden in the Law (Exod. 22:25–27; Deut. 24:12–13). These merciless creditors also drank wine purchased with money acquired through dishonest economic and legal practices or "fines" (NIV). If the altars and temple refer to idolatrous shrines (cf. Hos. 4:13–14), then the violation of the most basic covenant stipulation of all, the first commandment, compounded their sin.

Finally, the Lord condemned Israel's ingratitude, which He contrasted with His gracious acts on the nation's behalf (vv.9–12). The Lord delivered His people from Egypt, led them through the wilderness, and destroyed the powerful Amorites so that Israel might possess the land of Canaan (vv.9–10). The Lord also made provision for the nation's spiritual welfare by raising up prophets and Nazirites (v.11). The Nazirites consecrated themselves to the Lord by a vow for a specified period of time (Num. 6:2–21). This oath included abstinence from fermented drinks. However, the Israelites encouraged the Nazirites to break their vows and commanded the prophets to be silent (v.12; cf. Amos 7:10–17). In so doing, they demonstrated their own lack of commitment to the Lord and their disregard for His Word.

---

[23] Ibid., pp. 17–21.

[24] On the *marzēaḥ* institution, see ibid., pp. 127–42; and King, *Amos, Hosea, Micah,* pp. 137–61.

Following this expanded accusation, the Lord announced His intervention in judgment (vv.13–16). He was about to crush violently the rebellious Israelites, just as a cart filled with sheaves crushes objects over which its wheels pass (v.13). The figurative language refers to Israel's military defeat, which is depicted in verses 14–16. Even the bravest of Israel's warriors would flee for their lives, discarding any weapons or clothing (note "naked" in v.16) that might hinder their retreat. The sevenfold description of the warriors' demise in verses 14–16 emphasizes the completeness of Israel's defeat, as seven often serves as a number of completeness or fullness in Semitic and biblical literature.[25]

Israel's Social Injustice Denounced (3:1–6:14)

These chapters contain a series of judgment speeches directed primarily against the northern kingdom. The structure of chapters 3–4 may be outlined as follows:

I. Judgment sppech against the entire nation (3:1–15)
  A. Call to attention (v.1)
  B. Summary statement (v.2)
  C. Validation of prophetic message (vv.3–8)
  D. Judgment speech proper (focusing on Samaria; vv.9–15)
    1. Accusation (vv.9–10)
    2. Announcement of judgment (vv.11–15)

II. Judgment speech against the wealthy women of Samaria (4:1–3)
  A. Call to attention (v.1a)
  B. Accusation (v.1b)
  C. Announcement of judgment (vv.2–3)

III. Judgment speech against the Israelites in general (4:4–13)
  A. Accusation (vv.4–11)
  B. Announcement of judgment (vv.12–13)

[25] Cf. James Limburg, "Sevenfold Structures in the Book of Amos," *Journal of Biblical Literature* 106 (1987): 219.

The two judgment speeches of chapter 5 include calls to repentance. The elements of each speech are arranged chiastically.

I. Judgment speech against Israel (with calls to repentance; vv.1–17)

    A) Announcement of judgment (in funeral lament form; vv.1–3)

      B) Call to repentance (vv.4–6)

        C) Accusation and announcement of judgment (vv.7–13)

      B) Call to repentance (vv.14–15)

    A) Announcement of judgment (with funeral lament motifs; vv.16–17)

II. Judgment speech against Israel (with call to repentance; vv.18–27)

    A) Announcement of judgment (woe-oracle form; vv.18–20)

      B) Accusation (hypocritical worship; vv.21–22)

        C) Call to repentance (vv.23–24)

      B) Accusation (hypocritical worship; vv.25–26)

    A) Announcement of judgment (v.27)

Chapter 6 includes a woe oracle and a judgment speech. Though addressed to both Jerusalem and Samaria (6:1), the woe oracle focuses on the northern kingdom (note "Joseph" in 6:6).

I. Woe oracle (vv.1–7)
    A. Accusation (vv.1–6)
    B. Announcement of judgment (v.7)

II. Judgment speech (vv.8–14)
    A. Panel one (vv.8–11)
      1. Accusation (v.8a)
      2. Announcement of judgment (vv.8b–11)
    B. Panel two (vv.12–14)

1. Accusation (vv.12–13)
2. Announcement of judgment (v.14)

The Roar of the Lion Signals Judgment (3:1–15)

In a message addressed to the entire nation (Judah included), the Lord reminded His people that special privilege brings with it special responsibility. The Lord had graciously delivered them from bondage in Egypt and chosen them to be His covenant people (vv. 1–2a). However, as the preceding chapter plainly demonstrated (2:4–16), His people had rebelled against His authority and responded with ingratitude to His gracious acts. Consequently they would become the special object of His judgment (v.2b). Rather than making them unconditionally secure, their election had actually made them more accountable to God and vulnerable to His disciplinary acts.

Before describing this judgment in detail (beginning in v.9), Amos drew his audience's attention to some important principles (vv.3–8).[26] Through a series of rhetorical questions the prophet reminded his listeners of the principle of cause and effect (vv.3–6). When two individuals are seen walking together, it is because they have met, perhaps by appointment, sometime prior to that (v.3). The lion's roar indicates it has captured its prey, for otherwise it keeps silent so as not to frighten away a potential victim (v. 4). A bird does not swoop down on a baitless trap, nor does a trap spring up without being tripped (v.5). When the trumpet sounds, signaling an impending battle, people respond in fear (v.6a). When calamity overtakes a city, the sovereign Lord is responsible (v.6b).

Having laid this logical foundation, Amos made his main points in verses 7–8. Just as the related occurrences described in verses 3–6 are inextricably linked by the cause-effect principle, so divine action and revelation are joined. Before carrying out His plans, the Lord reveals His intentions to His prophets (v.7). Consequently the Lord's people should not discount a prophetic (in this case, Amos's) message. Divine revelation and human

---

[26]For literary studies of this section, see Yehoshua Gitay, "A Study of Amos's Art of Speech: A Rhetorical Analysis of Amos 3:1–15," *Catholic Biblical Quarterly* 42 (1980): 293–309; and Shalom M. Paul, "Amos 3:3–8: The Irresistible Sequence of Cause and Effect," *Hebrew Annual Review* 7 (1983): 203–20.

response are also closely related. When the Lord "roars" out His intent to judge, the prophet must announce that message, and the people should respond in fear (v.8).

In the context of chapter 3 the overall purpose of verses 3–8 is to validate Amos's message. The people should expect the Lord to reveal His purposes through His prophets (v.7). When the prophet by necessity speaks (v.8b), the people should fear (v.8a). Israel's failure to recognize these truths, which should have been as self-evident as the observations made in verses 3–6, demonstrated the degree of its spiritual blindness and heightened its guilt.

From a rhetorical standpoint Amos's development of thought is particularly effective. His selection of examples in verses 3–6 is not without purpose. The section begins peacefully enough with the picture of two individuals walking together. All of a sudden the audience is overwhelmed with visions of attacking lions, ensnared birds, and cities under attack. This creates an ominous tone that anticipates the roaring of the "Lion" (v.8; cf. 1:2) in judgment (vv.9–15, esp. v.12).

In a sarcastic and ironic gesture the Lord invited the Philistines and Egyptians, traditional enemies despised by Israel, to observe the social oppression within Samaria (v.9). Even to these pagan nations, who had historically been among Israel's worst oppressors, the degree of social injustice in Israel would be a spectacle to behold. Samaria's fortresses were filled with "plunder and loot" taken from the poor (v.10). The Hebrew text literally reads here, "who hoard *violence and destruction* in their fortresses," emphasizing the means by which the rich gathered their stolen goods.

The announcement of Samaria's judgment (vv.11–15) is filled with irony. Appropriately the storehouses filled with wealth taken by oppressive means (v.10) would themselves be plundered by an enemy army (v.11). The only salvation experienced by Israel, which was expecting a great day of deliverance from its enemies (5:18), would be the preservation of a few individuals from the Lord's judgment (v.12). This "salvation" would actually be like a shepherd's salvaging bits and pieces of a devoured sheep.[27]

The "LORD God Almighty" (lit. "LORD God of Armies")

---

[27] On the wordplay involved here, see Robert B. Chisholm, Jr., "Wordplay in the Eighth-Century Prophets," *Bibliotheca Sacra* 144 (1987): 47–48.

would unleash His military power against Israel, rather than fighting on her behalf (vv.13–14a). Appropriately He would cut off the horns of Bethel's altars (v.14b), a focal point of Israel's hypocritical "worship" (cf. 4:4–5). Since the horns of an altar were a place of asylum for fugitives (Exod. 21:14; 1 Kings 1:50–51; 2:28), their destruction would symbolically indicate that no refuge or asylum was available to these rebels against the Lord's covenant. The Lord would also annihilate their mansions, which symbolized their exploitation of the poor (v.15). The wealthy residents of the northern kingdom were "living like kings," possessing both winter and summer houses "adorned with ivory" (1 Kings 22:39; Jer. 36:22).[28]

Samaria's Wealthy Women Denounced (4:1–3)

The wealthy women of Samaria came under special fire from the prophet. Amos sarcastically called them "cows of Bashan" because they, like the well-known livestock of this district (cf. Deut. 32:14; Ps. 22:12; Ezek. 39:18), were pampered and well fed (v.1a). These women maintained their luxurious life style at the expense of the poor. They demanded that their husbands satisfy their cravings, thus encouraging them to continue their exploitation of the poor, whose stolen money and land was necessary to support such extravagance (v.1b).

The "Sovereign LORD" solemnly vowed by His own holy character that He would send these transgressors into exile (vv.2–3). The divine title used here is carefully chosen. "Sovereign" (v.2) and "husbands" (v.1) translate the same Hebrew word. Ironically, while these women demanded drinks from their "lords," the true Lord was announcing their destruction.

The precise meaning of verse 2b is uncertain. Paul, after a careful study of the terms involved, translates, "And you will be transported in baskets and the very last one of you in fishermen's pots."[29] In this case, the background of the imagery is not fishing per se but the packing and transporting of fish to market.[30]

---

[28] For archaeological evidence for winter and summer houses and for the use of ivory, see King, *Amos, Hosea, Micah,* pp. 64–65, 139–49.

[29] Shalom M. Paul, "Fishing Imagery in Amos 4:2," *Journal of Biblical Literature* 97 (1978): 190.

[30] Ibid., p. 188.

According to verse 3, these women would be led away through gaps in the destroyed city's walls and sent to a foreign land. "Harmon" should probably be changed to "Hermon," a mountain north of Israel in the direction of Assyria.

Israel's Obstinance Leads to Judgment (4:4–13)

The next judgment speech, addressed to the nation as a whole (v.12), begins with a series of ironic commands that highlight the people's hypocrisy (vv.4–5). According to Wolff, these verses are a parody of a priestly instruction in which the usual summons to religious pilgrims to enter the sanctuary is given an ironic twist.[31] The people regularly brought their sacrifices to Bethel and Gilgal, traditionally associated with worship and covenant. (On Bethel, see Gen. 12:8; 28:10–22; 35:1–15; 1 Sam. 7:16; 10:3. On Gilgal, see Josh. 4:19–5:10; 1 Sam. 7:16; 11:14–15; 15:21). However, the Lord regarded this as empty religious formalism because the life-style of these "worshipers" contradicted their professed devotion to Him (cf. 5:4–7, 10–15, 18–27). Consequently their religious acts only heightened their guilt by adding hypocrisy to their list of sins (note the commands "sin" and "sin yet more" in v.4). The association of Gilgal with ineffective, hypocritical worship recalls 1 Samuel 15:22–23, where Samuel rebuked Saul for disobediently sacrificing livestock at Gilgal and reminded him that the Lord requires obedience before sacrifice.

Verses 6–11 further heighten Israel's guilt by showing that time after time the nation failed to respond positively to God's discipline. Each of the specific acts of divine judgment corresponds to one of the covenant curses listed in Leviticus 26 or Deuteronomy 28: hunger (v.6; cf. Lev.26:26; Deut. 28:48), drought (vv.7–8; cf. Lev.26:19; Deut. 28:22–24), crop failure (v.9a; cf. Lev.26:20; Deut. 28:22, 40), insects (v.9b; cf. Deut. 28:38), plagues (v.10a; cf. Lev.26:16, 25; Deut. 28:21–22, 27, 35, 59–61), and military defeat (vv.10b–11; cf. Lev.26:25, 33, 36–39; Deut. 28:25–26, 49–57) as thorough as the destruction of Sodom and Gomorrah (cf. Deut. 29:23). Despite God's implementation of these covenant curses, Israel refused to repent, as the recurring refrain "yet you have not returned to me" (vv.6, 8, 9, 10, 11) emphasizes.

Because of Israel's obstinance the time for final judgment

---

[31] Wolff, *Joel and Amos*, p. 218.

had arrived (vv.12–13). "This is what I will do" (v.12) refers either to the disaster announced in the preceding chapter (3:11–15) or to the judgment alluded to in verse 13. Israel must come face-to-face with its God, the sovereign Creator and omnipotent Warrior whose march into battle is accompanied by the darkness of judgment. The phrase "treads the high places [i.e., mountains] of the earth" (cf. Mic. 1:3) pictures God descending in the storm clouds and moving along the high mountain peaks and ridges.

The Necessity of Genuine Repentance (5:1–17)

This next speech begins with a funeral lament comparing Israel to a young woman who has been mortally wounded and left to die (vv.1–2). The reality behind the metaphor is Israel's military defeat, which would decimate its fighting ranks by 90 percent (v.3).

Rather unexpectedly the Lord called Israel to repentance (vv.4–6). On the surface a call to repentance appears to be inconsistent with Amos's heretofore unconditional announcements of judgment. However, elsewhere in the Old Testament one finds that prophecies of apparently unconditional judgment can have an implied conditionality and be averted by repentance (Jonah 3:5, 10; cf. Mic. 3:12 with Jer. 26:17–20).

The basic call (vv. 4b, 6a) is to seek the Lord through repentance, demonstrated by obedience to God's ethical demands (vv.14–15, which correspond to vv.4–6 in the chiastic structure of this speech). The motivation attached to this call is a promise of life. Deliverance from military defeat is in view in this context (cf. vv.3, 6b). The promise recalls the basic covenantal principle that life (defined in terms of prosperity, fertility, and security) results from obedience, while disobedience brings death and curse (Deut. 30:6, 15, 19–20; 32:47).

The prohibitions of verse 5 give the negative side of the command to seek the Lord. To "seek" the Lord meant to reject religious formalism and hypocrisy, symbolized by the cult sites of Bethel, Gilgal, and Beersheba. The appearance of Beersheba, located in Judah, is unexpected in a message directed primarily to the north, but apparently northerners were worshiping there (cf. 8:14). Like Bethel, it had strong connections with patriarchal worship and divine covenantal promises (cf. Gen. 21:33; 26:23–25; 46:1–4).

These prohibitions against religious formalism are motivated by a warning (v.5b). Like all of Amos's prophecies of judgment, this warning of coming judgment has an unconditional tone. However, to take the warning in this way would be inconsistent with the context, which contains calls to repentance and promises of life and deliverance. Consequently the point of verse 5b seems to be this: *If* Israel failed to seek the Lord and reject its religious formalism, then the sites in which it trusted would surely be destroyed. Apart from genuine repentance, judgment was certain, for only the Lord (not religious formalism) could bring deliverance.

Wordplay and irony are prominent in verse 5. The warning about Gilgal's fate is highlighted by alliteration, the *g* and *l* sounds of the name being mirrored in the words *gālōh yigleh*, "will surely go into exile." Since Israel had celebrated and commemorated its entry into the land at Gilgal (Josh. 4:19–24), the threat of Gilgal's expulsion from the land would be highly ironic and forceful. As for Bethel (lit. "house of God"), it would become, ironically, nothing (or perhaps a place of grief (cf. NIV margin).

In verses 7–9 a description of the accused (v.7) stands in contrast to a hymnic-style description of the sovereign Judge (vv.8–9). Many scholars treat verses 8–9 as secondary because seemingly they relate loosely to their context and interrupt the development of the accusation in verses 7a and 10. However, these verses do fit formally and thematically in this context. As noted above, when juxtaposed with verse 7, their descriptive style establishes a formal contrast between the accused and their judge. Word repetition contributes to this contrast, as the word *hāpak*, "turn," appears in verses 7–8. Thematically verses 8–9 focus on the Lord's role as sovereign creator of the universe. In this role He possesses the authority and power to judge the evildoers described in verse 7.

Verses 8–9 include four illustrations of the Lord's sovereignty. He is the creator of the constellations and controls the daily cycle of light and darkness. The Lord has the waters of the sea at His disposal, depositing them as rain upon the earth. Finally, the Lord is fully capable of destroying human fortifications, no matter how strong they may be (cf. 3:10–11).

The accused were guilty of perverting justice (v.7). In their hands justice was like a plant transformed into wormwood, known for its bitter taste (cf. NIV "bitterness"). They had, as it were, hurled justice to the ground and shattered it.

Verses 10–13 expand this accusation. These sinners (v.12a) despised anyone who took a stand for justice or testified honestly in court (v.10; cf. Isa. 29:21; Mic. 3:9). Through the corrupt courts (v.12b) they exploited the poor economically (v.11a) and then used their ill-gotten gain to build extravagant houses and plant fine vineyards (v.11b). The situation had become so bad that the most prudent course of action was to refrain from involvement in legal matters (v.13). To take up the cause of the oppressed would only invite trouble and prove to be futile.

The coming judgment would be perfectly appropriate. These oppressive landowners would have their fine homes and vineyards taken away from them (v.11b; cf. Isa. 5:8–10; Zeph. 1:13). This judgment corresponds to the covenant curse threatened in Deuteronomy 28:30.

Verses 14–15, which correspond to verses 4–6 in the chiastic structure of this speech, contain a call to repentance. The antithetical word pair good/evil (v.14) refers to social justice/injustice, as verse 15 makes clear (cf. also Isa. 1:16–17; Mic. 3:2). To repent by establishing a just society would give substance to an otherwise empty confession. The Israelites claimed that the Lord was with them. If they repented, He truly would be.

The exhortation "Hate evil, love good" (v.15a) stresses that repentance would involve a total commitment to a new way of life. Israel must completely reject evil and express total devotion to good. For a nation characterized by love for hypocritical formalism (cf. 4:5) and hatred for the champions of justice (cf. v.10), this repentance would necessitate a complete reversal of attitudes and life style.

The concluding motivation (v.15b) reminds Israel that God's grace would not be an automatic consequence of repentance. "Perhaps" indicates that God reserves the sovereign right to dispense mercy to whom He wishes (cf. Exod. 33:19). Israel had fallen into religious formalism, which assumed that prosperity would be the automatic result of going through the right motions. Having offered these people the possibility of deliverance in exchange for genuine repentance, the prophet was careful to point out that sinful people, even if repentant, cannot approach the sovereign God with such a presumptuous attitude (cf. Joel 2:13–14; Jonah 3:9; Zeph. 2:3).

An announcement of judgment concludes this speech

(vv.16–17). (The introductory "Therefore" relates back to the accusation of vv.12–13, with the call to repentance of vv.14–15 being parenthetical.) This conclusion, with its portrayal of widespread mourning and lamentation in the Day of Judgment, corresponds thematically to verses 1–2. The references to farmers and vineyards suggest that a major agricultural disaster would occur, probably in conjunction with a military invasion. For wailing to take place in the vineyards would be both appropriate (cf. v.11) and ironic (cf. Isa. 16:10).

The Lord Himself would pass through the nation in judgment (v.17b). The language used here alludes to the Passover account, where the Lord said, "I will pass through Egypt" (Exod. 12:12). Ironically the Lord would treat Israel as He had Egypt. A motif associated for centuries with the judgment of Israel's enemies would now be associated with God's judgment of His own people.

The Day of the Lord (5:18–27)

The prophet introduced his next speech with the word "woe" (v.18a). This term, which has its origin in the funeral lament (cf. 1 Kings 13:30; Jer. 22:18; 34:5, where the same Heb. word is translated "Oh" or "Alas"), suggests impending doom for the addressee. The prophet was, as it were, acting out the addressees' funeral in advance. The addressees in this case were those "who long for the Day of the Lord." They were anxiously anticipating a day when the Lord would intervene militarily on their behalf and give them victory over their enemies. The word translated "long for" (v.18) expresses intense longing. It is used elsewhere of a craving for food (Num. 11:4, 34; Prov. 23:3, 6), water (2 Sam. 23:15), possessions (Deut. 5:21; Prov. 13:4; 21:26; Eccl. 6:2), and a beautiful woman (Ps. 45:11).

However, the Lord was ready to fight against them, not for them. The approaching Day of the Lord would be characterized by darkness (i.e., judgment and disaster), not light (i.e., deliverance and victory) (vv.18b, 20). This judgment would be inescapable, as the vivid simile of verse 19 emphasizes.

The Lord condemned Israel's hypocritical formal religion (vv.21–22), removing in the process any potential objection that Israel's judgment would be unfair. Ironically the Lord's hatred of Israel's hypocrisy (v.21) mirrored the nation's hatred of justice (cf. v.10).

The call to repentance (vv.23–24) is central to the structure of this message. The call contains a negative (v.23) and a positive (v. 24) side. First, Israel must reject its religious celebrations, which were characterized by singing and music. Second, Israel was to establish justice. In an obvious wordplay on Gilgal, one of the nation's prominent religious sites (cf. v.4), the Lord called for justice to "roll" (*yiggal,* from *gālal,* the verbal root of Gilgal) like a stream that never runs dry.

Once more the Lord denounced Israel's emphasis on formal religion (v.25; cf. vv. 21–22). The rhetorical question implies a negative answer. The Lord's point seems to be as follows: Since sacrifices did not characterize our relationship in its initial, relatively pristine period, why do you put such a premium on them now?

Some scholars have seen here (and in the similar statement of Jer. 7:22–23) evidence for the non-Mosaic character of the Pentateuchal sections dealing with sacrificial requirements. For those who hold to the historicity of the Pentateuchal accounts of the origin of the sacrificial system, such an explanation is not possible. It is better to see in verse 25 and in Jeremiah 7:22–23 an intentional overstatement designed to emphasize the *relative* insignificance of sacrifices in Israel's relationship to the Lord.

In addition to being hypocritical, Israel's religion had also been contaminated by pagan elements (v.26). (NIV interprets v.26 as a continuation of the accusation begun in v.25. Another possibility is to translate, "You *will* lift up . . . ," understanding this verse as part of the announcement of judgment that follows in v. 27.) Although the precise meaning of the Hebrew text is uncertain at this point, it appears that Israel was participating in some type of astral worship. (Cf. the phrase "star of your god" as well as the NIV marginal note. The latter offers an alternate translation that sees references in the verse to two Mesopotami-an gods, Sakkuth and Kaiwan.)[32]

This message concludes, as it began (cf. vv.18–20), with an announcement of judgment (v.27). Coming as a mighty warrior, the Lord would send His people into exile beyond Damascus (cf. 4:3; 5:5). The wordplay involving the similar sounding verbs "I will send (you) into exile" (*higlêtî,* v.27) and

---

[32]Cf. Barstad, *Religious Polemics,* pp. 118–26.

"let (justice) roll" (*yiggal*, v.24) effectively highlights Israel's two alternatives. They could either establish justice or experience the judgment of exile.

Judgment upon Israel's Carousing Wealthy Class (6:1–7)

Another woe oracle follows in chapter 6. The prophet specifically addressed the arrogant and self-confident residents of Zion (= Jerusalem) and Samaria (v.1a). Though the northern kingdom was the focal point of Amos's message, this particular oracle was especially applicable to Judah as well. Jerusalem was susceptible to the same kind of arrogance that Samaria exhibited. Many in Jerusalem held to the dogma of Zion's inviolability, which was based on a misunderstanding of the Davidic covenant and divine election. By addressing Zion, as well as Samaria, the prophet emphasized that Jerusalem's complacency was unwarranted if she followed Samaria's moral and ethical example.

Verse 2 is best understood as the boastful words that the leaders (addressed in v.1) spoke to those who came to them (v.1b). These proud leaders felt their kingdoms (i.e., Judah and Israel) were superior to others. Because of this sense of superiority these leaders refused to consider the possibility of calamity overtaking them (cf. "You put off the evil day," v.3a) and continued their oppressive measures (v.3b).

The upper classes enjoyed carousing (vv.4–6). They lounged around on beautiful "beds inlaid with ivory" and ate choice meats (v.4). They fancied themselves to be musicians (v.5), indulged in wine, and anointed themselves with the finest oils (v.6a). The scene described in these verses may be a religious banquet associated with the *marzēaḥ* institution, which is attested elsewhere in the ancient Near East.[33] If so, then the text condemns syncretistic and outright pagan religious activity, as well as carousing at the expense of the poor and oppressed.

This obsession with luxurious living had diverted the attention of the upper class from reality (v.6b). The "ruin of Joseph" refers either to the impending doom of the northern kingdom (cf. "Joseph" in 5:6) or to its socioeconomic disintegration brought about by the upper class's oppressive measures. In either case the reality of Joseph's ruin should have sickened

---

[33]Note that *mirzaḥ*, translated "feasting" by NIV, occurs in v.7. For fuller discussion, see ibid., 127–42; and King, *Amos, Hosea, Micah*, pp. 137–61.

these leaders and prompted them to repent. Their refusal to do so meant that judgment was certain (v.7).

Wordplay, used to highlight the theme of poetic justice, is prominent in the announcement of judgment (v.7). "First" (*rō'š*, v.7) is related to the word translated "foremost" and "finest" (*rē'šît*, vv.1 and 6). Those who considered themselves the first of nations (v.1) and demanded the best oils for their bodies (v.6) would, appropriately, be first in line (v.7) when the exiles were carried off. In verse 7b a series of repeated sounds draws attention to the message of judgment. In the phrase *wᵉsār mirzaḥ sᵉrûḥîm*, "your feasting and lounging will end," note the repetition of *s, r, m,* and *ḥ*. The word translated "will end" (*sār*) sounds like *sᵉrûḥîm*, "lounging," emphasizing that the ones who lounged would be appropriately punished.

Judgment upon the Proud (6:8–14)

The final judgment speech of this second major section of the book begins on a solemn note. Reference is made to the Lord's having sworn by Himself, which, of course, meant that His oath, recorded in verse 8, was certain of fulfillment. Before announcing Israel's judgment, the Lord expressed His extreme displeasure with Israel, thereby establishing her guilt as a basis for judgment (v.8a). The word pair translated "abhor/detest" appeared in 5:10 (NIV "hate/despise") to describe the sinners' attitude toward justice. Here, by way of contrast, the Lord declared what *He* detested, namely, Israel's proud self-confidence, symbolized by its fortresses.

The coming destruction of Samaria would be total (vv.8b–11). The Lord would deliver over to the invaders everything in the city (v. 8b) and smash to bits every house, no matter how big or small (v. 11). Only a handful of survivors would remain (vv.9–10). Those left would be afraid to invoke the Lord's name in prayer, for fear of bringing down a further outpouring of divine wrath.

The second panel of the judgment speech begins with two rhetorical questions that are designed to draw Israel's attention to the absurdity of its actions in the moral and ethical realm (v.12). Israel's perversion of justice (v.12b; cf. 5:7) was as irrational as riding a horse on a rocky cliff or plowing with oxen on a steep precipice (v. 12a). A healthy society is characterized by justice. The perversion of justice introduces a poison that causes society to self-destruct.

The theme of Israel's pride (cf. vv.1–3, 8) reemerges in verse 13. Allusion is made to Israelite military successes under Jeroboam II in which the Transjordanian sites of Lo Debar and Karnaim were conquered.[34] These two places are specified here for their wordplay value. The Israelites rejoiced in their victory over Lo Debar (lit. "nothing"), but this actually amounted to nothing, as the name suggests. Their mentioning Karnaim (lit. "two horns") illustrated their arrogance, for the horn was a symbol of military might (cf. Deut. 33:17).

Israel's success would soon be reversed (v.14). The LORD God Almighty (lit. "the LORD God of Armies") would raise up a nation to oppress Israel throughout the very borders He had allowed Jeroboam II to reclaim (cf. 2 Kings 14:25). The word here translated "oppress" is used frequently in earlier historical accounts, especially Judges, to describe Israel's oppression by foreigners (e.g., Exod. 3:9; Judg. 2:18; 4:3; 6:9; 10:12; 1 Sam. 10:18). This negative side of Israel's history was about to repeat itself. According to the Book of Judges, the Lord "raised up" deliverers to rescue His people from these oppressors (cf. Judg. 2:16, 18; 3:9, 15). However, verse 14 promises no such deliverer. In fact, ironically the word translated "raised up" in Judges is used here of God's "stirring up" the foreign oppressor. This reversal of the Judges pattern may be illustrated as follows:

| Judges 2:18 | Enemy *oppresses* | God *raises up* deliverer |
| Amos 6:14 | God *raises up* enemy | Enemy *oppresses* |

Israel's Judgment and Restoration (7:1–9:15)

A series of three visions introduces this final section of the book. The first two visions are almost identical in structure, but the third exhibits significant differences. The visions may be outlined as follows:

I. First vision (7:1–3)

[34]Cf. Yohanan Aharoni and Michael Avi-Yonah, *The Macmillan Bible Atlas,* rev.ed. (New York: Macmillan, 1977), p. 89.

    A. Introductory formula (v.1a)
    B. Description of scene (vv.1b–2a)
    C. Prophet's intercessory cry (v.2b)
    D. Divine response (v.3)

  II. Second vision (7:4–6)
    A. Introductory formula (v.4a)
    B. Description of scene (v.4b)
    C. Prophet's intercessory cry (v.5)
    D. Divine response (v.6)

 III. Third vision (7:7–9)
    A. Introductory formula (v.7a)
    B. Description of image (v.7b)
    C. Dialogue (question and response; v.8a)
    D. Divine decision (announcement of judgment; vv.8b–9)

A biographical narrative of Amos's encounter with Amaziah follows the introductory visions. This account may be outlined as follows:

  I. Amaziah's Opposition to Amos (7:10–13)
    A. Amaziah's accusation before Jeroboam (vv.10–11)
    B. Amaziah's confrontation with Amos (vv.12–13)

  II. Amos's Response to Amaziah (7:14–17)
    A. Amos's defense of his mission (vv.14–15)
    B. Amos's judgment speech against Amaziah (vv.16–17)

Chapter 8 includes another vision (vv.1–3), followed by a lengthy judgment speech (vv.4–14).

  I. Vision (8:1–3)
    A. Introductory formula (v.1a)
    B. Description of image (v.1b)
    C. Dialogue (question and response; v.2a)
    D. Divine decision (announcement of judgment; vv.2b–3)

II. Judgment speech (8:4–14)
    A. Accusation (vv.4–6)
    B. Announcement of judgment (vv.7–14)

The mood of chapters 7–8 continues into chapter 9, where the prophet sees a vision (note "I saw" in 9:1) of the Lord decreeing Israel's judgment (9:1–6). This announcement of judgment is expanded in verses 7–10, although the reference to the preservation of a remnant in verse 8b gives a hint that ultimately the Lord had a positive purpose in mind for His people. That purpose becomes readily apparent in verses 11–15, which describe the Lord's future restoration of Israel. Chapter 9 may be outlined as follows:

I. Introductory vision (9:1–6)
    A. Introductory description of the Lord (v.1a)
    B. Judgment decree by the Lord (vv.1b–4)
    C. Concluding description of the Lord (vv.5–6)

II. Judgment announcement (9:7–10)

III. Salvation announcement and portrayal (9:11–15)

Three Prophetic Visions (7:1–9)

In the first vision (vv.1–3) the prophet saw the Lord send a locust swarm that destroyed the land's vegetation. This invasion occurred as the later planting (probably involving legumes and vegetables)[35] was sprouting in conjunction with the rains of late winter and early spring. Troubled by the scene, Amos called upon the Lord to forgive His people and withhold this judgment. The prophet appealed to Jacob's (i.e., Israel's) relative weakness. The Lord responded positively to Amos's request and relented from sending the locusts.

Despite the Lord's willingness to relent in response to the prophet's intercessory prayer (vv.2–3), Israel's sin was so great that it again prompted a vision of judgment (vv.4–6). In this second vision the prophet saw a divinely ordained fire that consumed everything in its path, even the deepest sea. Once again Amos objected, appealing to Jacob's inability to withstand

---

[35]Cf. Oded Borowski, *Agriculture in Iron Age Israel* (Winona Lake, Ind.: Eisenbrauns, 1987), p. 34.

such punishment. Because of the urgency of the situation, Amos did not even ask for forgiveness (cf. v.2) but simply pleaded for an immediate cessation of the hostilities being planned by God (note "stop" in v.5). As before, the Lord patiently relented in response to His prophet's prayer.

The third vision (vv. 7–9) differs from the first two in at least three respects. First, the nature of the vision changes, being more like a snapshot than a movie. No longer do we see a scene involving an event and its outcome; rather, we have an isolated picture—of the Lord standing with a plumb line next to a wall (v.7)—carrying symbolic significance.

Second, the vision is followed by a question directed by the Lord to Amos (v.8), not by an objection directed by the prophet to the Lord (cf. vv.2, 5). The Lord asked Amos to identify what he saw. After the prophet answered, the Lord then explained to him the significance of the vision. The Lord had placed a "plumb line" alongside His people (who correspond to the wall in the vision) and found them to be slanted, not perfectly straight, in the moral-ethical realm. Consequently judgment must come with no further delay. The nation's special relationship to the Lord (note "my people," v.8) demanded discipline and could not be used as a basis for false confidence and security (cf. 3:2).

Third, the vision concludes with an announcement of judgment (v.9), rather than a gracious response (cf. vv.3, 6). Israel's places of worship, including "high places" (cf. 2 Kings 17:9, 11) and "sanctuaries" (cf. Amos 7:13), would be destroyed. The Lord Himself would rise up against Jeroboam's house (i.e., the dynasty of Jehu, Jeroboam's great-grandfather) and destroy it. This prophecy was fulfilled a few years later, ca. 752 B.C., when Shallum assassinated Zechariah, Jeroboam's son, and brought Jehu's dynasty to an end (2 Kings 15:8–12).

Amos's Encounter with Amaziah (7:10–17)

This biographical account of Amos's encounter with Amaziah, the priest of Bethel, seemingly interrupts the series of visions (7:1–9; 8:1–3). Nevertheless, the references to Jeroboam (vv.10–11) link it formally with the preceding vision (cf. v.9). The account demonstrates beyond all doubt the necessity of the judgment announced in the surrounding visions (cf. 7:8–9; 8:2–3).

Verses 10–11 record Amaziah's report to Jeroboam concerning Amos's activities. He charged the prophet with conspiring against the crown in the "very heart" of the northern kingdom. The statement "the land cannot bear all his words" refers to the negative impact of Amos's prophecies upon the inhabitants of Israel and to the potentially harmful political effects of his message. As proof of Amos's treason Amaziah reported the prophet's words (apparently in summary form), including his pronouncement of judgment upon the king and his prediction of the nation's exile. The words about exile were an accurate summary of Amos's prophecies in this regard (cf. 5:5, 27; 6:7). However, the report of Amos's prophecy about Jeroboam contained two significant alterations from the divine message of verse 9 (which was presumably repeated by Amos and formed the basis for Amaziah's accusation). First, no mention is made of the Lord's direct involvement (note "I will rise," v.9). Second, the Lord spoke of the *house* (dynasty) of Jeroboam, while Amaziah made the prophecy more pointed (*"Jeroboam* will die," v.11).

Verses 12–13 record Amaziah's words to Amos. Implying that Amos's motivation was primarily monetary, Amaziah commanded him not to preach at the royal sanctuary in Bethel and urged him to return to Judah.

Amos began his response by defending the legitimacy of his mission (vv.14–15). Verse 14a may be translated with the past tense ("I was neither a prophet . . . I was a shepherd" NIV) or the present ("I am not a prophet . . . I am a herdsman" NASB). According to the former, Amos was emphasizing that his prophetic ministry did not originate in a professional context. Rather, he received a special call to leave his vocation as a shepherd and dresser of sycamore-fig trees and become a prophet. If one understands the present tense, then Amos, while functioning as a prophet (cf. 3:8; 7:15b), was denying that he was a prophet in the technical, professional sense suggested by Amaziah (v. 13). Rather, he still viewed himself as a shepherd and dresser of trees.

Because of Amaziah's opposition to Amos's ministry, the Lord pronounced judgment upon the priest and reiterated the fact that Israel would go into exile (vv.16–17). Ironically, the Lord repeated verbatim Amaziah's summary quotation of Amos's warning (cf. v.17b with v.11b; although NIV has "surely" in v.11b and "certainly" in v.17b, the words are identical in the Heb. text.)

The judgment upon Amaziah and his family would be especially severe. His wife would have to resort to prostitution in order to stay alive. For a priest's wife to turn to such a life-style would be especially reprehensible, since priests were forbidden to marry women defiled by prostitution (Lev.21:7, 14). Amaziah's children, like Jeroboam's house (vv.9, 11) would fall by the sword. Amaziah himself would lose his landed property and die in exile ("in a pagan country," lit. "in an unclean land"). In light of a priest's responsibility to distinguish the clean from the unclean (Lev.10:10), the use of "unclean" with respect to Amaziah's eventual place of residence is quite ironic.

A Fourth Vision (8:1–3)

Another vision, similar in structure to the one in 7:7–9, now follows. In this vision the prophet saw "a basket of ripe fruit," which, like the plumb line (cf. 7:7), is an image, not a scene (cf. 7:1–6). The significance of this vision is primarily in its wordplay. The word *qayiṣ*, "ripe fruit," sounds like *qēṣ*, "end," which appears in the statement "The time is *ripe* [*qēṣ*] for my people Israel" (v.2b, lit. "the *end* has come for my people Israel," cf. NASB). Because of this similarity in sound the basket of "ripe fruit" was suggestive of Israel's approaching judgment, which would bring only grief and death in its wake (v.3).

Judgment upon the Dishonest and the Unjust (8:4–14)

This judgment speech is addressed to those who were guilty of socioeconomic dishonesty and oppression. Using language reminiscent of an earlier speech (cf. 2:6–7), Amos denounced those who mistreated the poor and sold debtors for financial gain (vv.4, 6a). This same group also used dishonest practices in the marketplace in order to make a greater profit (vv.5b, 6b). "Skimping the measure" (lit. "making small the ephah" [a dry measure]) resulted in giving customers less than they paid for. "Boosting the price" (lit. "making large the shekel") involved using a shekel (a weight used to measure the purchase price) that was heavier than standard. By then altering the scales (e.g., by bending the crossbar) and mixing chaff with the grain, the merchant was able to increase his profit even more. Of course, such dishonest practices were specifically forbidden in the Mosaic Law (Lev.19:35–36; Deut. 25:13–16).

Proverbs also speaks of the Lord's hatred for such exploitation (e.g., 11:1; 16:11; 20:10, 23).

Perhaps the attitude of these merchants toward holy days (the New Moon and the Sabbath, v.5a) best illustrated their perverse value system. On these days, when commercial activity was suspended, one's thoughts were to be directed toward the Lord. However, these greedy merchants impatiently longed for the day to end so that they might resume their dishonest, though highly profitable, practices.

The Lord would not tolerate this kind of activity within the covenant community, which was to be a model of justice and honesty. He solemnly vowed to bring severe judgment upon the land (v.7). To reinforce this oath He swore by "the pride of Jacob" (NASB). (NIV has "the Pride of Jacob," understanding the referent to be the Lord, viewed as the object of Jacob's pride. However, the usage of the phrase in 6:8 militates against this interpretation. Note also NIV's interpretation of the similar phrase, "pride of Israel," in Hos. 5:5 and 7:10.) Earlier in the book the Lord swore by His own unchanging character (4:2; 6:8a). Here, in biting sarcasm, He swore by something just as permanent and unchanging—Israel's arrogant trust in her own strength (cf. 6:8b).

Verses 8–10 picture this coming judgment as a time of cosmic disturbances and national mourning. The Lord's presence would cause the earth to quake and the sun to disappear. This darkness (cf. 4:13; 5:18–20) would be accompanied by bitter mourning, like the lamentation prompted by the death of an only child (cf. Jer. 6:26; Zech. 12:10).

In desperation Israel would search for a word from the Lord (vv.11–13). However, divine revelation would appropriately cease for those who had rejected God's prophetic word (cf. 2:12; 7:10–13, 16) and turned instead to false gods (v.14).[36]

A Concluding Vision and Message of Judgment (9:1–10)

Amos's series of visions culminated in a picture of violent and inescapable divine judgment (vv.1–6). The prophet saw the Lord decreeing the demolition of a temple and the destruction of the worshipers within it (v.1a). This temple probably symbolizes Israel's formal religious system, which God found

---

[36]The exact identity of the false gods alluded to in 8:14 is not certain. For a thorough discussion of this verse, see Barstad, *Religious Polemics*, pp. 143–201.

polluted by syncretism and social injustice (cf. 4:4–5; 5:5, 21–23, 25–26; 8:14). Rather than protecting Israel from judgment, her religion would be the object of divine wrath.

No one would escape the coming judgment (v.1b). Even if one were to go to the extremities of the universe (the underworld or heaven), the Lord would be able to find that one because the whole world is within His sovereign domain (v.2). Neither high mountains ("the top of Carmel") nor the depths of the sea can provide refuge from the Lord, whose instruments of judgment are seemingly everywhere (v.3; cf. 5:19 for another reference to the Lord's serpent/snake that bites). Not even those carried off to distant lands by conquering armies would find respite from the Lord's anger (v.4).

The vision concludes with a hymnic-style description of the Lord as Warrior and Creator (vv.5–6; cf. 4:13; 5:8–9). His intervention in judgment causes cosmic disturbances and fear. As the sovereign Ruler of the world, He possesses both the power and authority to judge evildoers.

Verses 7–10 are transitional in the structure of chapter 9. While expanding upon the preceding vision of judgment, they also pave the way for the following message of salvation (vv.11–15) by alluding to the preservation of a remnant (vv.8b–9).

Though Israel possessed a special relationship with the Lord (cf. 3:2), there was also a sense in which it was no different from other nations under His sovereign universal rule (v.7). The comparison with the Cushites, a distant people who lived on the edge of Israel's world, demonstrates this. Only the Lord's grace, not any qualities inherent in Israel, gave it special status. The historical movements of the Philistines and Arameans were just as much the result of the Lord's sovereign work as Israel's salvation history. The Israelites were relying on their special relationship to the Lord and their salvation history as guarantees of continued peace and prosperity. However, the Lord made it plain that His sovereignty transcended that relationship and history. He had every right to judge Israel because they, like the other nations, were subject to His absolute authority.

The Lord was keeping a close eye on Israel, ensuring that judgment would be inevitable and inescapable (v.8). However, this judgment would be neither indiscriminate nor final (vv.9–10). The Lord would destroy only sinners, whose self-confident words testified to their spiritual insensitivity (v.10). Verse 9b compares this judgment to separating grain from refuse with a sieve. The sieve in view was coarse-meshed, retaining the refuse and allowing the grain to fall into a container. The righteous remnant corresponds to the grain, while the pebbles symbolize the sinners who would be purged out of the covenant community by the coming judgment.

Israel's Restoration Foreseen (9:11–15)

Having purified the nation, the Lord would restore it to a place of prominence and blessing. He would suddenly transform the Day of Judgment into a day of salvation. (Contrast the use of the phrases "in/on that day" and "the days are coming" in earlier judgment speeches [2:16; 3:14; 8:3, 9, 11, 13] with their use in 9:11, 13.)

The Lord would restore the weakened Davidic dynasty (compared here to a "fallen tent") to its former glory (v.11). Of course, the implication here is that the northern kingdom, Amos's primary target group, would be reunited with the south (cf. Hos. 1:11; 3:5). Like David of old, this revitalized dynasty would subjugate Israel's enemies (v.12a). As elsewhere, Edom is singled out as Israel's archenemy and as an appropriate symbol for all its foes (cf. Ps. 137:7; Isa. 34:5–15; 63:1–6; Lam. 4:21; Obad. 1). In this Day of Restoration Israel would conquer and dispossess Edom (cf. Num. 24:18–19; Isa. 11:14; Obad. 18–21), following the example of David himself (2 Sam. 8:12–14).[37]

In fulfillment of His covenantal promise to David, the Lord would give the restored dynasty widespread dominion (Pss. 2:8; 72:8–11; 89:20–27). The Davidic king would extend his rule

[37] The original Greek text had " 'that the remnant of men and all the nations, over whom my name is called, might seek,' says the Lord who does all these things." Later Greek witnesses filled in the ellipsis after "seek" by supplying an object for the verb (either "me" or "the Lord"). The Old Greek corruption of the Heb. text resulted from taking (1) Heb. *yîrᵉšû*, "possess," as *yidrᵉšû*, "seek" (yod/daleth confusion is attested elsewhere; cf. Eugene C. Ulrich, Jr., *The Qumran Text of Samuel and Josephus* [Missoula, Mont.: Scholars Press, 1978], p. 91); (2) Heb. *'ᵉdôm*, "Edom," as *'ādām*, "humankind, nations"; and (3) "the remnant of all men and all the nations" as the subject of the verb, rather than its object. In Acts 15:16–17 James followed a text form close to one of the secondary Greek forms (note "seek the Lord"). He used the passage as a prooftext for his theological point, namely, that God had always meant to establish a closer and special relationship with the Gentiles.

over the surrounding nations, who were subject to the Lord's sovereign authority and destined to be a part of His theocratic kingdom (cf. 1:2–2:3; 9:7). The phrase translated "that bear my name" literally reads "over whom my name is called." The expression indicates ownership and possession, as 2 Samuel 12:28 clearly demonstrates. There Joab, having begun a campaign against Rabbah, exhorted David to complete the conquest of the city. He warned, "Otherwise I will take the city, and it will be named after me" (lit. "my name will be called over it").

Israel's exiles would also return to their land, rebuild the ruined cities, and enjoy the Lord's agricultural blessings (vv.13–14). The Lord used vivid hyperbole to picture the agricultural abundance of this coming day. Because of the bountiful nature of the crop, the plowman (who worked in November/December) would overtake the reaper of the previous harvest (who normally worked in April/May). The one treading grapes (normally done in late summer) would still be laboring away when sowing time (November/December) arrived (cf. Lev.26:5). The grape harvest would be so plentiful that, perhaps as a result of overflowing vats, the hills would seemingly drip with the fruit of the vine (cf. Joel 2:24; 3:18). In contrast to Amos's sinful generation (cf. 5:11), the restored community would enjoy the fruits of its labors.

In fulfillment of God's promise to Abraham, restored Israel's possession of the land would be permanent (v.15; cf. Gen. 17:8). Never again would the nation experience exile. Though the Lord would remove sinful Israel from "the face of the earth" (*'aḏāmâ*, v.8), He also promised to bring them back again to their "own land" (*'aḏāmâ*, v.15). The repetition of the Hebrew word draws attention to the reversal from exile to restoration.

THEOLOGY

Summary

The Lord, the sovereign Ruler of the universe, would come as a mighty warrior to judge the nations, who had rebelled against His sovereign authority. In particular, He would punish Israel for its breach of covenant, which was especially evident in its dishonest and oppressive socioeconomic dealings, empty religious formalism, and arrogant self-confidence. However, the Lord would eventually restore His people to a place of blessing under the leadership of a revitalized Davidic dynasty.

Analysis

The Lord's Positions and Roles

Amos portrayed the Lord as the Creator of the universe who controls the forces of nature. The Lord formed the mountains (4:13) as well as the heavens (9:6) and their starry hosts (5:8). He controls the wind (4:13), rain (4:6–8; 5:8; 9:6), drought (1:2; 4:6–8; 7:4), and pestilence (4:9–10; 7:1–2). The entire universe lies within His domain (9:2–4).

As Ruler of the universe, the Lord also controls nations. He determines their history and destiny (1:2–2:16; 3:1–2; 9:7, 12). When calamity comes to a city, the Lord is ultimately responsible (3:6), for armies are subject to His bidding (6:14).

The Lord is the Warrior *par excellence* (3:13; 4:13; 5:27; 6:8, 14; 9:5), who can annihilate His enemies. Like ancient Near Eastern warrior-kings, He is compared to a lion (1:2; 3:8), employs fire as an instrument of destruction (1:4, 7, etc.), comes in the storm (4:13; 5:8–9), and causes cosmic disorder and intense fear (8:8; 9:5).

The Lord and the Nations

The Lord held the nations accountable for violating the principles of His mandate to Noah. The Lord viewed the nations' disregard for their fellow humans as covenantal rebellion, which in turn necessitated the implementation of curses (1:2–2:3). Though the nations were objects of divine judgment, the Lord would eventually subject them to the Davidic throne and thereby incorporate them into His theocratic kingdom (cf. 9:12).

The Lord and Israel

Judgment. The Lord's judgment of Israel would be perfectly just, as the accusatory sections of Amos's judgment speeches make clear. Israel had rebelled against the Lord by breaking the principles of the Mosaic covenant. Specifically, Israel's sins included social injustice and economic dishonesty (2:6–7; 3:9–10; 4:1; 5:7, 10–12; 6:12; 8:4–6); luxurious living, often at the expense of the poor (2:8; 3:15; 6:4–6); disrespect for God's servants, especially the prophets (2:11–12; 7:10–17); ingratitude for the Lord's gracious salvific acts (2:9–12); pride and self-confidence (6:1–3, 8, 13; 9:10); religious hypocrisy (4:4–5; 5:21–25); and syncretism and idolatry (5:26; 8:14).

The coming judgment would culminate the implementation of the covenant curses, which were intended to lead Israel to repentance (4:6–12). Though the Lord had exhibited great patience in His dealings with Israel (7:1–6), the time for severe judgment, characterized by widespread slaughter and mass exile, had come. The judgment would be appropriate (note esp. 3:10–11; 5:11; 6:1–7; 8:11–12), inescapable (3:14; 5:5, 19; 9:1–4), and discriminating (9:8–10).

Amos's generation was relying on its elect position and special history as guarantees of future prosperity and success. They anticipated the Day of the Lord, expecting it to be another glorious episode in salvation history. To combat such thinking, the Lord used allusions to their election and covenantal traditions in the midst of His judgment speeches. He made it clear that their special position, because it carried with it grave responsibility, necessitated special punishment (3:1–2). Rather than being exempt from judgment, Israel would be the primary object of the Lord's wrath (1:2–2:16). The approaching Day of the Lord would be a time of divine warfare against Israel, not a repetition of His earlier holy wars on her behalf (5:18–20). In direct contrast to the Abrahamic ideal of numerous offspring, Israel would be reduced to an insignificant remnant (3:12; 6:9–10). The Lord would "pass through" Israel as He had Egypt (5:17), bringing death and destruction with Him. Ironically, Gilgal, a symbol of Israel's occupation of the Promised Land, would go into exile, and Bethel, a symbol of God's presence and promise, would be destroyed (5:5). The recent successes of Jeroboam, rather than marking a return to a Solomonic golden age, would be reversed (6:13–14).

Salvation. Despite the severity of this judgment, God would not abandon Israel forever. The Lord's yearning for His people, seen in His patience (4:6–12; 7:1–6) and exhortations to repentance (5:4–5, 14–15, 23–24), would move Him to preserve a remnant (9:8–9), which would form the basis for a restored and purified community (9:14).

The Lord would fulfill His ancient promises to David and Abraham. He would restore the Davidic dynasty to its former glory and strength, thus providing genuine leadership and protection for the nation (9:11–12). The Davidic ruler would subjugate Israel's enemies and bring the surrounding nations under his control. With its borders safe, Israel would enjoy the Lord's bountiful agricultural blessings and rebuild its cities (9:13–14). In fulfillment of His promise to Abraham, the Lord would never again remove Israel from its land (9:15).

4

OBADIAH

INTRODUCTION

Date

Since the book's heading does not indicate the date of authorship, scholarly opinion on the subject has varied greatly. Some would date the prophecy in the mid-ninth century B.C., arguing that verses 10–14 refer to the Philistine-Arab invasion of Judah during Jehoram's reign (ca. 853–841; cf. 2 Chron. 21:8–20).[1] In this case, the verbal and thematic parallels between Obadiah and Jeremiah 49 may be explained on the basis of the priority of Obadiah.[2]

At least two objections may be raised against this position. First, while an Edomite revolt did occur during Jehoram's reign (2 Kings 8:20–22; 2 Chron. 21:8–10), the Edomites are not mentioned as participating in the invasion of Judah at this time (cf. 2 Chron. 21:16). Second, while the royal palace was looted (2 Chron. 21:17), there is no indication that Jerusalem suffered to the degree reflected by Obadiah 10–14.

Obadiah 10–14 is best explained against the background of the Babylonians' destruction of Jerusalem in 586 B.C.[3] The

[1] See, for example, Hobart E. Freeman, *An Introduction to the Old Testament Prophets* (Chicago: Moody Press, 1968), pp. 140–41.
[2] Cf. Obad. 1–4 with Jer. 49:14–16, Obad 5–6 with Jer. 49:9–10, Obad. 8 with Jer. 49:7, and Obad. 16 with Jer. 49:12.
[3] Cf. Leslie C. Allen, *Joel, Obadiah, Jonah, and Micah* (Grand Rapids: Eerdmans, 1976), pp. 129–30; Carl E. Armerding, "Obadiah," in *The Expositor's Bible Commentary*, ed. Frank Gaebelein (Grand Rapids: Zondervan,

language of the text, with its repeated emphasis on the extremely disastrous nature of the event and its reference to lots being cast over the city, strongly supports this interpretation. Psalms 137:7, Lamentations 4:21–22, and Ezekiel 25:12–14; 35:5, 12–15 specifically refer to Edomite involvement in this calamity. In this case, the verbal parallels between Obadiah and Jeremiah 49 must be attributed to Jeremianic priority or to a common source.

The book should be dated sometime between Jerusalem's fall in 586 B.C. and the destruction of Edom, which it anticipates. The precise date of the latter is uncertain. Probably by the mid-fifth century B.C. Edom had experienced, at least to some degree, the divine judgment prophesied by Obadiah (cf. Mal. 1:3).

Structure

This short prophecy consists of three closely related sections (vv.1–9, 10–14, and 15–21). The first of these is a judgment speech against Edom that emphasizes the Lord's intervention and its results. This section may be further subdivided into three parts (vv.1–4, 5–7, and 8–9).

Verses 1–4 include a heading (v.1a), an introduction that illustrates the Lord's sovereign control over international affairs (v.1b), and a judgment speech proper (vv.2–4). The divine announcements of intervention ("I will make you small," v.2a, and "I will bring you down," v.4b) form an inclusio for this speech. Within this framework, a general summary of the results of judgment (v.2b) and an accusation (vv.3–4a) appear.

Verses 5–7 expand upon verse 2b, describing Edom's demise in greater detail. Verses 5–6 display two corresponding panels, with a shift in the order of elements occuring in the second of these.

I. Panel 1 (v.5a)
   A. Conditional clauses ("If . . . if . . .")
   B. Exclamatory statement about Edom's destruction ("Oh ['êk] . . .")
   C. Rhetorical question ("Would they not . . . ?")

1985), 7:350–51; and C. Hassell Bullock, *An Introduction to the Old Testament Prophetic Books* (Chicago: Moody Press, 1986), p. 260.

II. Panel 2 (vv.5b–6)
   A. Conditional clause ("If . . .")
   B. Rhetorical question ("Would they not . . . ?")
   C. Exclamatory statement about Edom's destruction
      ("But how [*'êk*] . . .")

The placement of the exclamatory statement at the end of the second panel (it was merely parenthetical in the first panel) highlights Edom's demise, which is further developed in verse 7. The structure of the parallelism in verses 5–6 also emphasizes this theme. In the first panel synonymous parallelism is employed in the conditional clauses ("If thieves come to you" // "if robbers in the night"), while the exclamation and the question are single statements. In the second panel, the conditional clause and question are individual statements, while synonymous parallelism draws attention to the exclamation ("But how Edom will be ransacked" // "his hidden treasures pillaged!").

Verses 8–9 appropriately conclude this section of the book by utilizing formal and thematic elements from verses 1–7. As in verses 1–4 the Lord's intervention (v.8; cf. vv.2a, 4) and its destructive results (v.9; cf. v.2b) receive attention. The rhetorical questions (v.8), which continue the style of verses 5–6, and the repetition of *t^eḫûnâ*, "detect" in verse 7 and "understanding" in verse 8, link the conclusion with verses 5–7.

The second major section of the prophecy (vv.10–14) develops in detail the accusatory element of the previous section (cf. vv.3–4a). While verses 3–4a speak in general terms of Edom's pride, verses 10–14 make it clear that Edom would be judged because of the way it had mistreated its "brother."

The major portion of this section contains a series of ironic commands directed to Edom, which reveal exactly how Edom had taken advantage of Judah (vv.12–14). The commands are arranged in two panels.

I. Panel 1 (vv.12–13a)
   A. "You should not *look down* . . . in the day of his misfortune" (v.12a)
   B. "Nor *rejoice* . . . in the day of their destruction" (v.12b)
   C. "Nor *boast* . . . in the day of their trouble" (v.12c)

    D. "You should not *march* through . . . in the day
       of their disaster" (v.13a)

II. Panel 2 (vv.13b–14)
    A. "Nor *look down* . . in the day of their disaster"
       (v.13b)
    B. "Nor *seize* . . . in the day of their disaster"
       (v.13c)
    C. "You should not *wait* . . . to cut down their
       fugitives" (v.14a)
    D. "Nor *hand over* . . . in the day of their trouble"
       (v.14b)

While both panels begin in the same way, there is an
increasing intensity in Edom's hostility within each panel and in
verses 12–14 as a whole. In the first panel, Edom observes
Judah's plight (v.12a), displays an improper attitude (v.12bc),
and initiates hostile action (v.13a). In the second panel observation (v.13b) is followed by the completion of the hostile deeds
described at the end of the first panel (vv.13c–14).

One should also note that, with one exception, each
command concludes with a reference to Judah's "day of
misfortune/destruction/trouble/disaster." The exception to the
pattern comes toward the end of the second panel, where the
phrase "to cut down their fugitives" (v.14a) replaces a reference
to the character of the day. This alteration in the structure draws
attention to the degree of hostility expressed by Edom, which
did not show pity even on helpless, terrified refugees.

Verses 15–21 anticipate the Day of the Lord, which would
bring a reversal in the nations' (especially Edom's) and Judah's
fortunes. Within this framework of universal judgment (vv.15a,
16), Edom's punishment is announced (v.15b). Verses 17–21
then elaborate on Edom's downfall and envision the restoration
of Israel. Key words and themes are arranged chiastically.

  A) There will be safety for God's people on Mount
     Zion (v.17a)

    B) The house of Jacob takes possession of its land
      (v.17b)

      C) The house of Jacob annihilates Edom (v.18)

B) Israel takes possession of its land (vv.19–20)

A) God's people rule over Edom from Mount Zion (v.21)

ANALYSIS

Edom's Pride (1–9)

The prophecy opens on an ominous note as an unidentified group (perhaps Obadiah and the faithful remnant of God's people) announces it has heard a message from the Lord Himself. This message may be the call to war at the end of verse 1 ("Rise, and let us go against her for battle"), in which case the Lord is pictured directly summoning the nations to war through His envoy. It is possible that the message is the judgment speech of verses 2–4 or even the rest of the prophecy. If so, this message coincided with another one sent among the nations by a human envoy (cf. v.1b). Unbeknown to the nations, they were already working in concert with God as He prepared to bring judgment upon Edom. No matter how one understands the "message" of verse 1, God's absolute sovereignty over international affairs is apparent.

Following this reference to the instruments of divine judgment (v.1), the Lord addressed Edom directly, announcing His intent to bring the proud nation low (vv.2–4). Edom was arrogant and self-assured because of its impregnable natural defenses. The Edomites considered their dwelling places, located in the rocky highlands south-southeast of the Dead Sea, to be as unassailable as an eagle's nest. The comparison to an eagle, in addition to illustrating Edom's inaccessibility, also alludes to its predatory character, emphasized later in the prophecy (vv.12–14; cf. Job 39:27–30). However, Edom's pride had lulled it into a false sense of security. Despite its seemingly secure position, the Lord would tear Edom from its nest, making the proud nation an insignificant object of scorn.

In a most effective manner the questions and exclamations of verses 5–6 draw attention to the totality of Edom's coming destruction. No matter how greedy they might be, even thieves usually leave something in the house. No matter how efficient they are, grape pickers invariably miss or drop some of the grapes (cf. Lev.19:10; Deut. 24:21). By contrast, Edom's greedy invaders would be abnormally thorough and efficient. Edom would be so completely "ransacked" and "pillaged" (both words, lit., "searched out") that even its hidden treasures would not escape the plunderers.

The Edomites' allies would turn against them in their time of need (v.7). These deceitful treaty partners would thrust away Edomite envoys and, in violation of past agreements and promises, take hostile action against Edom. Edom's mistreatment by its friends would be appropriate, since it had dealt with its "brother," Israel, with similar deceit and hostility (vv.10–14).

The Lord would destroy Edom's wise men and warriors, who embodied the nation's pride and self-confidence (vv.8–9a). Irony predominates here. The announcement of the Lord's judgment against Edom's wise men takes the form of a rhetorical question, a stylistic feature typical of wisdom literature. Despite their reputation for discernment, these wise men were self-deceived (v.3) and incapable of detecting the deception of others (v.7).

With its wisdom undermined by the Lord's sovereign decisions and its military strength annihilated before His invincible power, Edom's entire population would be killed (v.9b). Ironically the supposedly inaccessible "mountains of Esau" would be covered with the corpses of their inhabitants.

Edom's Mistreatment of Its Brother (10–14)

A more detailed description of Edom's sins now appears. Disregarding its ancient blood ties with Israel, Edom treated its "brother" with violence (v.10). The Edomites' hostility initially took a passive form, as they stood aloof while Jerusalem was looted (v.11). This passivity quickly gave way to gloating (v.12) and aggressive action (vv.13–14). Ironically Edom's relationship to Israel was more like that of a foreigner than a brother. Just as foreigners entered Jerusalem's gates to plunder its wealth (v.11), so the Edomites marched through them in anxious anticipation of sharing the spoils (v.13).

Edom's prominent role in Jerusalem's demise is highlighted by a subtle wordplay. In verse 13 "disaster" (which appears twice) and "calamity" both translate the word 'ê*d*. This word, especially when suffixed with the third-person plural masculine pronoun 'ê*d*ām (as it is here in the first instance), sounds like Edom ('e*d*ôm). Through this similarity in sound the Lord hints at Edom's active involvement in and responsibility for Judah's disaster.[4]

Because of the Edomites' role in the fall of Jerusalem, the Lord would bring irreversible destruction upon them (v.10b). God's poetic justice is emphasized through wordplay. "Destroyed" (v.10; cf. also "cut down" in v.9) translates the same Hebrew word as does "cut down" in verse 14. The Lord would treat Edom as it had treated His people.

The Day of the Lord (15–21)

The principle of appropriate divine justice is clearly stated and illustrated in verses 15–16. The nations that had participated in Judah's "day" of calamity (cf. vv.11–14) would have a special "day" set aside for them, in which the Lord would repay them for the harm done to His people.

In verse 15b ("As you have done . . . your own head") Edom is addressed, as the second-person *singular* masculine pronominal and verbal forms in the Hebrew text indicate. Elsewhere in the book such forms are used without exception in addresses to Edom. As already vividly illustrated (vv.7, 14), the Lord would treat Edom as it had treated others.

In verse 16a the second-person form translated "you drank" is plural, suggesting Edom (at least solely) is no longer in view. Because verse 16b uses drinking imagery for judgment and refers to the nations in the third person, it is possible that God's people are here addressed. Just as the residents of Jerusalem had to experience God's judgment, so the nations would be forced to drink the cup of His wrath, resulting in their destruction. However, since the people of Judah and Jerusalem are never addressed elsewhere in the book, this interpretation is problematic.

Another possibility is that the nations are addressed, with the drinking referred to in verse 16a being their carousing as they celebrated their victory over Jerusalem. In this case, the use of the drinking motif in verse 16b in a different sense (judgment) is a very effective way of bringing out the appropriate nature of their punishment. Those who drank in celebration would now drink the cup of judgment. However,

---

[4]Cf. Allen, *Joel, Obadiah Jonah, and Micah,* p. 158.

the second half of the verse speaks of the nations in the third person, suggesting the addressee here is distinct.

A final option is to read a singular verb here and understand this as a continuation of the address to Edom in verse 15b.[5] In this case, Edom's carousing on Zion ironically foreshadowed its and the nations' judgment.

At any rate, verse 16b compares judgment to drinking an intoxicating drink; the drunkard's disorientation, manifested in his staggering, provides an apt illustration of the panic and confusion experienced by the objects of divine judgment (cf. Pss. 60:3; 75:8; Isa. 51:17, 22; Hab. 2:15–16). In this case, their judgment would be especially severe (note "drink continually" and "drink and drink") because they had violated holy ground.

Verses 17–21 emphasize the coming reversal in both Judah's and Edom's fortunes. While Edom had gloated over and exploited Judah's weakness (vv.10–14), the Day of the Lord would completely transform the situation. Although Edom and the other nations had cut down Jerusalem's "fugitives" (pᵉlîṭāyw, v.14) and treated the inhabitants of God's holy hill severely (v.16), the city would experience "deliverance" (pᵉlêṭâ) and be a holy sanctuary once more (v.17a). As in the original conquest under Joshua, the Lord would give His restored people the Promised Land as their inheritance (vv.17b, 19–20). In conjunction with this reoccupation of the land, Israel would totally annihilate Edom, just as fire completely devours stubble (v.18). In contrast to God's people, who were preserved despite Edom's attempts to destroy their "survivors" (śᵉrîḏāyw, v.14), no Edomite "survivors" (śārîḏ, v.18) would remain. Jerusalem's leaders would then incorporate the territory formerly held by Edom into the Lord's kingdom (v.21).

THEOLOGY

Summary

In the coming Day of the Lord, He would judge the nations for their mistreatment of His covenant people. In particular, He would totally destroy Edom because of its pride and its participation in Judah's downfall. Ironically, when the

---

[5] Taking the final mem as enclitic, one could repoint the verb as šātîtā (second person singular masculine). On enclitic mem, see P. Kyle McCarter, Jr., *Textual Criticism* (Philadelphia: Fortress Press, 1986), pp. 52–53.

Lord restored Judah to its land, He would also give His people the territory of the Edomites as well.

Analysis

As in Joel and Zephaniah, the Day of the Lord plays an important role in Obadiah's vision of the future. The Lord, who exercises sovereign control over international political developments (v. 1), would judge the nations severely and appropriately (vv. 15–16). Edom would be the focal point of this judgment. Although their father, Esau, was Jacob's brother (vv.10, 12), the Edomites repudiated this ancient blood tie with God's people and instead participated with the nations in Jerusalem's destruction (vv.10–14). Underlying this hostility was Edom's pride in its security (vv.2–4).

Edom's judgment would be complete (vv.5–6, 9, 18) and appropriate (v.15b). Since Edom had betrayed its "brother," it would in turn be deceived by its allies (v.7). Because the Edomites had turned Israelite survivors over to their oppressors (v.14), they would have no survivors in the day of retribution (v.18). Edom's seemingly invincible natural defenses and vaunted wisdom would be of no avail on the Lord's Day (vv.2–9). Proud Edom would become "small among the nations" (v.2). Through His judgment of Edom, the Lord would once more reveal His abhorrence of the proud (cf. Prov. 6:16–17).

Because of the Lord's faithfulness to His covenant, whereby He promised Abraham and his descendents possession of the land of Canaan (Gen. 15:18–21), He would rescue His exiled people and restore them to the Promised Land (vv.19–20). Mount Zion would gain prominence over the mountains of Esau (v.21) as God's people destroyed Edom and incorporated its land into the Lord's kingdom (vv.18, 21). In its eschatological dimension Edom becomes a symbol for all who oppose God's chosen people.

5

JONAH

INTRODUCTION

Literary Type and Historicity

The Book of Jonah differs from the other Minor Prophets in that it is an account of the prophet's experiences, rather than a collection of his prophetic speeches. Other Minor Prophets do contain biographical material (e.g., Hos. 1–3 and Amos 7:10–17), but it is relatively rare. Jonah's narrative style, including its focus upon supernatural occurrences, makes it more akin to the biographical accounts of the prophets (esp. Elijah and Elisha) recorded in 1 and 2 Kings.

Scholars have labored to categorize the book and have debated its historicity. Though many regard the book as a parable or allegory, the traditional view understands it as a historically accurate account of Jonah's experiences, albeit one with a theological purpose. For support, adherents of this view have pointed to the reference in 2 Kings 14:25, which attests to the existence of the prophet Jonah, and to the geographical details of the story, such as the references to Joppa and Nineveh. Of primary importance to this view is Jesus' testimony to the book's historicity. Jesus drew upon the book for illustrative purposes, mentioning the repentant men of Nineveh in the same breath as the Queen of Sheba (Matt. 12:39–42; Luke 11:29–32).

The book's historicity has been questioned for several reasons. The primary barrier relates to the miraculous events it records, especially Jonah's being swallowed alive by the great fish, in which he survived (and even prayed!) for three days before being spit up on the shore. Some have tried to make this particular element less objectionable by appealing to supposed modern parallels of sailors who were preserved alive inside large marine creatures. However, the accuracy of many of these accounts is questionable.[1] It is better to affirm the unique and miraculous nature of this specific event and to defend its historicity on the basis of general parallels with the experiences of Jonah's prophetic predecessors Moses, Elijah, and Elisha, all of whom witnessed and participated in some truly unusual occurrences.[2] While some point out that Jonah is an antihero, not a hero, and consequently dismiss these parallels,[3] one should note that miraculous occurrences were sometimes associated with antiheroes as well (e.g., Balaam's experience with the donkey, Num. 22:21–35). It would seem that the prophets of the Old Testament, whether heroes or antiheroes, often experienced the work and power of God in unique and miraculous ways.

The book's portrayal of Nineveh has also given rise to skepticism about its historicity. Some contend that the reference to the "king of Nineveh" (3:6) betrays an inaccurate understanding of the Assyrian empire in the eighth century B.C. The Assyrian ruler reigned over an entire empire, not just a single city. In addition, Nineveh was not even the capital of the empire at this time. Furthermore, it is argued, the book's portrayal of the city's size (3:3; 4:11) is inaccurate, and its account of the Ninevites' repentance highly improbable.[4]

Each of these objections has received an adequate response. There are other biblical examples of kings of nations being identified as well with a major city of their empire. For example, Sihon is called both "king of the Amorites" (Deut. 1:4) and "king of Heshbon" (Deut. 2:24); Jabin, "king of Canaan" (Judg. 4:2) and "king of Hazor" (Judg. 4:17); and

---

[1] R. K. Harrison, while dismissing many of these accounts, does feel that some are accurate. However, he points out that Jonah was "fully conscious and coherent" while in the fish, in contrast to the sailors in modern accounts, who "were recovered unconscious, and sometimes dead." See his *Introduction to the Old Testament* (Grand Rapids: Eerdmans, 1969), pp. 907–8.

[2] Cf. ibid., p. 905; and C. Hassell Bullock, *An Introduction to the Old Testament Prophetic Books* (Chicago: Moody Press, 1986), pp. 45–46.

[3] Terence E. Fretheim, *The Message of Jonah* (Minneapolis: Augsburg, 1977), p. 63.

[4] Ibid., pp. 63–65.

Ahab, "king of Israel" (1 Kings 20:13) and "king of Samaria" (1 Kings 21:1).[5] Though Nineveh may not have become the single capital of Assyria until later, it was a major royal city and residence even before the time of Jonah.[6] As for the city's size, Jonah 3:3 is capable of various interpretations, and the population figure of 120,000 seems consistent with archaeological evidence.[7] Finally, while there is no extrabiblical reference to a spiritual awakening in Nineveh in the early eighth century B.C., there was political turmoil in the Assyrian empire at this time, and evidence exists of an earthquake and an eclipse, all of which would have made the Assyrians ripe for repentance.[8] The Assyrians' subsequent sinful behavior (they conquered both Israel and Judah before the century was over) does not mean they could not have repented for a brief period of time.

Date and Authorship

The date and author of the book are unknown. Arguments for a late date of the sixth century or later include the presence of Aramaic linguistic influence, alleged dependence on Jeremiah 18 and Joel 2, and supposed allusions to distinctly Persian customs.[9] Each of these points, however, has been satisfactorily countered.[10]

Structure

The book is divided into two main sections. The first (chs. 1–2) tells of Jonah's attempt to run away from his prophetic commission and of God's rather drastic measures to set him back on track. The second section (chs. 3–4) records Jonah's ministry in Nineveh and his response to the Lord's forgiveness of the Ninevites.

[5]Douglas Stuart, *Hosea–Jonah* (Waco: Word Books, 1987), p. 441.

[6]Ibid., pp. 441–42.

[7]Ibid., pp. 487–88; Harrison, *Introduction,* p. 909; Bullock, *Introduction,* pp. 46–47.

[8]Stuart, *Hosea–Jonah,* p. 440.

[9]Leslie C. Allen, *Joel, Obadiah, Jonah, and Micah* (Grand Rapids: Eerdmans, 1976), pp. 186–88.

[10]Stuart, *Hosea–Jonah,* pp. 432–33.

ANALYSIS

God Retrieves His Runaway Prophet (1:1–2:10)

Jonah Runs from God (1:1–16)

The story begins with Jonah's commission to go to the great city of Nineveh and denounce its wickedness (vv.1–2). The city's sinful deeds had "come up before" the Lord in the sense that they had reached excessive proportions and could no longer go unpunished. Though the book never specifies these evil deeds, the king's decree, recorded later (3:8), suggests that social injustice within Nineveh was in view.

One would expect a prophet of the Lord to respond in obedience (cf. 1 Kings 17:8–10). However, Jonah took off in the opposite direction in an effort to escape his commission (v.3).[11] Rather than going to Nineveh, located northeast of Palestine, he went down to the port of Joppa and boarded a ship bound for Tarshish, located in the distant west across the Mediterranean Sea. The precise location of Tarshish is uncertain and really unimportant.[12] The name, like our Timbuktu, would have been associated with the outskirts of the civilized world. The author does not reveal the reason for Jonah's disobedient response at this point of the story but reserves this information for a later scene (cf. 4:1–3).

The Lord did not let Jonah shirk his duty. He sent (lit. "hurled" or "threw") a violent storm that threatened to destroy the ship (v.4). The terror-stricken sailors cried out to their respective gods and began throwing cargo overboard to make the ship lighter and thereby reduce the amount of water taken in (v.5a).

During all of this turmoil Jonah slept soundly below deck (v.5b). However, the ship's captain, not about to leave any stone unturned, awakened Jonah and urged him to pray to his god (v.6). In the Hebrew text the captain's exhortation, "Get up [*qûm*] and call [*q^erā'*]" echoes the Lord's commission to Jonah in

---

[11] The irony inherent in Jonah's disobedience is highlighted in the Heb. text. In commissioning Jonah, the Lord said, "Arise, go" (v.2). In relating Jonah's response, the text says, "But Jonah arose to flee" (v.3).

[12] Among other sites, scholars have identified it with Tarsus in Asia Minor or with Tartessus in Spain. For discussion see Allen, *Joel, Obadiah, Jonah, and Micah*, pp. 204–5 n. 10; and Hans W. Wolff, *Obadiah and Jonah*, trans. Margaret Kohl (Minneapolis: Augsburg, 1986), pp. 100–102.

verse 2: "Go [*qûm lēk*] . . . and preach [*qᵉrā'*]." As Allen observes, "Jonah must have thought he was having a nightmare" as he heard this pagan unwittingly remind him of the Lord's commission.[13]

In the meantime the sailors, assuming correctly that someone had angered his god, decided to cast lots to determine who was responsible for bringing the storm upon them (v.7a).[14] Casting lots should not be viewed as an appeal to chance (like our drawing straws or flipping a coin). Rather, it was an accepted means of gaining information from God (1 Sam. 14:41–42; Prov. 16:33).

The sailors' statement, "Come, let us cast lots to find out who is responsible for this calamity," (v.7a) is filled with irony. The Hebrew word translated "calamity" (*rā'â*) appears in verse 2, where it is rendered "wickedness." Jonah had been sent to denounce *rā'â* (in the moral sense) in the pagan world; instead he had become a source of *rā'â* (in the nonmoral sense) among the pagans.

When the lot fell on Jonah (v.7b), the sailors demanded more information about his identity and background (v.8). Jonah identified himself as a Hebrew (a designation often used of Israelites by foreigners) who worshiped (lit. "feared") the Lord (v.9a). In pious fashion he included a theological credo, affirming that the Lord was "the God of heaven, who made the sea and the land" (v.9b). Once again irony is present. Why would one who feared the creator of the sea try to run away from that same God via the sea?

Terrified by the thought that one who dared to run away from a god was aboard ship (v.10), the sailors asked Jonah's advice (v.11). Jonah instructed them to throw him into the sea (v.12), but the sailors initially refused, undoubtedly being fearful that God would punish them for taking a human life (cf. v.14). Following an unsuccessful last-ditch effort to row to shore, the sailors realized they had no other alternative than to follow Jonah's advice (v.13). Having begged God not to hold them accountable for Jonah's life (v.14), they hurled him overboard (v.15a). Though the sea immediately grew calm (v.15b), the sailors were taking no chances. Trembling with fear, they sacrificed and made vows to the Lord (v.16).

[13] Allen, *Joel, Obadiah, Jonah, and Micah*, p. 207.
[14] On the technique involved, see Stuart, *Hosea–Jonah*, pp. 459–60.

The stark contrast between Jonah and the sailors should be apparent. The pagan sailors had been willing to do everything in their power to save Jonah's skin. Jonah was unwilling to make such an effort for the pagan Ninevites. Jonah, although orthodox in creed, responded to God in disobedience. He claimed to fear God, but his actions contradicted his confession. By way of contrast, the sailors, though polytheistic pagans, responded submissively to God's will and power as revealed through the casting of lots and the storm. Unlike Jonah, their actions demonstrated their genuine fear of the Lord. The Hebrew text of verse 16a emphasizes the sailors' fear of the Lord. It reads literally, "And the men feared the LORD with great fear."

Jonah in the Fish (1:17–2:10)

The Lord arranged for a great fish to swallow Jonah. Jonah remained inside the fish for three days and three nights (1:17) before it finally spewed him up on dry land at God's command (2:10). A Sumerian mythological text views the underworld as being a three-day journey from the land of the living. In light of this, the time reference may indicate that Jonah had gone all the way to the land of the dead, his return via the fish requiring the usual three days.[15] Jonah's own description of his experience is consistent with this interpretation. He felt he had descended "into the very heart of the seas" (v.3) and had been imprisoned in the underworld itself (v.6).

Jonah offered up a song of thanksgiving from the belly of the fish (2:1–10). The song, which contains several standard formal elements found in thanksgiving psalms, includes (1) an opening summary statement (v.2a); (2) a recollection of the time of need, the cry for help, and God's deliverance (vv.2b–7); (3) an affirmation of loyalty combined with a vow of praise, sacrifice, and renewed devotion (vv.8–9a); and (4) a concluding statement of praise (v.9b).

Jonah recalled in vivid detail his descent into the underworld (vv.3, 5–6). Jonah's statement, "I sank down [yārad]" forms an ironic conclusion to the pattern of descent begun in 1:3–5. Three times in those verses yārad appears, describing how Jonah went down to Joppa (v.3), went aboard (lit. "went

---

[15]George M. Landes, "The Kerygma of the Book of Jonah," *Interpretation* 21 (1967): 11–12.

down into") the ship (v.3), and went below deck (v.5). The Lord brought this descent to an appropriate conclusion by bringing him all the way down to Sheol itself!

Despite his circumstances Jonah cried out to the Lord in confidence that he would one day stand in the Lord's presence again (vv.2, 4, 7). Convinced that God had answered his prayer, Jonah affirmed his devotion to the Lord. Contrasting himself with the worshipers of idols (v.8), he promised to thank God publicly for his deliverance (v.9a). He then concluded his song with the rousing confession, "Salvation comes from the LORD" (v.9b).

What is the reader to make of all this? On the surface it appears that Jonah experienced a genuine change of heart, especially in light of his subsequent obedience to his original commission (cf. 3:1–3). However, a closer examination of the text and the following context suggests otherwise. Nowhere in Jonah's prayer did he mention his rebelliousness and sin. In fact, he still piously considered himself better than the pagans (cf. 2:8–9), though, as we have seen, a comparison with the sailors suggests otherwise. Jonah also made an enormous assumption when he determined that the fish was God's instrument of salvation. How did he know the fish was giving him a return trip to the land of the living? How did he know that being swallowed by the fish was not some cruel prolongation of his agony? Imagine it—to arrive in the land of the dead and then have insult added to injury by being submerged in the stomach juices of a denizen of the deep! However, Jonah assumed (rightly, by God's grace) the fish was his savior. The final proof that Jonah had not really changed comes in the book's last chapter, where the prophet expresses his rage at God's decision to spare Nineveh (4:1–3).

Why did the author include this account of Jonah's experience inside the fish? Rather than indicating some positive change in the prophet's character, this account contributes to the author's negative portrayal of Jonah. This becomes more apparent in chapter 4, when one finally realizes the reason for Jonah's unwillingness to go to Nineveh. In Jonah's opinion the wicked, pagan Ninevites deserved punishment. He refused to be part of their reclamation. When God finally spared them, Jonah was outraged. Without this account of Jonah's experience in the fish, his anger would still be unjustified. Against the background of chapter 2, however, Jonah's attitude appears even more inexplicable and irrational. Jonah had come face-to-face with death, had experienced God's grace toward an obstinate rebel, and had affirmed that "salvation comes from the LORD." Yet he still had the audacity to deny certain groups (namely, the pagans whom he disparages in 2:8), faced with the same reality of death, that same mercy. Thus chapter 2 plays a vital role in the author's characterization of Jonah by showing, in the larger context of the book, just how inconsistent his double standards really made him.

Jonah and the Ninevites (3:1–4:11)

Nineveh's Response to Jonah's Message (3:1–10)

Having gained Jonah's attention, albeit through radical means, the Lord repeated His commission (vv.1–2). This time Jonah obeyed, apparently without hesitation or complaint (v.3). As Jonah started through Nineveh he announced that the city would be destroyed in forty days (v.4).

Before Jonah had gone very far into the city, the Ninevites responded positively to his message (vv.4–5). As a sign of contrition, they fasted and put on sackcloth. When the king heard the news, he also exchanged his royal robes for sackcloth (v.6) and officially decreed a fast that was to include both humans and animals (v.7). With a touch of hyperbole he also commanded that both man and beast don sackcloth and cry out to God. In the Hebrew text of verse 8, "man and beast" appears to be the subject of both "be covered" and "call." The lowing, braying, and bleating of the hungry animals could, of course, be viewed poetically as praying to God. All Ninevites were to abandon their evil, violent ways in hopes that God might yet relent from sending judgment (vv.8–9).

Nineveh's sincere repentance had its intended effect upon the Lord. He decided to spare the city from the judgment He had threatened through Jonah (v.10). Though Jonah's message had appeared to be an unconditional announcement of judgment (cf. v.4), it really possessed an implied conditionality, as suggested by the ambiguous term "overturned."[16]

As in chapter 1, Jonah finishes a distant second when compared with the pagans and their fear of God. The Ninevites responded immediately and positively to God's revelation, in

---

[16]Stuart, *Hosea–Jonah*, p. 489.

contrast to rebellious Jonah, who obeyed God only after being subjected to the most drastic divine measures. Jonah presumed upon God's mercy; the Ninevite king humbly submitted to God's sovereign authority, recognizing that God was not obligated to spare the city (cf. 3:9).

Jonah's Reaction to Nineveh's Deliverance (4:1–11)

Jonah was outraged by God's compassionate treatment of Nineveh (v.1). At this point in the narrative the author reveals for the first time the reason for Jonah's earlier disobedience and for his displeasure over the sparing of Nineveh. Jonah knew the Lord was "a gracious and compassionate God, slow to anger and abounding in love, a God who relents from sending calamity" (v.2). Consequently he suspected that the Lord would spare Nineveh if it repented. Because Jonah desired Nineveh's destruction, not its deliverance, he had tried to escape his commission and was distraught over the apparent success of his preaching. Rather than live with the realization that he had helped Nineveh escape punishment, Jonah requested that the Lord take his life (v.3).

Why did Jonah harbor such ill-will against Nineveh? Though the text never tells us, we can venture a guess based on historical developments prior to Jonah's time. By Jonah's day (ca. 780 B.C.) Assyria, represented here by one of its prominent cities, had fallen upon difficult times. However, in the previous century Assyria had carried out imperialistic policies that had been accompanied by cruel atrocities. Shalmaneser III (ca. 858–824) had campaigned as far west as the Mediterranean, forcing several western states, including Israel, to submit to his authority and pay tribute. An Assyrian monument from the time even portrays Israel's king Jehu bowing down before the Assyrian king. The thought of God extending mercy to this pagan empire, just as it was about to be destroyed, was undoubtedly repulsive to patriotic Israelites like Jonah.

Though one might understand, at least from the human perspective, why Jonah resented the Assyrians, Jonah's response to Nineveh's deliverance was ironic in at least two ways. First, God had sent him to denounce Nineveh's wickedness (*rā'â*, 1:3). However, when God used Jonah's preaching to turn Nineveh from its "evil [*rā'â*] ways" (3:10), Jonah was "greatly displeased [*rā'â* once more]" (4:1). Though the book began with Nineveh being characterized as wicked, by its conclusion the word *rāʿâ* (though now used in a different semantic sense) is more applicable to Jonah!

Second, Jonah once again recited a credo (4:2; cf. 1:9; 2:9), demonstrating his orthodoxy and theological awareness. The basis for this credo was God's past mercies to Israel. Almost identical words appear in Exodus 34:6–7, where mention is made of God's mercy toward rebellious Israel following the golden calf incident. A shorter form of the credo occurs in Numbers 14:18 in Moses' prayer on behalf of sinful Israel. In other words, Jonah knew these theological facts about God's gracious nature because God had revealed His grace to Jonah's disobedient ancestors, as well as to the prophet himself not too long before this. The Ninevites, it seems, were really no different than Israel (or Jonah, for that matter). Both were rebellious sinners deserving only punishment. Yet God had graciously decided to show mercy to both. Jonah was willing to accept this in Israel's (and his own) case, but not in Nineveh's.

The final verses of the book (vv.4–11) record God's efforts to reason with His pouting prophet. When Jonah asked to die (v.3), God responded with a brief question, designed to move Jonah to reflect upon his attitude (v.4). Instead of continuing the dialogue, Jonah, hoping against hope that God might change His mind and destroy Nineveh after all, sat down outside the city (undoubtedly a safe distance away in order to escape any brimstone from heaven!) to see what might transpire (v.5). Though inconsistent with his death wish (cf. v.3), he built a shelter to protect himself from the hot Mesopotamian sun.

As in chapter 2, Jonah was in a position to learn a lesson. The Lord made a vine sprout up, providing extra shade for the sweaty, sulking prophet (v.6). No sooner had Jonah expressed joy over the appearance of the plant than God caused a worm to destroy it (v.7). To make matters worse, He then sent a "scorching east wind" that, in combination with the blazing rays of the sun, prompted Jonah to repeat his request to die (v.8). The Lord now repeated His question, though in a slightly different form (v. 9a; cf. v.4). When Jonah quickly replied that his anger was justified, the Lord was ready to make His point. Jonah felt concern over a vine, which he had not even produced. His concern was, of course, based solely on self-interest, seeing that the vine had given him protection from the elements (v.10). If Jonah could feel such concern over the loss of a flimsy, short-lived plant, then how much more should God be allowed to feel concern over thousands of people, who were the products of His creative work (v.11). To drive the point home, God also emphasized the moral and ethical ignorance of the Ninevites. In the moral realm they were like small children, unable to distinguish right from left. Yet despite their limitations, they had responded positively to God when confronted for the first time by His revealed word. With a final note of sarcasm the Lord reminded Jonah that the city also contained "many cattle" (the phrase with which the Heb. text of v.11 ends). If Jonah could not feel compassion for human beings, perhaps this plant-lover might acknowledge that the city should be spared for the sake of the animals, partners with plants in the natural realm.

THEOLOGY

Summary

By extending His grace to wicked Nineveh (and to rebellious Jonah!), God revealed His concern for sinful human beings. As the sovereign Creator of all persons, God has the right to show mercy to whom He wills, no matter how unworthy the object might appear to be. God's servants are not to resist or question His decisions in these matters but are to submit obediently to His wishes.

Analysis

The Book of Jonah teaches a great deal about God's character. Throughout the book God appears as the omnipotent Ruler of the world (cf. 1:9). He stirs up and calms the sea, determines the outcome of the sailors' lot-casting, commands a great fish to do His bidding, causes a plant to grow and then die, employs a worm and hot east wind to accomplish His purposes, and controls the fate of even the mightiest cities.

God exerts all of this power toward a particular goal—the reclamation of sinful, rebellious human beings. In so doing He demonstrates that He alone is the source of deliverance from death (2:9). He also reveals Himself to be a gracious, compassionate, and patient God whose devotion to men and women prompts Him to relent from judgment (4:2). God's grace is not limited to the Israelites (represented by Jonah) but extends to the pagan world and even brutish animals (4:11).

Through the negative example of its main character, the book also teaches God's servants how they should respond to His sovereign decisions. In the name of justice Jonah attempted to limit God's sovereignty by denying His grace to the wicked pagans. From a merely human perspective one might argue he was justified. However, from the divine perspective Jonah was guilty of applying a double standard. Though he was well aware of God's past mercy to Israel (cf. 4:2) and had himself experienced that same mercy (cf. ch. 2), he was unwilling to let pagans receive it. By trying to put God in a box, Jonah became a confused, depressed walking contradiction, whose attitudes and actions were a practical denial of his pious theological confessions. Jonah's negative example is a reminder to God's servants that they must accept God's sovereign decisions, even if they do not appear to correspond to one's own ideas of what is just and proper.

6

MICAH

INTRODUCTION

Authorship and Date

Micah, the author of this prophetic book, came from the town of Moresheth, which should probably be identified with Moresheth Gath (mentioned in 1:14), located southwest of Jerusalem. He prophesied during the reigns of Jotham (ca. 750–731 B.C.), Ahaz (ca. 735–715), and Hezekiah (ca. 715–686). Some of his messages clearly predate the fall of Samaria in 722 (e.g., 1:6–7), while others appear to reflect the Assyrian crisis of 701 (cf. 4:9–5:1).

Unity

Many have denied the unity of the book. Generally speaking, such critics attribute chapters 1–3 to Micah (with the exception of 2:12–13) and chapters 4–5 and 7:8–20 to later authors/editors. No consensus has emerged with respect to 6:1–7:7.[1] For the most part, sections dealing with the salvation of God's people are considered secondary, while the judgment speeches and accusations are regarded as genuine.

The salvation passages are denied to Micah for various reasons. First, each salvation section (2:12–13; 4:1–5:14; 7:8–20) is rather loosely related to its context, the transition from

[1] For a survey of views, see Brevard S. Childs, *Introduction to the Old Testament as Scripture* (Philadelphia: Fortress Press, 1979), p. 430.

judgment to salvation being abrupt and awkward. Second, some of the passages presuppose the Exile (2:12–13) and reflect an exilic perspective (7:8–20). Third, 4:10 prophesies an exile to Babylon, which would appear to reflect the international situation of the late seventh and early sixth centuries B.C., not that of the eighth century, when Assyria, not Babylon, was the dominant power in the Near East.

In response to these points, we may note the following factors. In the first place, the salvation sections are introduced quite abruptly and, on the surface at least, appear to be the product of a sloppy editorial process. However, from a rhetorical standpoint, one could view them as part of an intentional juxtapositional technique used to contrast sharply the present/immediate future described in the preceding or following context(s) with the ultimate restoration portrayed in the salvation messages themselves.

Several literary clues support this understanding. The promise of a return from exile in 2:12–13 contrasts sharply with the threat of exile in the preceding context (cf. 1:16; 2:4, 10). The phrase "at their head" ($b^e r\bar{o}'\check{s}\bar{a}m$, 2:13), which refers to the Lord as Israel's eschatological Ruler (note "their king" in the parallel line), contrasts with 3:1, where the Lord denounces the "leaders" ($r\bar{a}'\check{s}\hat{e}$, "heads") of Micah's generation. The passage 4:1–4, which introduces the central salvation section of the book, contrasts sharply with 3:12. In the latter the "temple hill" ($har\ habbayi\underline{t}$) is reduced to a wasteland; in 4:1–4 this same hill (note $har\ b\hat{e}\underline{t}yhwh$, "the mountain of the Lord's temple," 4:1) is elevated above all others. Within the chiasmus of chapter 7 (see analysis below) the prophet's lament (7:1–7) contrasts with the nation's hymn of praise (7:18–20), which concludes the book's final salvation section.

One should note that this contrasting technique occurs elsewhere in the book, especially within the chiastic structure of 4:5–5:15 (cf. esp. 4:8 with 4:9–10; 4:9–10 with 4:11–13; 4:11–13 with 5:1; 5:1 with 5:2–6). Perhaps such a chiasmus exists in chapters 1–3, with the pivotal salvation notice of 2:12–13 contrasting with the surrounding elements.

A) Immediate future: Jerusalem conquered like Samaria (1:2–16)

B) Present: Judah's sin denounced (2:1–11)

C) Ultimate future: Restoration from exile
   (2:12–13)

B) Present: Judah's sin denounced (3:1–11)

A) Immediate future: Jerusalem conquered (like Samaria;
   3:12 [cf. 3:12 with 1:5–6])

Second, since Micah anticipated the nation's exile, he could also anticipate its release. In a highly poetic manner he even projected himself into the future situation of the exiles, dramatically representing suffering, but hopeful, Zion (7:8–13), as well as the future exilic generation (7:14–20). In so doing, he made it possible for this future remnant to appropriate his message more easily and draw encouragement from it.

In response to the third objection above, several explanations for the reference to Babylon (4:10) may be offered. One could label this line a later gloss without necessitating a late date for the entire context. However, if 4:10 is a gloss, why were 5:5–6 and 7:12, which view Assyria as Judah's enemy and place of exile, not altered by the proposed editor for the sake of consistency? Another possibility is that Micah, like Isaiah (cf. 39:6–7), foresaw a distant Babylonian exile beyond the Assyrian crisis of his own day. However, if so, why did he picture Assyria as Judah's eschatological enemy (cf. 5:5–6) and view it as the place where Zion's people would be exiled (7:12)? A third possibility is that Micah, in mentioning Babylon, was referring (from his perspective at least) to the Assyrians, who conquered Babylon and regarded it as an important religious center. Micah may have chosen the name "Babylon" for its symbolic value[2] or because of its association with Nimrod (cf. Gen. 10:10), whom the prophet names in 5:6 in conjunction with Assyria. Since Genesis 10:8–12 identifies Nimrod as the founder of both Assyria and Babylon, the two were probably closely related in Israelite thought.

---

[2]See Thomas E. McComiskey, "Micah" in *The Expositor's Bible Commentary*, ed. Frank E. Gaebelein (Grand Rapids: Zondervan, 1985), 7:425.

Structure

The juxtaposition of judgment and salvation provides the book with a three-paneled structure, which may be outlined as follows:[3]

Panel	Judgment	Salvation
1	1:2–2:11	2:12–13
2	3:1–12	4:1–5:15
3	6:1–7:7	7:8–20

ANALYSIS

Judah's Exile Envisioned (1:2–2:13)

Micah faced the difficult tasks of denouncing a potentially hostile audience for its sin and announcing its impending doom. Like Amos, Micah captured his audience's attention by first describing the judgment of its enemies. He began with a vivid portrayal of the Lord coming in power to judge the nations (1:2–4). He then included the northern kingdom and its capital, Samaria, within the scope of this judgment (1:5a). At this point his Judahite audience must have been nodding its approval. With his listeners' guard down, Micah quickly delivered the knockout blow, pointing out that Judah and Jerusalem would not escape divine punishment (1:5b, 8–16). The structure of chapter 1 may be outlined as follows:

I. Judgment speech against the nations (vv.2–4)
   A. Call to attention (v.2)
   B. Description of the Judge's coming (vv.3–4)

II. Judgment speech against the northern and southern kingdoms (vv.5–16)
   A. Accusation (v.5)
   B. Announcement of judgment (vv.6–16)

[3]The structural relationship between 3:1–12 and chapters 4–5 does not invalidate the chiasmus proposed above for chapters 1–3. Two or more structures can sometimes run concurrently.

1. Against the north (vv.6–7)
2. Against the south (vv.8–16)

The announcement of judgment against the south takes the form of a lament, which exhibits the following structure: introduction (1:8–9), lament proper (vv.10–15), and conclusion (call to lament, v.16). The mourning terminology and animal similes of verses 8 and 16 form an inclusio for the lament.

Micah elaborated on Judah's sin in 2:1–11, which may be outlined as follows:

I. Woe oracle (vv.1–5)
   A. Accusation (vv.1–2)
   B. Announcement of judgment (vv.3–5)

II. Judgment speech (vv.6–11)

References to the people's attitude toward true and false prophecy (2:6, 11) form an inclusio for the judgment speech. The verb *nāṭap,* "to prophesy," occurs three times in verse 6 and twice in verse 11.

Chapter 2 concludes with an abrupt shift in tone, as the Lord is described as leading His people home from exile (vv.12–13).

God's Judgment on the Nations (1:2–4)

Micah began by warning the nations that the Lord was about to come in judgment against them (v.2). He then described the Lord departing from His heavenly temple, descending to earth, and moving along the high mountain peaks (v.3). The whole earth, represented here by its extremities (mountains and valleys), disintegrates before Him (v.4).

Judah Follows in Samaria's Footsteps (1:5–16)

Surprisingly, Micah announced that the sin of God's people had occasioned this outburst of divine wrath (v.5a). More specifically, he singled out Samaria and Jerusalem because both cities epitomized the spiritual unfaithfulness of their respective kingdoms (v.5b). Both cities had become centers of false religion, Samaria because of its Baal temple (cf. 1 Kings 16:32) and Jerusalem because of its pagan high places (cf. 1 Kings 11:7; 2 Kings 23:5; 2 Chron. 34:3).

Micah is at his rhetorical best here, as he artfully makes the transition from the nations to the northern kingdom to Judah. By mentioning Samaria before Jerusalem in verse 5b, he seems to identify the ambiguous Jacob/house of Israel, mentioned in verse 5a, with the northern kingdom. When one compares the structure of his initial question-answer sequence ("What is Jacob's transgression? Is it not Samaria?") with the parallelism of the first half of verse 5, one expects the verse to conclude, "What is the house of Israel's sin? Is it not Samaria?" However, Micah replaces "the house of Israel" with Judah and then substitutes Jerusalem for Samaria. He even specifies the offense(s) he had in mind by replacing "sins" with "high place." Much to the chagrin of the original audience, Judah is sudddenly thrust to center stage in Micah's indictment.

The repetition of "high place(s)" (vv.3, 5) links the accusation against Jerusalem with the universal judgment described in verses 3–4. According to verse 3, the earth's "high places"—mountains (cf. v.4)—though symbols of permanence and stability, would disintegrate before the Lord. If these cosmic high places could not withstand His anger, then Jerusalem, a "high place" of pagan worship, was certainly doomed for destruction.

Before elaborating on Jerusalem's fate (vv.8–16), Micah announced the Lord's judgment upon Samaria (vv.6–7). The Lord would reduce the city to a heap of ruins, making it suitable only for agricultural pursuits. Samaria's stones would go tumbling into the valley below, leaving the very foundations of the city exposed. Samaria's idols, symbols of her rebellion against the Lord, would be crushed to bits and burned, just as Moses had smashed and burned the golden calf (Deut. 9:21).

Because Judah had followed Samaria's sinful example (vv.5, 13), Micah bitterly lamented Samaria's demise. He realized that the destruction of Samaria portended disaster for Judah as well (vv.8–9). The prophet foresaw a future invasion of Judah (probably that of Sennacherib in 701 B.C.) that would have especially disastrous effects upon several cities located southwest of Jerusalem and would threaten the capital itself (vv.10–15). The prophet's lament is characterized by irony and wordplay involving the names of these cities.

The lament proper begins with words taken from David's lament over Saul and Jonathan following their death in battle (v.10a; cf. 2 Sam. 1:20). Whether Gath was controlled in

Micah's day by Judah (cf. 2 Chron. 26:6) or Philistia is immaterial. By the eighth century B.C. these words had probably become idiomatic, meaning, "Don't broadcast the news of our defeat in a foreign town."

Though sorrow should not be expressed in foreign territory (cf. v.10a, "weep not at all"), where news of Judah's defeat would be welcomed, lamentation was quite appropriate in the towns of Judah. The inhabitants of Beth Ophrah (lit. "house of dust") should "roll in the dust" as a sign of their sorrow (v.10b; cf. Jer. 6:26; 25:34; Ezek. 27:30).

Such irony permeates the remainder of the lament. The prophet urged the inhabitants of Shaphir (meaning "pleasant" or "beautiful") to file away into exile "in nakedness and shame," the antithesis of beauty (v.11a). He also observed that the residents of Zaanan (which sounds like the Heb. word for "come out") would not be able to leave their city, probably due to its being besieged by the enemy (v.11b). Unfortunately, Beth Ezel ("the house next door") would be of no assistance (v.11c). The people of Maroth (which sounds like a Heb. word for "bitter"), though anticipating "relief" (lit. "something good"), would be disappointed, for the Lord would send a "disaster" (lit. "something bad," v.12). Micah urged the residents of Lachish (which sounds like *reḵeš,* translated here "team") to harness their teams of horses to their chariots, for a battle was imminent (v.13). (Lachish is singled out as having followed the northern kingdom's sinful practices and as having a negative influence upon Jerusalem.)

The prophet compared Judah's loss of Moresheth Gath to giving "parting gifts" (i.e., a dowry) to a newly married daughter (v.14a). The similarity in sound between the name Moresheth and *mᵉʾōrāśâ,* "betrothed," facilitates this comparison. Aczib (v.14b, which apparently means "deception" or "disappointment") would in some way "prove deceptive," or disappointing, to the royal house. A conqueror would attack Mareshah (which sounds like *yōrēš,* translated "conqueror" in v.15a). Finally, the "glory of Israel" (probably referring to its leaders and wealthy citizens) would be forced to go into hiding in Adullam (v.15b), associated in Israelite thought with David's humiliating experience as a fugitive (1 Sam. 22:1; 2 Sam. 23:13).

The invasion would culminate in the exile of Judah's children (v.16). In anticipation of such horrifying prospects

Micah urged his countrymen to shave their heads as a sign of lamentation and sorrow (cf. Jer. 7:29; 16:6; 47:5; 48:37; Ezek. 27:31).

Judgment upon Land Robbers (2:1–5)

Micah pronounced a woe oracle against those who treated their countrymen unjustly. The term translated "woe," used elsewhere in funeral laments (1 Kings 13:30; Jer. 22:18; 34:5; Amos 5:16), suggested the coming doom of those addressed. These sinners characteristically spent their nights devising evil plans (v.1a). These plans became reality at sunrise because they had the financial and legal power to carry them out successfully (v.1b).

According to verse 2, these plans involved robbing others of their possessions. Covetousness, which was prohibited in the Ten Commandments, led to fraudulent acquisition of property, in blatant contradiction of the principles of covenant life (Lev.19:13). In the theocratic structure of ancient Israel, the land belonged to the Lord (Lev.25:23), who assigned it to individual families. Land was not to be transferred permanently (cf. Num. 36:7–9; 1 Kings 21:3), for this would be a practical denial of the Lord's ownership of the land and would be antithetical to the spirit of covenantal brotherhood.

The Lord announced judgment upon the perpetrators of these crimes (vv.3–5). This judgment would be appropriate, a fact emphasized by wordplay and irony. The Lord was "planning disaster" (v.3) against those who had done the same (cf. v.1). The words translated "evil" (v.1) and "disaster" (v.3) are virtually identical in Hebrew. On that day bystanders would ridicule (lit. "lift up a taunt song over") those who had stolen from others ("take" in v.2 is lit. "lift up," the same word translated "ridicule" in v.4). This taunt song, the words of which are quoted in verse 4, takes the form of a mocking lament, in which the mockers quote the words of the mourning rich people. Ironically the rich, who had stolen the fields of others (v.2), would now lament the fact that these fields were being stolen from them. The words translated "we are utterly ruined" (*šādôd nᵉšaddunû*) sound like the word for "fields" (*šādôt*), emphasizing the appropriate nature of these field-robbers' punishment. Not only would those who disregarded the Lord's division of the land have their land stolen, but they would also be excluded from participating in any future redivision of the land among the Lord's people (v.5).

Several other wordplays in verses 1–5 deserve mention. "Save" (v.3) and "takes" (v.4) translate the same Hebrew word (*mûš*, lit. "remove"). The repetition draws attention to an ironic contrast. The sinners would not be able to "remove" themselves from the Lord's judgment, but their enemies would be able to "remove" them from their property. Several other words in verses 3–5 contain *m* and *s* sounds, including *mišpāḥâ* ("people," v.3), *māšāl* ("ridicule," v.4), and *mašlîḵ* ("one . . . to divide," v.5). This repetition of *m* and *s* sounds mimics *miškᵉḇôtām* ("their beds," v.1) and drives home the fact that those who planned evil on their beds would be justly punished.[4]

Judah's Rejection of the Lord's Word (2:6–11)

Verse 6 contains a quotation from the people (or perhaps the false prophets; cf. NIV) that exhibits their attitude toward the Lord's true prophets. They refused to accept a message of judgment, insisting they were immune to punishment. They did not believe the Lord's patience had run out or that He would do to them the things threatened by prophets like Micah (v.7a).

In verses 7b–10 the Lord corrected this faulty thinking. He reminded them that He deals well only with the upright (v.7b). Unfortunately for the sinful people addressed here, they did not fall into this category. Rather than showing concern for their covenant brothers, they attacked them like an enemy would (v.8a). This hostility took the form of social injustice against the unsuspecting, including even women and children (vv.8b–9). Appropriately, the Lord commanded those who had "risen up" (v.8) in such hostility to "get up" (v.10) and leave the land, with both verbs translating forms of the same Hebrew verb. Their sense of security was unjustified, for the land of Judah would not be a "resting place" (contrast Deut. 12:9). Instead it was contaminated by the evil of its people and doomed for destruction.

This speech closes, as it began, with a reference to prophecy (v.11; cf. v.6). Those who rejected God's true prophets and their warnings of impending judgment would

---

[4]On this passage, see Leslie C. Allen, *Joel, Obadiah, Jonah, and Micah* (Grand Rapids: Eerdmans, 1976), p. 287.

accept only one kind of "prophet"—namely, a liar promising them wine and beer (perhaps symbols of blessing here). Ironically these self-proclaimed experts on the subject of the Lord's Spirit (cf. v.7) were unable to discern truth and error. Wordplay in the Hebrew text highlights this irony: "If a liar and deceiver comes" reads literally, "If one comes in wind [*rûaḥ,* the word translated "Spirit" in v.7] and falseness."

Restoration from Exile (2:12–13)

Having warned that judgment and exile were inevitable if Judah continued in its sinful ways, the Lord suddenly looked ahead to a day beyond the judgment when He would restore His exiled people. Though the coming judgment would reduce the nation to a remnant (v.12a; cf. 4:6–7), the Lord, like a shepherd, would lead them out of their captor's city and bring them to His own fold (vv.12b–13).

Since this interpretation of verses 12–13 entails an abrupt shift in tone from judgment (cf. vv.1–11) to salvation, some have understood them as an announcement of judgment. However, several factors point to the salvific nature of verses 12–13. First, the motif of regathering from exile is prominent in the prophets, including Micah (cf. 4:6–7, 10). In 4:6 "gather" and "assemble" translate the same Hebrew words rendered "gather" and "bring together" in 2:12. Second, the remnant is viewed in a positive light elsewhere in Micah (cf. 4:7; 5:7–8; 7:18). Third, the royal-shepherd motif is applied elsewhere to a return from exile, viewed as a second exodus (cf. 7:14–15, as well as Jer. 23:3 and Ezek. 34:11–15).

Zion's Fall and Rise (3:1–5:15)

This second major section of the book, like chapters 1–2, exhibits a movement from judgment to salvation. Chapter 3 contains a series of three judgment speeches, the structure of which may be outlined as follows:

I. Judgment speech against the rulers of the land (vv.1–4)
  A. Call to attention (v.1a)
  B. Accusation (vv.1b–3)
  C. Announcement of judgment (with accusation summarized; (v.4)

II. Judgment speech against false prophets (vv.5–7)
   A. Accusation (v.5)
   B. Announcement of judgment (vv.6–7) (Micah's affirmation of confidence, v.8)

III. Judgment speech against rulers, false prophets, and priests (vv.9–12)
   A. Call to attention (v.9a)
   B. Accusation (vv.9b–11)
   C. Announcement of judgment (v.12)

In chapter 4 the mood of the prophecy suddenly shifts. Verses 1–4 picture the elevation of Zion/Jerusalem and the submission of the nations to the Lord's sovereign rule. However, the nations were not following the Lord in Micah's day (4:5), and Zion was in desperate straits (4:9; 5:1), ready to experience judgment (cf. 3:12) and the exile of its citizens (4:10). The question therefore arises, "How will the situation described in 4:1–4 come about?" The section 4:6–5:15 outlines the process. Following the exile of Zion's people and the humiliation of her king, restoration would come. A new Davidic ruler would arise (4:8; 5:2–6), the land would be purified (5:10–14), and a remnant would be regathered and strengthened (4:6–7; 5:7–9).

The arrangement of themes in 4:5–5:15 is chiastic:

A) The nations do not follow the Lord at present (4:5)

  B) Judah is restored (4:6)

    C) A remnant becomes a great nation under the Lord's rule (4:7)

      D) Rulership returns to Zion (4:8)

        E) Zion and its king are humiliated (4:9)

          F) Zion is exiled and redeemed (4:10)

          F) Zion is protected (4:11–13)

        E) Zion and its king are humiliated (5:1)

      D) A ruler arises in power (5:2–6)

> C) The Lord's power makes a remnant a
>   superior nation (5:7–9)
>
> B) Judah is purified (5:10–14)
>
> A) The Lord judges the disobedient nations (5:15)

Judah's Leaders Denounced (3:1–12)

Micah accused the rulers of Jacob/Israel (i.e., Judah; cf. v.12) of the grossest forms of social injustice. These leaders were responsible for maintaining justice in the land (v.1b). Instead they perverted all proper standards of right and wrong (v.2a) in their exploitation of the poor (vv.2b–3). Micah compared this social injustice to cannibalism. The oppressors of the poor had, as it were, stripped off the skin of their victims, crushed and chopped up their bones, cooked them in a pot, and eaten them for dinner. Though used elsewhere of social oppression (e.g., Ps. 14:4; Prov. 30:14; Hab. 3:14), this eating motif is developed most vividly here. The realities behind this figurative description include theft of property (2:2; cf. Isa. 5:8–9), refusal to recognize the legal rights of the poor (cf. Isa. 1:23; 5:23; 10:2), and acts of violence (3:10; 7:2; cf. Isa. 1:15–17, 21–23; 5:7). The judicial leaders addressed here participated in this unjust system primarily by their acceptance of bribes in exchange for favorable decisions on behalf of the rich (3:11; 7:3; Isa. 1:23).

Because of their evil deeds against the helpless, these rulers would be helpless in the Day of Judgment (v.4). They would cry out to the Lord for help, but He would hide His face from them. The punishment is fitting. Since the rulers had refused to respond to the cries of the oppressed and had hidden their faces from them, the Lord would treat them in the same manner (cf. Prov. 21:13).

Micah next addressed the false prophets. He accused them of misleading the people through greed (v.5). Instead of giving an accurate word from God, they devised their own messages. To those who gave them food to eat, they pronounced a word of blessing. Those who did not pay the prophets heard a message of calamity and were treated as enemies.

The Lord would judge these false prophets in an appropriate manner. Since they had misused the prophetic office, they would be deprived of their abilities and access to God (vv.6–7). Night and darkness symbolize the cessation of revelation, whether through visions or divination. Since the latter was forbidden in Israel (cf. Deut. 18:10), the language may merely reflect the prophets' view of how the divine will was revealed; it need not imply that they actually received divine messages through divination. Verse 7 probably anticipates the time of calamity that would come upon the nation (cf. vv.4 and 12). At that time these prophets would desperately seek a word from God concerning the nation's future but would find the channels of communication cut off. In despair and shame they would cover their mouths, a sign of mourning (cf. Lev.13:45; Ezek. 24:17, 22) that here also ironically symbolizes the cessation of their function as spokesmen for God.

In contrast to the false prophets, Micah affirmed his own credentials to serve as God's spokesman (v.8). Energized by the Lord's Spirit, Micah's prophetic ministry and message were characterized by power and a concern for justice. With courage and honesty he exposed the nation's covenantal rebellion.

The use of *mišpāṭ* ("justice") in verse 8 is especially significant in light of its use in verses 1 and 9. Although Judah's leaders were to promote justice (v.1), they despised and perverted it (v.9). Instead they oppressed God's people, stripping off their skin, as it were. The word *hipšîṭû* ("strip off," v.3) sounds like *mišpāṭ*, which draws attention to this perversion of justice.

In the final judgment speech of the chapter, Micah again addressed the nation's rulers, although the announcement of judgment mentions the priests and prophets as well (v.11). Once more he condemned social injustice (vv.9–10; cf. vv.1–3), using strong language to stress the leaders' perversion of justice and its consequences. These sinners abhorred (NIV "despise") justice and twisted (NIV "distort") the correct ethical standards. The picture is that of a straight, level road being transformed into a tortuous and bumpy one. Violence accompanied this social injustice. The rulers built Jerusalem with violence in the sense that they used the wealth obtained by violent methods to finance building projects in the city.

Micah also condemned the greed of the nation's leaders (v.11; cf. v.5). The judicial leaders made unjust decisions for bribes. The priests, though responsible for teaching the people the Law (Deut. 33:10), were motivated by profit as well. Since priests were involved in settling legal disputes (Deut. 17:8–13), they may have been accepting bribes in exchange for favorable verdicts. The prophets too were in business for financial gain.

Despite their blatant practical denial of the principles of covenant life, these leaders had the audacity to trust in the Lord for protection (v. 11; cf. 2:7). They were confident of the Lord's presence in their midst, boasting, "Is not the LORD among us?" With these words they were laying claim to a traditional affirmation of the Lord's covenant people (cf. Num. 11:20; 14:14; Deut. 7:21). One of the songs of Zion, Psalm 46, affirms, "God is within her, she will not fall; God will help her at break of day" (v.5). In claiming the Lord's promises of protection as absolutely unconditional, these covenant breakers overlooked the fact that obedience was foundational to receiving the Lord's blessing and protection (cf. Deut. 28).

The sins of the nation's leaders would bring destruction upon Jerusalem, the nation's capital (v.12). Like Samaria, whose sins she had followed (1:6), Jerusalem would be reduced to a heap of ruins. The picture of plowing suggests that everything in the city would be uprooted and overturned. The temple mount would become a forest, the habitation of wild beasts.

Because of Hezekiah's faithfulness and repentance, this prophecy of judgment was postponed, as the elders of the land recalled in Jeremiah's day (Jer. 26:17–19). Though held in suspension for a century or so, it eventually was fulfilled when the Babylonians sacked Jerusalem and burned the temple (2 Kings 25:9; 2 Chron. 36:19; Pss. 74:1–8; 79:1).

Jerusalem's Glorious Future (4:1–5)

The tone of Micah's message suddenly shifts from judgment to salvation. He portrayed the coming golden age as a time of peace and prosperity for Israel, whose major city, Jerusalem, would serve as the center of the Lord's worldwide rule. The elevation of Zion to a position above all other mountains (v.1) stands in stark contrast to the destruction predicted for the city at the end of chapter 3. The language is hyperbolic, physical height symbolizing prestige and honor.

Once-hostile nations, which had been the Lord's instruments in the destruction of Jerusalem (1:8–16), would stream toward Jerusalem for a completely different reason (4:1–2). They would now come to the city to receive instruction from the Lord so that they might live in accordance with His principles and rules for human society. The prophet pictured the Lord as a universal king whose laws and decrees are binding upon all people.

One of the Lord's royal functions would be to settle disputes between nations (v. 3). The mention of "many peoples," "strong nations," and "far and wide" stresses the universal scope of His jurisdiction. With the sovereign King making perfectly just legal decisions, nations would no longer go to war to settle differences. They would reforge their metal weapons into agricultural implements. Military training would become obsolete.

In verse 4 the prophet portrayed the consequences of this universal peace and disarmament. Each man would be able to enjoy the fruit of his labors without worrying about military invasion bringing death and starvation. Sitting under one's own vine and fig tree pictures prosperity and security. Similar language is used of the Solomonic era (1 Kings 4:25). The motif is probably traditional, since Sennacherib promised such conditions to the inhabitants of Jerusalem if they rebelled against Hezekiah (2 Kings 18:31). The absence of a terrorizer (note "no one will make them afraid") is also a traditional motif associated with divine blessing (Lev. 26:6) and restoration (Jer. 30:10; 46:27; Ezek. 34:28; Zeph. 3:13). This promise of universal peace and prosperity was certain of fulfillment because it was made by the Lord Almighty, whose awesome power would deter any militarism on the part of the nations.

Appended to this salvation portrayal is an affirmation of loyalty by the faithful among the Lord's people (v.5). Present conditions contrasted with the picture of the future drawn by the prophet in verses 1–4. The nations followed their own gods, not the Lord. However, through the faithful the eschatological ideal could be realized in the present, at least in part. To "walk in the name of" might be paraphrased "to give allegiance to." "Name" here represents the one possessing it and symbolizes the Lord's authority over those who acknowledge His sovereignty.

Crisis and Restoration (4:6–5:15)

4:6–7. The Lord next announced salvation for the remnant of Judah. He emphasized that He would personally intervene on behalf of His people (note the repetition of the first person). The exiles are described as injured, their grief having been caused by the Lord Himself, who is here cast in the role of an adversary.

However, a reversal in the Lord's relationship to the nation would take place. In fulfillment of the Mosaic promise (Deut. 30:4), the Lord would regather the exiles and make them into a remnant who would form the nucleus of the Lord's mighty restored nation of the eschaton. The establishment of a "strong nation" would fulfill the Lord's promise to Abraham (Gen. 18:18; cf. also Exod. 1:9; Num. 22:6; Isa. 60:22).

4:8–5:6. This section deals with the issue of Zion's future in relation to the Davidic throne. Zion would again become the center of Davidic rule (4:8; 5:2–6), but only after she suffered without a king (4:9; 5:1) and experienced the exile of her people (4:10).

The prophet addressed the ancient fortified city of David, located within Jerusalem (4:8). As the traditional home of the Davidic ruler, who was viewed as Israel's shepherd (cf. Ps. 78:70–72), this citadel could be appropriately called the "watchtower of the flock." The Lord promised the ancient royal site that its former glory would be restored.

In contrast to the future, Zion was in distress in Micah's day (4:9). The rhetorical questions suggest that the Davidic ruler had become relatively ineffective in thwarting the aggressive nations. Before the threat of her enemies Zion was like a woman in labor, whose intense pain causes her to writhe, cry out, and even panic.

The ironic command of 4:10 stresses that this panic was justified because the exile of the city's population was imminent. The reference to leaving the city and camping in the open field pictures the loss of security and protection. More specifically, the language depicts the people's deportation to Babylon. It is unlikely that the prophet meant this to be a reference to the Chaldean empire that would succeed the Assyrians as the dominant political force in the ancient Near East. During Micah's time Assyria controlled Babylon. For the prophet and his contemporaries a reference to Babylon would have suggested the Assyrian empire (cf. 5:5–6; 7:12). Nevertheless, the specific reference to Babylon does anticipate subsequent historical developments in a more precise way than the prophet probably realized (see on 3:12 above).

For Zion, called in 5:1 a "city of troops" (i.e., a city under attack), ritual mourning was appropriate. The verb translated "marshal your troops" is better rendered "slash yourselves in mourning." This ritual act of self-mutilation is mentioned elsewhere in the Old Testament (Deut. 14:1; 1 Kings 18:28; Jer. 16:6; 47:5; Hos. 7:14 [NIV margin and Septuagint]). Such an extreme emotional expression was fitting in this case because Zion was surrounded by troops. The reference to a siege recalls the covenant curses of Deuteronomy 28:52–57.

As already noted in 4:9, to which 5:1 corresponds in the chiastic arrangement of themes (see above), Zion's king was humiliated. Striking another on the cheek was an insult (cf. 1 Kings 22:24; Job 16:10; Lam. 3:30). The fact that this blow is struck with a "rod" (i.e., the royal scepter), an instrument that the ideal Davidic king is pictured as using to subdue the nations (cf. Ps. 2:9), makes the insult even worse. A wordplay draws attention to the irony of this development: Israel's ruler (*šōpēṭ*) is struck with a rod (*šēḇeṭ*).

The precise historical background of this passage is uncertain, although the language accurately reflects the position of Judah and her king relative to Assyria during the latter part of the eighth century and most of the seventh century (cf. 2 Kings 16:7–8, 17–18; 18:13–16; 2 Chron. 33:11). Since the distress, according to 4:9–10, would culminate in exile, the humiliation of the Davidic rulers before the Chaldeans may even be included (cf. 2 Kings 24–25).

Although the crisis described here would end in exile and humiliation, the Lord would not forget His people. Using language reminiscent of Israel's deliverance from Egypt, the prophet promised that the Lord would rescue His people from Babylon (4:10b). In 4:11–13 he pictured the future deliverance of Jerusalem from enemy armies. He saw the present crisis (cf. "but *now* . . ." in v.11), which epitomized gentile hostility toward God's people, as foreshadowing a final eschatological attack upon Jerusalem. He jumped ahead to that final time in verses 12–13. This blending of the temporal and eschatological perspectives, while confusing to modern readers, is typical of the prophets and attests to the unity of God's sovereign work in history. It is possible that the Lord's destruction of Sennacherib's armies outside the walls of Jerusalem in 701 B.C. contributed to the eschatological hope expressed here.

Wordplay is used in 4:11–13 for purposes of contrast and irony. In contrast to 4:9, where there is reason to believe that Jerusalem's human "counselor" has perished, the Lord Himself here plans the deliverance of the city. The words translated "counselor" (v.9) and "plan" (v.12) are derived from the same

Hebrew root word. The one who, according to 4:6, would gather and assemble the exiles of Judah here gathers the nations together in order to destroy them (cf. vv.11–12, where the same Heb. words used in v.6 appear again). "Gathered" in verse 11 (*ne'espû*) is an example of double entendre. From the nations' perspective they are gathered for war with the purpose of destroying Jerusalem. However, the word *'āsap*, "gather," is used rather frequently in harvesting and threshing contexts (e.g., Exod. 23:10, 16; Lev.23:39; 25:3, 20; Deut. 11:14; 16:13; 28:38), and this agricultural nuance is suggested by verses 12–13. From God's perspective the nations would be "harvested" or "heaped up" in order that they, not Jerusalem, might be destroyed.

The restoration of God's people would be accomplished through the reestablishment of the Davidic throne to its former glory (5:2–6). Bethlehem Ephrathah is identified as the place of origin of this coming ruler (Ephrathah is an alternate name for Bethlehem; cf. Gen. 35:19; 48:7; Ruth 1:2; 4:11; 1 Sam. 17:12). Though the town was small among the clans of Judah, the Lord's ruler would arise from it.

The emphasis on Bethlehem's relative insignificance is consistent with a pattern seen elsewhere in the Old Testament. The Lord predicted that Jacob, though the younger of the sons born to Rebekah, would become the more prominent of the two. A similar prediction was made concerning Ephraim (Gen. 25:23; 48:14–19). Gideon, though the youngest in the smallest family in Manasseh, was used mightily by God (Judg. 6:15). Saul was chosen to be Israel's first king, although he was from the smallest family of Benjamin, the smallest of the tribes of Israel (1 Sam. 9:21). The word translated "small" in Micah 5:2 is used in each of these texts.

The mention of Bethlehem reminds one of David. In riddlelike fashion the reference to the ruler's origins being from antiquity hints that David himself would return.[5] Other

---

[5] In this context the Heb. expressions translated "from of old" and "from ancient times" refer to antiquity, not eternity past. The former clearly refers to antiquity in Isa. 45:21 and 46:10. In other texts it refers more specifically to the early periods of Israel's history (cf. Pss. 74:12; 77:11), including the time of David (Neh. 12:46). In Hab. 1:12 the phrase may be used of eternity past, however, although even here the contextual emphasis is on the Lord's involvement in Israel's early history (cf. Hab. 3). The expression translated "from ancient times" in Mic. 5:2 also refers elsewhere to former periods in

prophets are more direct and actually call the coming ideal ruler "David" (Jer. 30:9; Ezek. 34:23–24; 37:24–25; Hos. 3:5). The language is probably to be taken idiomatically, not literally. By presenting this future ruler as David himself, these prophets emphasized that he would spring from the ancient Davidic line (cf. Isa. 11:1, 10; Jer. 33:15), reign in the spirit and power of his illustrious ancestor, and fulfill the ideals of the Davidic covenant. In the progress of biblical revelation the Lord Jesus Christ, the perfect and ideal Son of David, emerges as this new Davidic ruler.[6]

Picking up the imagery of 4:9–10, the prophet pointed out that Zion's suffering would eventually come to an end (5:3a). The Lord would give His people over to exile (4:10) until Zion finally "gives birth." In 4:9–10 Zion's horror in the face of impending exile and defeat is compared to a woman experiencing unrelenting labor pains. In 5:3 the cessation of exile is likened to birth, which finally brings the pains to an end.

With the return from exile the nation would be reunited (5:3b). "The rest of his brothers" most naturally refers to the coming king's fellow Judahites, in which case the "Israelites" mentioned would be the returning exiles of the northern tribes. The reunification of north and south is a prominent motif in prophetic eschatology (cf. Isa. 11:12–13; Jer. 31:2–6, 15–20; Ezek. 37; Hos. 1:11; 3:5).

Micah next described the reign of this ideal Davidic king over the reunified nation (5:4–5a). The description contains several standard motifs associated with the royal figure in the ancient Near East. This king would be a shepherd who rules by the power of God. His widespread fame and success would bring peace to his realm. The language is also reminiscent of the historical David, who was God's appointed shepherd over his people (2 Sam. 5:2; Ps. 78:71–72) and experienced God's energizing power (2 Sam. 22:30–46). National security and widespread fame were also associated with the Davidic ideal

history (cf. Isa. 63:9, 11; Mic. 7:14; Mal. 3:4), including the time of David (Amos 9:11).

[6]Some have seen in 5:2 a supernatural figure (i.e., the preincarnate Christ) who was active in Israel's early history. This interpretation requires a different translation of the text to avoid the implication that the second person of the Trinity had a beginning in time. The word *môṣā'ōṯ* (lit. "goings out"; cf. NIV "origins") must be understood as meaning "appearances" or "activities" in this view.

(2 Sam. 7:10; Ps. 72). This ideal would finally be fully realized in the new David, the Messiah.

In 5:5b–6 the prophet stressed Israel's invulnerability to enemy attack and its ascendency over its enemies in the end times. Assyria here epitomizes and represents Israel's historical enemies. During the latter half of the eighth century B.C., Assyria invaded Palestine at will, forcing the small western states to submit to her harsh tyranny. However, in the new era to come such aggressors would be unsuccessful. Under the military leadership of her mighty king (note "*he* will deliver us" in v.6), Israel would not only suppress any attacks but also extend its suzerainty over the attackers. "Seven shepherds"/"eight leaders of men" suggests an ideal defensive force. In the x/x + 1 pattern (here 7/8) the focus can be on the first number, which is likely here, the number "seven" suggesting realization of an ideal or completeness. Assyria is also referred to as "the land of Nimrod" here, probably because Nimrod, the founder of Assyria, was renowned as a warrior and hunter. However, in the eschaton Israel would violently suppress all who seek to war against and prey upon it.

5:7–9. Micah next developed the remnant theme, introduced earlier (cf. 4:7). The meaning of 5:7 is debated. Some see this as a reference to the positive effect the Israelite remnant would have upon the surrounding nations. In this case verse 7 contrasts with the following verses. However, the structural correspondence between verses 7 and 8 suggests they are complementary. Some see the emphasis in verse 7 as being the divine origin of dew and rain. Like the dew and the rain, the remnant would be the product of God's sovereign work. Another possibility is that the dew simile is used to picture hostile action, as in 2 Samuel 17:12, where a surprise attack is likened to dew appearing on the ground. In this case the similes of verses 7–8 correspond thematically, the emphasis in each being upon the irresistible might of the remnnant. Just as people are unable to control dew and rain, and as the beasts of the forest and flocks of sheep are unable to resist the powerful lion, so the nations would be unable to combat the military power of Israel's remnant. Verse 9 includes a blessing addressed to this remnant. The hand, lifted up over one's enemies, is a symbol of power (Ps. 89:13; Isa. 26:11).

5:10–14. These verses, which in isolation have the tone of a judgment speech, must be viewed more positively in the larger context of the chapter. The Lord here described how He would purify Judah of its symbols of self-sufficient pride and paganism. The repetition of the first-person verb forms draws attention to the Lord's personal involvement in the matter. Horses and chariots had no place in the theocratic ideal because Israel was to rely solely on the power of the Lord for deliverance and victory (Exod. 14:9, 23; 15:1, 3–4; Deut. 17:16; 20:1; Josh. 11:4–9; 2 Kings 6). This principle appears as well in other genres of Old Testament literature: hymnic (Pss. 20:7; 33:16–19), wisdom (Prov. 21:31), and prophetic (Isa. 2:7; 31:1–3; Hos. 14:3). Fortified cities also symbolized the nation's pride and sense of self-sufficiency (Isa. 2:15; Jer. 5:17). Judah would also be purged of false religious practices. The Mosaic Law prohibited divination (Lev. 19:26; Deut. 18:10) and the worship of idols, sacred pillars, or Asherah poles (Exod. 20:4, Deut. 7:5, 25; 12:2; 16:21–22).

5:15. This verse complements 4:5 in that it shows how the nations, which in Micah's day followed their own gods, would come to a place of total subservience to the true God (cf. 4:1–4). The Lord would lash out in anger against the nations like a mighty universal sovereign taking punitive action ("vengeance") against His rebellious servants.

Covenants Broken and Fulfilled (6:1–7:20)

This final major section of the book, like the two sections preceding it, moves from judgment (6:1–7:7) to salvation (7:8–20). Chapter 6 may be divided into two units, a covenant lawsuit (vv.1–8) and a judgment speech (vv.9–16).

I. Covenant lawsuit (vv.1–8)
   A. Introduction (vv.1–2)
      1. Challenge to people to present their case (v.1)
      2. Summons to mountains to appear as witnesses (v.2)
   B. Divine challenge to the people (vv.3–5)
      1. Challenge to bring an accusation against the Lord (v.3)
      2. Challenge to remember the Lord's saving deeds (vv.4–5)

    C. Conclusion (a prophetic reminder of the Lord's requirements) (vv.6–8)

II. Judgment speech (vv.9–16)
    A. Call to attention (v.9)
    B. Accusation (vv.10–12)
    C. Announcement of judgment (vv.13–15)
    D. Summary of judgment speech (v.16)
        1. Accusation (v.16a)
        2. Announcement of judgment (v.16b)

Chapter 7 may be divided into three formal units, the structure of which is reflected in the following outline:

I. Prophetic lament (vv.1–7)
    A. Lament proper (vv.1–6)
    B. Statement of confidence (v.7)

II. Zion's statement of confidence/oracle of salvation (vv.8–13)
    A. Confidence (vv.8–10)
    B. Oracle of salvation addressed to Zion (vv.11–13)

III. National prayer (vv.14–20)
    A. Petition (v.14)
    B. Oracle of salvation directed to nation (v.15)
    C. Nation's statement of confidence (vv.16–17)
    D. Concluding hymn of praise (vv.18–20)

At the same time, the chapter as a whole displays a chiastic arrangement.

A) Prophet's lament (vv.1–7)

    B) Zion confident of her enemies' defeat (vv.8–10)

        C) Zion assured of salvation (vv.11–13)

            D) The nation's prayer (v.14)

        C) The nation assured of salvation (v.15)

    B) The nation confident of her enemies' defeat (vv.16–17)

A) The nation's hymn of praise (vv.18–20)

The B and C points correspond thematically around the pivotal prayer (D). The A points correspond in a contrastive sense, the contrast highlighting the reversal in the nation's fortunes that the chapter emphasizes. At the beginning of the chapter a lone prophet bemoans the situation around him. By the end of the chapter a restored nation praises its forgiving and faithful God.

A Divine Lawsuit (6:1–8)

The lawsuit opens with a challenge to the people to present their case against the Lord before the mountains, which appear here in the role of divinely summoned witnesses (vv.1–2). In other biblical divine lawsuits the heavens and earth, having been present at the ratification of the Lord's covenant with His people (Deut. 4:26; 30:19; 31:28), appear as witnesses (Deut. 32:1; Ps. 50:4; Isa. 1:2). Consequently the appearance of the mountains in this role may seem surprising. However, mountains appear as witnesses in secular treaties in the ancient Near East. These treaties provide the background for the biblical covenant model. As permanent fixtures in the physical world, the personified mountains were, in a poetic sense, constant witnesses to the actions of God's people. To appeal to them in a lawsuit is a powerful rhetorical device that lends solemnity to the proceedings.

The Lord began His accusation with two questions and a direct challenge (v.3). His disobedient people were acting as if He had mistreated them in some way. Elsewhere the word translated "burdened" is used of wearing out another physically (Job 16:7; Jer. 12:5), frustrating one's efforts to accomplish a task (Ezek. 24:12), or exhausting another's patience (Isa. 7:13). A related noun is used of Israel's exhaustion under the oppression of the Egyptians (Num. 20:14) and of their hardships during the period of wandering in the wilderness (Exod. 18:8), from which the Lord had delivered them. The question of Micah 6:3 implies that Judah was accusing the Lord, its Savior, of being an oppressor like Egypt!

In verses 4–5 the Lord demonstrated that Judah's complaint was unfounded by rehearsing the events of Israel's early history. He had not burdened Israel; rather, He had brought them up out of Egypt, the land in which they had been enslaved. A wordplay between "have I burdened you" (*hel'ēṭîḳā*) and "I brought you up" (*he/ᵉliṭîḳâ*) draws attention to the stark contrast between their warped view of God's dealings with them and historical reality.

The Lord also provided the nation with leadership. Moses and Aaron are mentioned together in other salvation traditions (Josh. 24:5; 1 Sam. 12:8; Pss. 77:20; 105:26). The inclusion of their sister Miriam (cf. Num. 26:59) in such traditional formulas is unique but certainly understandable in light of her role as a prophetess and contributor to Israel's early hymnic tradition (Exod. 15:20–21).

The Lord also supernaturally protected His people as they approached and entered the Promised Land. He thwarted Balak's attempts to curse Israel through Balaam (Num. 22–24; Josh. 24:9–10) and led the people safely from Shittim, where they camped before crossing the Jordan, to Gilgal, where they commemorated the miraculous crossing, submitted to circumcision, and celebrated the Passover (Josh. 2:1; 3:1; 4:19–5:10). All of these salvific deeds are called "righteous acts of the LORD" because they demonstrated the just character of the Lord, which had been impugned by Micah's generation.

In the conclusion to the lawsuit the prophet focused on the requirements of the Lord, emphasizing that He desires loyalty, not mere ritual (vv.6–8). The prophet employed a series of questions designed to raise the issue of access to God and point out the inadequacy of ritual (vv.6–7). In essence, he asked, "How is one to approach the Lord, the sovereign, transcendent God?" Because the people would have thought in terms of ritual and sacrifice, the prophet proposed several potential offerings in the order of increasing value. Would burnt offerings of year-old calves be appropriate? Some might think so (cf. Lev.9:3), but the prophet's next question suggests otherwise. Surely thousands of rams and infinite quantities of oil would suffice. Such offerings would rival those of Solomon (cf. 1 Kings 3:4; 8:63). However, the appearance of yet another question indicates that not even these vast offerings would be adequate. One would think that with his final question the prophet hits the nail on the head. Certainly the offering of one's firstborn son, the ultimate act of devotion, would satisfy the Lord (cf. 2 Kings 3:27). However, as shocking as it might be to one thinking in terms of ritual sacrifices, not even this sacrifice would be satisfactory

Actually the Lord had already told the people what He required most of all (v.8). Sacrifice was not even a part of the Lord's essential covenant demands. To gain the Lord's favor one must first of all meet certain ethical requirements. The essence of covenantal life is summed up in the words "act justly" and "love mercy." To love mercy results in acting justly. More specifically, being committed to one's fellow Israelites (devotion or commitment is the basic idea behind the word *ḥesed*, translated "mercy" in NIV) would mean doing everything in one's power to ensure their just treatment and would absolutely preclude any acts of socioeconomic injustice. To promote justice is, in turn, the way in which one walks "humbly" with God. The people of Judah, despite their heavy involvement in religious activity, had miserably failed to live up to this ethical standard (cf. Isa. 1:10–20; Mic. 2:1–5, 8–9; 3:1–3, 9–11; 6:10–12; 7:2–3, 6). Consequently their ritual was totally unacceptable to God and only heightened their guilt by adding hypocrisy to injustice.

Injustice Denounced (6:9–16)

This judgment speech is addressed to "the city," which is probably a reference to Jerusalem (cf. 3:10–12; 4:2, 7–13). Appended to the call to attention is a didactic observation intended to remind the audience of the necessity of wise submission to the Lord, who threatens judgment.

The accusation proper begins in verse 10 with a probing question that makes it clear that the Lord was fully aware of the socioeconomic injustice going on inside the city. Verses 10b–11 mention specific devices used by merchants to cheat their customers. The Mosaic Law prohibited such dishonest business practices (Lev.19:35–36; Deut. 25:13–16), as did wisdom literature (Prov. 11:1; 20:10, 23) and other eighth-century prophets (Hos. 12:7; Amos 8:5). The Lord's strong disapproval of this economic dishonesty is apparent from the rhetorical question of verse 11 and from the strong language used to describe the merchants ("O wicked house," v.10a), their profits ("ill-gotten treasures," v.10a), and the tools of their trade ("accursed," "dishonest," "false," vv.10b–11). Verse 12 either elaborates on the true character of the economic practices mentioned in verses 10–11 or, more likely, moves on to even more injurious crimes involving seizure of property or false legal testimony.

The Lord announced His intent to intervene violently against the sinners of Jerusalem (v.13). His judgment would bring loss of fertility (vv.14–15). There would not be enough food to satisfy the people's hunger, for invaders would steal both the crops stored up in the barns and those growing in the fields and vineyards.

The summary statement of the speech (v.16) accuses the guilty of having followed the practices of the Israelite Omride dynasty. Ahab, the most well known of the Omride rulers, epitomized the greed and power that resulted in the grossest forms of socioeconomic injustice (1 Kings 21). Like Ahab, the individuals denounced in verses 10–12 had exploited the social and economic weakness of others for selfish purposes. The Lord, through His devastating judgment (vv.13–15), would make these sinners the object of reproach among the surrounding nations, as He had threatened in the covenant curses (e.g., Deut. 28:37).

Micah's Lament (7:1–7)

The prophet's lament is a logical response to the sin and impending judgment described in the preceding chapter. Micah began with an agricultural metaphor, comparing himself to one who walks through an orchard or vineyard after the harvest and can find no fruit to satisfy his appetite (v.1). In the same way faithful and upright men could no longer be found in Judah (v. 2a).

Instead violence and dishonesty had permeated society (vv. 2b–3). The prophet vividly pictured the hostility existing between his countrymen. He portrayed them as setting ambushes for one another and as hunting down their fellow Judahites with nets. They directed all their energies (note "both hands," v.3) to evil deeds, which they successfully carried out. The expression translated "are skilled" (*lᵉhêṭîḇ*, v.3; lit. "to do well") is dripping with sarcasm. Elsehwere this phrase is used in a moral/ethical sense ("to do what is right/proper") and stands in contrast to doing evil (Isa. 1:16–17; Jer. 4:22; 13:23). Here the phrase simply has a neutral sense ("to do diligently or thoroughly") and describes how these sinners efficiently carried out their evil plans and deeds.

Returning to agricultural imagery, Micah declared that even the best of these sinners were like briers and thorns (v. 4a). The language contrasts with that of verse 1. When one looked out over the ethical landscape of Judah, one found, as it were, sharp thorns, not tasty fruit.

Such a society was doomed for destruction (v.4b). Some see the watchmen mentioned by Micah as the succession of prophets who had predicted a Day of Judgment upon sin. It is more likely that "the day of your watchmen" refers to the calamity that the city's guards would soon see approaching on the horizon in the form of an invading army. This calamity is called a time of "confusion" (*mᵉbûkâ*; cf. Isa. 22:5). This word was chosen because it sounds like the word translated "thorn hedge" (*mᵉsûkâ*) in verse 4. The similarity in sound draws one's attention to the correspondence between sin and punishment and the appropriate nature of the latter.

In verses 5–6 the prophet returned to the theme of societal disintegration. Relationships normally characterized by faithfulness and trust, such as friendships and marriage, had been disrupted. Within the home children and servants ("the members of his own household") rebelled against those in authority over them.

Despite the corruption all around him and the certainty of divine judgment, Micah expressed his trust in the Lord as the source of his deliverance (v.7; cf. Hab. 3:18). He stressed his personal relationship to God (note "my Savior" and "my God"). This expression of trust sets the tone for the remainder of the chapter, in which Jerusalem and then the entire nation speak confidently of the Lord's eventual intervention on their behalf once the smoke of judgment has lifted.

Zion's Confidence (7:8–13)

Although Jerusalem/Zion is not specifically designated as the speaker in these verses, such a conclusion is supported by (1) the feminine singular forms of the pronouns in the phrases "your God" (v.10) and "your walls" (v.11), (2) the reference to the rebuilding of the walls (v.11), and (3) the conceptual parallels between these verses and 4:8–13, where Jerusalem is also personified as a woman. The perspective in 7:8–13 is that of the exile prophesied by Micah in 4:10.

In verse 8 Jerusalem defiantly tells her enemies not to gloat over her humiliation. Though fallen and suffering the effects of judgment, she is certain of restoration when the Lord intervenes on her behalf. While she acknowledges her past sins and submits herself to the Lord's angry judgment, she is confident that the end of her chastisement is in sight and that the Lord is about to reverse her situation as well as that of her enemies (vv.9–10). The Lord would lead Jerusalem out of the darkness of judgment into the light of salvation. The background for the imagery may be release from a dark prison (cf. Isa. 42:7). The enemies would also experience a reversal of fortunes, their mocking pride being turned to shame.

The salvation oracle addressed to Zion (vv.11–13) continues the theme of a reversal of situation. For Jerusalem, which would stand desolate and abandoned during the Exile, the Lord's intervention would result in the city's being rebuilt and expanded in preparation for the arrival of its exiled citizens. On the other hand, the rest of the earth would lie desolate because of God's judgment upon the wicked deeds of its sinful inhabitants.

The Nation's Prayer (7:14–20)

In its petition, which is central in the chiastic structure of this chapter, the exiled nation asks the Lord to come like a shepherd and lead His people to fertile pastures (v. 14; cf. 2:12–13). The nation pictures itself as an isolated and therefore vulnerable flock trapped in a thicket where dangerous predators lurk. To make matters worse, this forest is surrounded by tantalizing fertile fields. In contrast to its present situation, the nation longs for the blessings of the "good old days" to be restored. Continuing the pastoral imagery of the first half of the verse, it likens this restoration to grazing in Bashan and Gilead, two well-known grazing regions (cf. Num. 32:1–5; Deut. 32:14; Jer. 50:19).

In response the Lord announces that Israel would again experience the miraculous salvation that highlighted its early history (v.15). The Lord would repeat the wonders that accompanied the Exodus. "Wonders" refers elsewhere to the plagues with which the Lord afflicted Egypt (Exod. 3:20) and to His miraculous deliverance of Israel at the Red Sea (cf. Pss. 78:12–13; 106:22).

Having heard this brief, but powerful, oracle from the Lord, the nation responds with confidence that its enemies, like Egypt of old, would be humiliated by the Lord and forced to submit to His sovereign power and authority (vv.16–17). Viewing this mighty display of God's might would cause the nations to be ashamed of their own power, which falls far short of the Lord's. They would be speechless, covering their mouths with their hands. The gesture is ironic, since the hand is often used in Scripture as a symbol of power. The expression "lick dust" vividly depicts the nations' humiliation and submission. The double simile, likening the nations to serpents, is highly derogatory.

The picture of the conquered nations' utter terror (v. 17b) has striking parallels in ancient Near Eastern literature and art. For example, an Egyptian text says of Ramses III, "As for the rebels who know not Egypt forever, they hear of his strength, coming with praise, trembling in their limbs at the (mere) mention of him, saluting with their hearts for terror of him."[7] The Assyrian annals frequently record how a military victory results in various city-states voluntarily submitting to the king's yoke. For example, Sargon recalled, "[The kings of Appatar and Kitpatai] heard of the approach of my expedition, the fear of my awe-inspiring splendor fell upon them, terror overcame them in their (own) land . . . they begged me to spare their lives, and that I should not destroy their walls, they kissed my feet."[8]

The book concludes with a hymn praising the incomparable God of Israel for His grace and covenantal faithfulness (vv. 18–20). Israel's experience of forgiveness forms the basis for its affirmation of God's uniqueness. The Lord's restoration of exiled Israel would demonstrate that ultimately His "mercy" (ḥesed, "loyal love, devotion") takes precedence over His wrath in His dealings with His covenant people. Though He lashes out in anger against His sinful people, His compassion prompts Him to forgive and restore them (cf. Hos. 11). His energies are then directed to discarding His people's sins, which is compared here to subduing an enemy and to hurling an object into the depths of the sea.

The foundation for God's gracious dealings with Israel is the unconditional covenant of grace given to Abraham and inherited by his offspring through Isaac and Jacob. Because of His irrevocable oath to Abraham and his seed (Gen. 22:16; 26:3;

[7]William F. Edgerton and John A. Wilson, *Historical Records of Ramses III: The Texts in Medinet Habu,* vols. 1–2 (Chicago: University of Chicago Press, 1936), p. 50.

[8]Daniel D. Luckenbill, *Ancient Records of Assyria and Babylonia,* 2 vols. (Chicago: University of Chicago Press, 1926–27), 2:78, par. 149.

50:24), whereby He promised the land of Palestine and numerous offspring, the Lord would restore His people, thus demonstrating His faithfulness to the fathers.

THEOLOGY

Summary

The Lord God of Israel stands at the center of Micah's theological message. Micah presented God as the sovereign Lord of the earth who controls the destinies of nations, including His covenant people Israel. The Lord appears primarily in the roles of judge, warrior, and (shepherd-)king.

The sovereign Lord would judge the nations of the earth, subduing them and incorporating them into His kingdom. This judgment would also include Israel, for God's people had violated His covenant demands. The Lord's thorough, but appropriate, judgment would purify His people. Because of His unconditional promise to Abraham, the Lord would forgive the sins of His people and deliver a remnant from exile. He would form them into a mighty nation under the rulership of the messianic king. Jerusalem, so badly humiliated by the nations in the past, would be elevated to a place of prominence, serving as the center for the Lord's worldwide rule of peace.

Analysis

God and the Nations

The introduction to Micah's prophecy (1:2–4) makes it clear that the God of Israel is sovereign over the nations. Using the language of the law court, the prophet announced to the nations that the "Sovereign LORD" was about to witness against them. He then described in vivid theophanic language the Lord's descent upon the mountains as He comes to judge.

In subsequent passages the prophet further developed this theme of universal judgment. According to 4:11–13, the Lord would gather many nations against Jerusalem so that they might be destroyed. Victorious Israel would then devote the wealth of the nations "to the Lord of all the earth" (4:13). The disobedient nations would be the object of the Lord's angry vengeance (5:14), which would leave the earth desolate (7:13). The nations who mocked the Lord's people (v.10) would crawl in fear before the Lord (vv.16–17), acknowledging His power and sovereignty.

This subjugation of the nations would usher in the millennial age, during which the Lord would reign over the earth from His royal palace in Jerusalem (4:1–4). The nations would look to Him for guidance and resolution of their disputes. Peace, an unrealized ideal throughout the bloody history of humankind, would prevail in human society, allowing men and women to devote their energies to purposes more useful than warfare.

God and His People

Judgment. Within the framework of God's universal dealings, the bulk of the prophecy concerns Israel, God's special covenant people. Israel's rebellion against the Mosaic covenant would actually set in motion God's universal judgment (1:5–7). This judgment would have as its primary target the kingdom of Judah, which had followed in the footsteps of the northern kingdom (1:5–7, 9, 13; 6:16).

Various reasons are given for the coming judgment upon God's people. Socioeconomic oppression of the poor receives special attention in the accusatory sections of Micah's judgment speeches (2:1–2, 8–9; 3:1–3, 9–10; 6:10–11; 7:2–3). This exploitation of one's fellow Israelites was antithetical to the Lord's basic covenantal demand for justice (6:8). The leaders of the nation, including the prophets and the priests, are singled out for their greed, dishonesty, unjust treatment of the poor, and complacency (2:6–11; 3:1–12).

The Lord's judgment of these sinners would be harsh, but perfectly fair and appropriate. Those who robbed their fellow Israelites of their land would be deprived of their own property and excluded from any future land allotments (2:1–5). Those who mercilessly oppressed others would find no mercy from the Lord in the Day of Judgment (3:1–4). The false prophets, who were motivated by greed, would be deprived of genuine prophetic revelation and would stand ashamed and silent (3:5–7).

The ultimate goal of God's judgment was the purification of His people (5:10–14). By destroying the nation's defenses and cultic system, the Lord would eliminate its sources of false security and pave the way for its restoration.

Salvation. The remnant theme is one of the most prominent

motifs in Micah's prophecies of Israel's future restoration. The Lord's merciful forgiveness of the remnant of His people would establish the foundation for Israel's restoration (7:18). The Lord promised to lead this remnant of exiles back to their homeland (2:12–13; 4:6, 10; 5:3) and form them into a mighty nation (4:7) that prevails over its foes (5:7–9).

In delivering this remnant from exile, the Lord would repeat the mighty acts that He performed at the beginning of Israel's history. Just as the Lord delivered Israel from Egypt and led them into the fertile Promised Land (6:4–5), He would again intervene in power to bring about their restoration (7:14–15). In so doing, the Lord would exhibit His ongoing concern for His people and demonstrate that His power is not diminished with the passing of time.

Jerusalem plays a central role in Micah's portrayal of Israel's future. Although subjected to humiliation because of its people's sin (3:12; 4:9–10; 5:1; 7:8–9), Jerusalem could look forward to a glorious future. A day would come when the city would be rebuilt and its people would return from exile (7:11–12). The Lord would restore the Davidic throne (4:8), protect the city from enemy attack (4:11–13), and make it the center of His universal kingdom (4:1–4).

The Messiah is an important figure in Micah's vision of the future. Micah placed this king's emergence against the background of the humiliation of the Davidic throne in his own day (4:9; 5:1). This ideal king's association with Bethlehem and with Israel's ancient past indicates that Micah, like other prophets (cf. Jer. 30:9; Ezek. 34:23–24; Hos. 3:5), envisioned the second coming of David. Isaiah and others provide clarification on this point. This coming ruler would not actually be David; rather, he would be a descendent of David who would rule in the spirit and power of his royal ancestor and would fulfill the ideal expressed in the Davidic covenant (cf. 2 Sam. 7:9–11). Under this king reunited Israel would be victorious over its enemies and experience peace and prosperity (5:3–6). According to Micah, within the theocratic structure of the eschaton the Messiah would be a vice-regent of the Great King, the Lord Himself (cf. 5:4 with 4:1–4). Like the Lord, he would be a shepherd-king who, in turn, would have other rulers (also called "shepherds") functioning under him (5:4–5).

The Abrahamic covenant is a foundational element in Micah's eschatology. God would forgive and restore Israel because He promised Abraham and his descendents by oath that He would multiply their offspring and give them the land of Palestine as an eternal possession. In Genesis 22:16–18, where the Lord formally ratified by oath the seed aspect of the Abrahamic covenant in response to Abraham's faithfulness (the land aspect of the covenant is formally ratified in Gen. 15), the Lord stated:

> I swear by myself . . . that because you have done this and have not withheld your son, your only son, I will surely bless you and make your descendants as numerous as the stars in the sky and as the sand on the seashore. Your descendants will take possession of the cities of their enemies, and through your offspring all nations on earth will be blessed, because you have obeyed me.

The promise contains three elements. First, Abraham would have numerous offspring, which is the same as saying his offspring would become a mighty nation (cf. Gen. 18:18). Second, his descendents would be victorious over their enemies. Third, through Abraham's offspring all the earth would eventually be blessed. Micah envisioned the fulfillment of each element in this promise. In 4:7 the Lord said He would form the remnant into a mighty nation. In several places in Micah the nation's future superiority to its enemies is stressed (4:12–13; 5:5–9; 7:10, 16–17). Finally, through Israel God's blessings would be extended throughout the world (4:1–4).

In short, a proper understanding of the relationship of the Davidic and Abrahamic covenants to the Mosaic covenant provides the interpretive key to Micah's theology and explains why he could move so abruptly from judgment to salvation. Micah denounced his contemporaries for their failure to obey the Mosaic covenant and announced that harsh judgment was about to fall, culminating in exile. Yet he also saw a light beyond the darkness of judgment (7:8). The basis for this hope was God's faithfulness to Abraham and David, which assured that His mercy would replace His anger (vv.18–20).

7

NAHUM

INTRODUCTION

Date

Nahum prophesied sometime between 663 and 612 B.C. He regarded as historical fact the fall of Thebes, an event that occurred in 663 (cf. 3:8–10). At the same time, he prophesied the fall of Nineveh, which occurred in 612. Within these rather broad limits, some attempt a precise dating of the book. However, the internal evidence cannot be pressed so far.

Unity

Detecting an original acrostic poem in 1:2–8, some deny these verses to Nahum. However, the presence of an acrostic here is highly questionable. Even if one were able to isolate such a poem, its authorship, or at least its inclusion in the book (possibly in an adapted form), could still be attributed to Nahum. On a more positive note, Carl Armerding has demonstrated the thematic and stylistic unity of the book.[1]

Structure

The Book of Nahum consists of two major sections: 1:2–11 and 1:12–3:19. The first of these contains two parallel parts

[1] See Carl E. Armerding, "Nahum," in *The Expositor's Bible Commentary*, ed. Frank E. Gaebelein (Grand Rapids: Zondervan, 1985), 7:451–52.

(1:2–6, 7–11), each of which is introduced by an affirmation about the Lord's character ("The LORD is a jealous and avenging God," v.2; and "The LORD is good," v.7). Both of these statements focus on the Lord's concern for His people. He vindicates (v.2) and protects (v.7) them. Verses 2–6 are a hymn that describes the Lord's awesome theophanic appearance in judgment against His enemies. Verses 7–11 begin in a similar descriptive fashion (vv.7–8) but then switch to direct address (vv.9 [NIV margin more accurately translates the Heb. second-person forms] and 11). Judgment is announced directly to Nineveh and its inhabitants, specified as the addressees by the heading of the book (1:1) and by the following context (2:8; 3:7). The second- and third-person plural forms in the Hebrew text of verses 9–10 indicate the residents of Nineveh are in view there, while the second-person singular feminine form at the beginning of verse 11 ("from you") suggests personified Nineveh is addressed at that point (note NIV's explanatory addition "O Nineveh").

The second major section of the book (1:12–3:19) begins with the introductory formula "This is what the LORD says." Sections 1:12–15 and 3:18–19 correspond thematically and form an inclusio around 2:1–3:17, which contains seven distinct formal units, arranged chiastically.[2]

Introduction: Judah urged to celebrate the demise of Assyria and its king (1:12–15)

A) Call to alarm (2:1–10)

   B) Taunt (2:11–12)

      C) Announcement of judgment (2:13)

         D) Woe oracle (3:1–4)

      C) Announcement of judgment (3:5–7)

   B) Taunt (3:8–13)

A) Call to alarm (3:14–17)

---

[2]I owe most of the following observations concerning the structure of 2:1–3:17 to my colleague, Gordon Johnston.

Conclusion: All who hear of the demise of Assyria and its king celebrate (3:18–19)

The passage 1:12–15 contains three parts: an announcement of salvation to Judah (vv.12–13), an announcement of judgment addressed to the king of Assyria (v.14), and a call to Judah to celebrate its deliverance from its enemy (v.15).[3] The conclusion 3:18–19 has the tone of a taunt directed to the king of Assyria. Despite these formal distinctions between 1:12–15 and 3:18–19, several motifs and key words tie the two passages together. Both include addresses to the king of Assyria and refer to Assyria's victims celebrating the news of its demise (cf. 1:15 with 3:19). Mountains figure prominently in both passages. In 1:15 the messenger bringing the good news of Assyria's defeat is seen approaching on the mountains. In 3:18 the defeated Assyrians are scattered upon the mountains. Other verbal connections can be seen in the Hebrew text.[4]

In 2:1–3:17 four types of speeches are employed in a detailed description of Assyria's demise. In the calls to alarm (2:1–10; 3:14–17) the prophet assumes for poetic purposes the role of a watchman on the walls of Nineveh. He excitedly calls upon the city's inhabitants to prepare for an enemy attack, the details of which he then vividly describes. The taunts (2:12–13; 3:8–13), which are introduced by rhetorical questions, allude in a derogatory way to Nineveh's pride. The judgment announcements (2:13; 3:5–7), which include a series of pronouncements by God Himself, are introduced by the formula " 'I am against you,' declares the LORD Almighty." Finally, the woe oracle (3:1–4), which is highlighted by its central position in the chiasmus, summarizes the reasons for judgment (vv.1, 4) and provides a vivid description of Nineveh's destruction (vv.2–3).

[3]The content of v.14 indicates that it is addressed to an enemy, not Judah. This is even more apparent in the Heb. text, where the second-person pronominal forms in vv.12–13 and 15 are feminine and those in v.14 are masculine. NIV's addition of "Nineveh" in v.14 is misleading. Elsewhere in the book Nineveh is addressed with the feminine singular form of the pronoun and her residents with the masculine plural. In v.14 the second-person pronominal forms are masculine singular, suggesting that the king of Assyria/Nineveh is in view, as in 3:18–19 (cf. NASB marginal note to 1:14).

[4]The appearance of the word 'ā̱bar, "to pass through" (translated "pass away" in 1:12, "invade" in 1:15, and "felt" in 3:19) and the root šbr (translated "break" in a verbal form in 1:13 and "wound" in a nominal form in 3:19) also tie the two passages together.

ANALYSIS

God Avenges His People (1:2-11)

God the Angry Warrior (1:2-6)

The opening theophanic hymn affirms that the Lord is a God of vengeance (vv.2-3a) and describes in detail His terrifying appearance and the cosmic reaction it evokes (vv.3b-6). The affirmation begins with the words "The LORD is a jealous and avenging God" (v.2). In this context, in which the Lord vindicates His people by judging their enemies, the Lord's jealousy is His zealous devotion to His people, which makes Him lash out in angry vengeance against those who have harmed them (cf. 2 Kings 19:31; Isa. 59:17; 63:15; Ezek. 36:6; Zech. 1:14).

Following this description of the Lord's intense anger, verse 3a, with its assertion that "the LORD is slow to anger," seems out of place. However, Nahum took a traditional confession about the Lord's patient character and altered it in such a way as to emphasize the inescapability of judgment. The traditional form of the confession, which states that "the LORD is slow to anger and *abounding/rich in love*," associates God's patience with His faithful and forgiving love (cf. Exod. 34:6; Num. 14:18; Neh. 9:17; Pss. 86:15; 103:8; 145:8; Jonah 4:2). Nahum substituted "power" for "love" and placed the altered confession in a context of judgment. In so doing, he indicated that forgiveness does not automatically or indefinitely flow from God's patience. A time can come when God's great patience is exhausted by unrepentant sinners, and a revelation of divine power in judgment becomes inevitable. For Assyria, the specific enemy to which the generalized references to "enemies" point, such a time had arrived. In Exodus 34:6-7 and Numbers 14:18, where the traditional confession appears to originate, the statement about God's patience and forgiving love is followed by a stern warning that God "will not leave the guilty unpunished." Nahum also appended this statement to his altered form of the confession, further emphasizing the inevitability of Assyria's judgment.

In verses 3b-6 Nahum pictured God as a powerful warrior. He employed several typical ancient Near Eastern warrior motifs, including those used by Assyrian kings to describe their military exploits. In so doing, Nahum affirmed that the Lord was the Warrior *par excellence.*

The description begins with the Lord's marching into battle in the midst of the whirlwind, storms, and cloud (v.3b). In ancient Near Eastern literature and art, gods—especially storm deities—were often portrayed as using the wind, storm, and clouds as vehicles, often in battle contexts.[5] Several Old Testament texts picture the Lord doing the same (Deut. 33:26; 2 Sam. 22:10–11; Pss. 68:4, 33; 104:3; Isa. 19:1). Assyrian kings frequently emphasized their power in battle by comparing themselves to storm winds. In similar fashion the Lord uses the storm winds as His weapon (Isa. 29:6; Jer. 23:19; Ezek. 13:13).

When the Lord utters His loud battle cry, all nature responds with terror (vv.4–5). In passages describing the Lord's theophanic appearance, the translation "rebukes" (NIV, v.4) is too mild for the Hebrew verb used here. It fails to express adequately the physical aspect that is clearly present in these texts. For example, in Psalm 104:7 the related noun, translated "rebuke" in NIV, corresponds to "sound of your thunder" in the parallel structure of the verse. In 2 Samuel 22:16 it stands parallel to "the blast of breath from his nostrils." Job 26:11 states that the "pillars of the heavens" (a poetic reference to the mountains) quake and are aghast at the Lord's rebuke. According to Psalm 76:6, the Lord's rebuke casts His enemies into a stupor. Here in Nahum 1:4 it causes both the sea and the most fertile regions of the earth to dry up. These strong physical reactions suggest a physical cause more powerful than a mere verbal rebuke. The Lord's rebuke is actually His powerful battle cry, which is so deafening and frightening that it incapacitates and routs His enemies.

The warrior's powerful battle cry is a common motif in ancient Near Eastern literature. For example, in Canaanite mythology the storm-god Baal is depicted as follows:

> Baal uttered his holy voice,
> Baal repeated the [issue] of his lips;
> (he uttered) his [holy] voice [(and)] the earth did
> quake,
> [(he repeated) the issue of his lips (and)] the rocks (did
> quake);

[5] See Moshe Weinfeld, " 'Rider of the Clouds' and 'Gatherer of the Clouds,' " *Journal of the Ancient Near Eastern Society of Columbia University* 5 (1973): 421–26.

peoples afar off were dismayed [   ] the
   peoples of the east;
the high places of the earth shook.
The foes of Baal clung to the forests,
the enemies of Hadad to the hollows of the rock.[6]

According to an Egyptian inscription, the battle cry of Thutmose III (ca. 1490–1436 B.C.) caused his enemies to hide in holes.[7] The Assyrian king Sennacherib (ca. 704–681) boasted, "Against all the hosts of wicked enemies, I raised my voice, rumbling like the storm. Like Adad [the storm-god] I roared."[8]

The severe effects of the Lord's battle cry illustrate its awesome power. The sea and rivers dry up, as well as such fertile regions as Bashan, Carmel, and Lebanon (cf. Isa. 2:13; 35:2; 60:13; Jer. 50:19; Mic. 7:14). The mountains, symbols of the earth's stability, shake and disintegrate, while the world's inhabitants tremble with fear.

Identical or similar imagery is typical in ancient Near Eastern battle accounts. In Baal's theophany, a portion of which is quoted above, the god's thunderous voice makes the earth's "high places" (i.e., mountains) shake. Widespread fear was a typical response to the Assyrian warrior-kings. For example, Ashur-nasir-apli II (ca. 883–859 B.C.) claimed that at his approach "all lands convulse, writhe, (and) melt as though in a furnace."[9] In light of the widespread ancient Near Eastern use of this imagery, it is not surprising that the Old Testament, in affirming the Lord's military might, frequently associates the shaking of the mountains and earth with His theophanic appearance (e.g., Judg. 5:4–5; 2 Sam. 22:8; Ps. 97:4–5; Amos 9:5; Mic. 1:4; Hab. 3:6).

Nahum concluded this hymn by returning to the theme of divine anger, which forms an inclusio for verses 2–6 (note "wrath" in both vv.2 and 6). The rhetorical questions in verse 6 provide a fitting conclusion to the preceding theophanic

[6] For this translation, see J. C. L. Gibson, *Canaanite Myths and Legends,* 2d ed. (Edinburgh: T. & T. Clark, 1978), p. 65.

[7] See Miriam Lichtheim, *Ancient Egyptian Literature,* 3 vols. (Berkeley: University of California Press, 1975–80), 2:36.

[8] Daniel D. Luckenbill, *Ancient Records of Assyria and Babylonia,* 2 vols. (Chicago: University of Chicago Press, 1926–27), 2:126, par. 253.

[9] A. K. Grayson, *Assyrian Royal Inscriptions,* 2 vols. (Wiesbaden: Otto Harrassowitz, 1972–76), 2:184, par. 714.

portrayal. Certainly no one is capable of effectively resisting such a mighty warrior once His fierce anger is aroused. That anger, which has the destructive power of fire, is capable of destroying even the most stable substances ("rocks"; cf. Job 18:4; 19:24).

God's Protection of His People (1:7–11)

This section, like the preceding one, begins with an affirmation about the character of the Lord (v.7a). Once again the prophet focused on God's concern for His people, asserting, "The LORD is good, a refuge in times of trouble. He cares for those who trust in him." The Lord's allegiance to His covenant people is in view. The verb translated "cares for" (lit. "knows") is a covenantal term. In ancient Near Eastern treaties the idiom "to know" was sometimes used of a superior party's recognition of his obligations to a faithful subject. For example, Abdi-Ashirta, an Amorite ruler, when threatened by an enemy army, asked his overlord, "May the king my lord know me?"[10] The word translated "trust" (lit. "seek refuge") in verse 7 points to the covenantal loyalty of the Lord's subjects. In the Psalms the one who "seeks refuge" in the Lord is often contrasted with rebels (Pss. 2:12; 5:9–12; 31:17–20; 34:21–22). "Seeking refuge" in the Lord is associated with loving His name (Ps. 5:11), fearing Him (Ps. 31:19), and serving Him (Ps. 34:22). Thus the very act of seeking the Lord's help in a crisis demonstrates one's loyalty to Him. According to verse 7, the Lord takes special notice of such faithfulness and protects His devotees from harm.

In contrast to His treatment of His faithful followers, the Lord destroys His enemies (v.8).[11] He pursues (the Heb. form is

[10]Cf. Herbert B. Huffmon, "The Treaty Background of Hebrew YĀDA'," *Bulletin of the American Schools of Oriental Research* 181 (1966): 32.

[11]Two textual problems make a precise interpretation of v.8 difficult. First, NIV follows the verse division in MT and understands "overwhelming flood" as an instrument of the Lord's judgment upon His foes. However, some prefer to take the first line of v.8 with v.7, reading, "He cares for those who trust Him when the flood passes through." Cf. Kevin J. Cathcart, *Nahum in the Light of Northwest Semitic Studies* (Rome: Biblical Institute Press, 1973), p. 56. This latter interpretation makes for tighter parallelism, the phrase "when the flood passes through" corresponding to "in times of trouble." Second, the phrase translated "[Nineveh]" in NIV is literally "in its place" (cf. NASB "its site"). NIV assumes the pronoun "its" refers to Nineveh, although Nineveh has not yet been mentioned specifically in the body of the prophecy (cf. the heading, however). It may be better to follow the Septuagint and other ancient versions

repetitive, "chases and chases") them into "darkness," which symbolizes death and destruction (cf. Job 18:18).

Verses 9–11 display a typical judgment-speech structure, containing both an announcement of judgment (vv.9–10) and an accusation (v.11). After informing the enemy that the Lord would frustrate their plot against Him (v.9), Nahum described their demise in figurative terms (v.10). Though the precise meaning of verse 10 is uncertain, the second part of the verse clearly indicates that the enemies' destruction would be swift and complete—like that of dry stubble when ignited by fire. Resuming his direct address (v.11; cf. v.9), the prophet identified the basis for judgment as the enemy's evil schemes, a reference to the Assyrian king's plans to destroy Judah (cf. 1:12–15).

Repetition of key words and phrases links verses 9–11 to the preceding context thematically. The word "trouble" appears in verses 7 and 9. The Lord promised that "trouble," which prompted His people to seek His protection (v.7), would "not come a second time" (v.9). The Assyrians would never again torment Judah as they had in the days of Sennacherib. The phrases "he will make an end" (v.8) and "he will bring to an end" (v.9) are virtually identical in Hebrew. The repetition serves to identify the enemies of verse 8 more specifically with the addressee of verse 9. The allusion to fire in verse 10 associates the punishment announced there with the theophanic judgment depicted earlier (cf. "like fire" in v.6).

Nineveh's Demise (1:12–3:19)

Judah Released from Oppression (1:12–15)

The Lord announced to the people of Judah (v.15) that He was about to deliver them from Assyrian oppression (vv. 12–13). Though the Lord had used the Assyrians as an instrument to punish sinful Judah (v.12b), He would now remove Judah's yoke and shackles, poetic symbols of Assyria's oppressive lordship (v.13). Despite Assyria's great military strength, they would "be cut off and pass away" (v.12a). The Hebrew verb translated "cut off," which usually refers elsewhere to shearing

(which presuppose a slightly different Heb. text) and read "adversaries" here (cf. RSV).

sheep, pictures the Assyrians as weak sheep unable to resist the mighty God of Israel.

In His bold address to the king of Assyria (v.14), which is placed between His statements to Judah (vv.12–13, 15), the Lord announced He would destroy the king's offspring, idols, and tomb.[12] Eradication of a king's offspring, which would bring his dynasty to an end, is a common judgment motif in the Bible (cf. 1 Sam. 24:21; 1 Kings 14:10; Isa. 14:20) and in ancient Near Eastern literature, being particularly prominent in curse lists.[13] The Lord's destruction of the king's idols would demonstrate His absolute superiority over the Assyrian gods. The desecration of the royal tomb would also prove the impotence of these gods. In the ancient Near East tombs often had attached to them curses calling upon the gods to punish anyone who might violate the sepulchre.[14] Thus the Lord's assertion that He would destroy the tomb of the Assyrian king shows His disdain for the gods responsible for protecting the grave.

In anticipation of Assyria's certain demise, the Lord urged the people of Judah to celebrate their deliverance from oppression (v.15). In times of crisis a petitioner would often make a vow to the Lord in order to motivate a positive response (Judg. 11:30; 1 Sam. 1:11; Pss. 22:25; 61:5; 66:13–15; 116:14, 18). Judah had apparently made such vows in their prayers for deliverance from Assyrian rule. Now the time had come to fulfill these promises, for the wicked Assyrians would never again invade Judah. Repetition of the word ʿāḇar, "pass (through)," draws attention to the reversal in Assyria's fortunes. They would never again "invade" (lit. "pass through," v.15) Judah; instead they would "pass away" (v.12) before the Lord's destructive judgment.

---

[12]The last line of v.14 is better translated (with a slight emendation of the Heb. text), "I will make your grave desolate, for you are vile." See ibid., p. 67.

[13]See James Pritchard, ed., *Ancient Near Eastern Texts Relating to the Old Testament*, 3d ed. (Princeton: Princeton University Press, 1969), pp. 534–41. Note specifically pars. 45, 66, and 67 of Esarhaddon's vassal treaties. See also F. C. Fensham, "Common Trends in Curses of the Near Eastern Treaties and *kudurru*-Inscriptions Compared with Maledictions of Amos and Isaiah," *Zeitschrift für die alttestamentliche Wissenschaft* 75 (1963): 158–60.

[14]Pritchard, *Texts*, pp. 661–63.

Nineveh Invaded (2:1–10)

Assuming the role of a watchman on Nineveh's walls, Nahum described in detail the fall of the city.[15] The account begins with the observation that an enemy army stood outside the city walls (v.1a). This attacking force is called "the scatterer" (cf. NASB), alluding to the fact that it would take the city's inhabitants into exile (v.7). Nahum, in his imaginary role as watchman, urged the city's populace to be alert and brace itself for the onslaught (v.1b).

As noted in 1:12–15, Nineveh's destruction would bring deliverance to God's people. In 2:2 the prophet interrupted his description of Nineveh's fall to reaffirm this fact. Though Judah (here called "Jacob") was like a ruined vineyard (cf. Jer. 5:10; Ezek. 19:10–14), the Lord would restore its splendor. Within the agricultural figure used here, "splendor" refers to renewed fertility and luxuriant growth (cf. Isa. 4:2). The agricultural figure, in turn, pictures the nation's restoration to a place of divine favor and blessing.

Returning to the battle scene, Nahum described the swift and relentless advance of the attacker (vv.3–5). The enemy soldiers carried red shields and wore scarlet clothing, the foreboding color suggesting the bloodshed about to overtake the city. The chariots, flashing in the sun, raced like lightning bolts through the streets outside the main fortress. Brandishing their spears, infantrymen hurried forward to the wall of the fortress and prepared to breach the city's defenses. The statement "yet they stumble on their way" probably implies that they fell over the numerous Assyrian corpses in their haste to advance (cf. 3:3).

Having gained control of the outlying areas of Nineveh, the attackers opened the canal gates (v.6a). The rushing flood waters damaged the city's walls and buildings, including the royal palace (v.6b). The verb translated "collapses" (lit. "melts") is also used in the theophanic account that begins the book (cf. 1:5). This verbal repetition links the specific judgment detailed in chapter 2 with the generalized picture of cosmic judgment described in chapter 1.

The invading soldiers, having gained entry to the city proper through its damaged walls, spread terror as they plundered Nineveh's vast wealth (vv.7–10). The city's inhabi-

[15] A Babylonian account of Nineveh's fall may be found in ibid., pp. 304–5.

tants reacted in consternation and panic (v.10b). Slave girls wept bitterly (v.7b), while others fled like water draining from a pool (v.8). To heighten the emotional impact of the scene and lend vividness to his description, Nahum included the actual words of some of the participants (vv.8–9). Amid the confusion and din of the massacre one can hear the shout "Stop! Stop!" directed to the fleeing Ninevites, and the excited cry "Plunder the silver! Plunder the gold!" spoken by the wide-eyed and greedy conquerors. The statement "She is pillaged, plundered, stripped!" (v.10a), highlighted in Hebrew by the similarity in sound between the words used (*bûqâ ûmᵉḇûqâ ûmᵉḇullāqâ*) emphasizes the totality of Nineveh's destruction.

Nahum's fourfold description of the Ninevites' intense, panic-stricken physical reaction to their defeat (v.10b) rounds off the section, corresponding to the fourfold appeal at the beginning of this speech (cf. v.1). In the Hebrew text repetition contributes to the inclusio and draws attention to the reversal in Nineveh's situation. The phrases translated "brace yourselves" (v.1; lit. "strengthen the loins") and "bodies tremble" (v.10; lit. "anguish in all the loins") correspond. At the beginning of the speech there was still time to "strengthen the loins," but by its conclusion fear has overtaken "all the loins," as panic sweeps away resolve.

Divine Opposition to the Assyrian "Lion" (2:11–13)

With a taunting rhetorical question Nahum drew attention to the stark contrast between Assyria's past and present. In the past the Assyrians had overcome their helpless victims with ease. Just as powerful lions bring back prey for their cubs, so the Assyrians had brought great wealth back from their military conquests. However, now the lions' lair (Nineveh) would be destroyed.

The application of lion imagery to the Assyrians is appropriate. In their role as warriors Assyrian kings often compared themselves to lions. For example, Esarhaddon (ca. 680–669 B.C.) boasted that he "roared like a lion."[16] Old Testament prophets also used lion imagery to describe Assyrian military power (Isa. 5:19; Jer. 50:17).

In verse 13 the Lord Himself bursts on the scene,

[16]See A. Spalinger, "Assurbanipal and Egypt: A Source Study," *Journal of the American Oriental Society* 94 (1974): 324–25.

reminding Nineveh that He would be the one ultimately responsible for the city's destruction. The series of first-person pronouns emphasizes the Lord's personal involvement. The divine title "LORD Almighty" is appropriate in that it pictures the Lord as the mighty military commander who leads His forces into battle (cf. Amos 3:13).

Combining battle imagery with the figurative lion motif, the Lord announced He would destroy Nineveh's chariots, symbolic of Assyrian military might, and its "young lions," referring to its population. The threat "I will leave you no prey on the earth" alludes to the fact that the Assyrians' source of wealth, the plunder and tribute taken from their vassal states, would be eliminated. The voices of Assyria's messengers, through whom the king carried on relations with subject peoples and had insulted the God of Israel (2 Kings 19:23; Isa. 37:9–14), would be silenced. In short, Assyria's vast empire would disappear, eliminating the flow of booty and need for messengers.

A Woe Oracle (3:1–4)

The woe oracle, highlighted by its central position in the chiastic structure of 1:12–3:19, summarizes the reasons for Nineveh's judgment (vv.1, 4) and describes her downfall in graphic detail (vv.2–3). Through violence and deceit (note "blood" and "lies") the Assyrians had filled Nineveh with plunder (v.1). The reference to "victims" continues the lion imagery of 2:11–13, where the same Hebrew word is translated "prey." Nineveh was like a seductive harlot who used her charms to exploit others for personal profit (v.4). The imagery may allude to Assyria's ability to exploit nations through its deceitful promises of economic prosperity (cf. Isa. 36:16–17; Hos. 5:13). Once these nations were committed to her by treaty, Assyria systematically drained them of their wealth (cf. 2 Kings 15:19–20; 16:8; 18:14–16).

Because of its crimes Nineveh would be overrun by hostile forces (vv.2–3). As in 2:3–10, the prophet supplies a vivid word picture of the battle scene. One sees the chariot drivers cracking their whips and hears the chariot wheels as they race through the streets (cf. 2:4). The heavily armed invaders leave in their wake a huge pile of Assyrian corpses.

Nahum emphasized the reversal in Nineveh's fortunes through three subtle wordplays, which are apparent only in the

Hebrew text. While Nineveh contained a seemingly "endless" (*'ên qēṣeh*) supply of gold and silver (2:9), she would soon be covered with bodies "without number" (*'ên qēṣeh* again; 3:3). "Piles" (*kōḇeḏ*) of corpses (3:3) would replace her abundant "wealth" (*kāḇōḏ*, 2:9). Because of her "wanton lust," literally "many [*rōḇ*] harlotries" (3:4; cf. NASB), Nineveh would be filled with "many [*rōḇ*] casualties" (3:3).

Nineveh's Humiliation (3:5–13)

Once again the Lord Himself spoke directly to Nineveh in His role as Lord of Armies, emphasizing His personal involvement in her destruction (vv.5–7; cf. 2:13). Drawing on the imagery of the previous verse, He announced He would publicly expose Nineveh's nakedness (v.5a) and subject her to the grossest forms of humiliation (v.6). Public exposure was a typical punishment for a prostitute or an adulteress (cf. Jer. 13:26; Ezek. 16:37; 23:10; Hos. 2:10). Appropriately the nations who had been exploited by Nineveh (cf. 3:4) would look upon her shame (v.5b). Her appearance would be so repulsive that all who see her would rush away in horror (v.7a; cf. Ps. 31:11). Of course, the reality behind this imagery is Nineveh's destruction, which no one would mourn (v.7b).

A taunting rhetorical question introduces the next formal unit in the prophecy (vv.8–13; cf. 2:11). Alluding to the Assyrians' conquest of the Egyptian city of Thebes in 663 B.C., Nahum reminded Nineveh that Thebes's seemingly unassailable position and numerous allies had not prevented it from being captured (vv.8–10). The Assyrians sacked the city, slaughtering its infants and carrying its inhabitants, including the most prominent citizens, into exile.[17]

As the rhetorical question implies, Nineveh's defenses were no stronger than those of Thebes had been. Despite her arrogant self-confidence, Nineveh could and would be conquered (vv.11–13). Nahum likened Nineveh's judgment to drunkenness, a common comparison in the Old Testament (Pss. 60:3; 75:8; Isa. 51:17, 21–23; Jer. 25:27; 51:7; Lam. 4:21; Ezek. 23:32–34; Hab. 2:15–16) in that the confusion, helplessness, and shame of a drunkard is like that of a defeated nation or city. Nahum compared Nineveh's fortresses to fig trees filled with ripe fruit. One simply has to shake the limbs and the figs

---

[17] See Luckenbill, *Ancient Records,* 2:351, para. 906.

fall right into one's mouth. Nineveh's defenses would be overcome with similar ease. Nineveh's troops, likened to women (cf. Isa. 19:16; Jer. 50:37; 51:30), would lack the courage and physical strength to resist the invaders. Consequently the city's environs would be wide open before the enemy.

The Watchman Speaks Again (3:14–17)

Once more assuming the role of a watchman on the city's walls (cf. 2:1), Nahum tauntingly urged the Ninevites to make hasty preparations for a siege (v.14). Of course, such efforts would be futile, for the city would be destroyed thoroughly, like crops before a horde of locusts (v.15a).

In verse 15b Nahum applied the locust imagery, used of Nineveh's enemies in the first half of the verse, to the city itself. He sarcastically challenged the city to multiply like locusts. Verses 16–17 suggest he was alluding to Nineveh's numerous merchants, guards, and officials. All of these groups, symbols of Nineveh's wealth and importance, would desert the city in the Day of Judgment. Like locusts that strip the land and then fly away, the merchants, having exploited the ill-fated city's economic possibilities to the maximum, would move on to greener pastures. The guards and officials, whose sense of security in Nineveh's prosperity is compared to locusts' settling "in the walls on a cold day," would also disappear.

Assyria's Victims Celebrate Its Demise (3:18–19)

Nahum concluded with a reproach addressed to the king of Assyria (cf. 1:14). The prophet observed that the leaders of Assyria, likened to shepherds, would fall asleep, leaving their people to be scattered like sheep on the mountains, with no one to deliver them from predators (v.18). Sleep and rest here depict death (cf. Job 3:13–15; 14:11–12; Ps. 76:5; Isa. 26:19; Jer. 51:39; Dan. 12:2), while the scattering of the sheep pictures the exile of the population (cf. Jer. 10:21–22; Ezek. 34:5–6).

In verse 19 the imagery shifts, the Assyrian king being compared to a man suffering from an incurable, fatal wound. Because of his past cruelty, his victims would celebrate the news of his demise (cf. 1:15).

THEOLOGY

Summary

The sovereign Lord, who is the most powerful of all warriors, would avenge the harm done to His covenant people by appropriately and thoroughly judging their Assyrian oppressors.

Analysis

Sovereign King

Nahum pictured God as the sovereign Ruler of the universe who controls both nature and nations. The Lord employs the elements of the storm as His vehicle (1:3). With His powerful battle cry He can dry up seas, rivers, and the most fertile regions of the earth (1:4). All of nature responds in fear when He appears in theophanic splendor (1:5). The Lord controls nations, judging them and using them as instruments of judgment in accordance with His will. Not even mighty Assyria, the most powerful nation on earth in Nahum's day, would be capable of withstanding the Lord's judgment. The Lord would also destroy Nineveh's idols (1:14), demonstrating His sovereignty over the Assyrian gods.

Warrior

For Nahum the Lord was, first and foremost, the divine Warrior *par excellence*. The book begins with a terrifying portrayal of the angry, avenging warrior who comes in the storm and frightens all of nature with His battle cry (1:2–6). In this opening theophany Nahum employed many of the same motifs used by Assyrian kings to describe their prowess and exploits in battle. In so doing he emphasized that the Lord, not the king of Assyria, was the most powerful of all warriors. Twice in the book (2:13; 3:5) the Lord, in His role of "LORD Almighty," or "Lord of Armies," personally announced He would defeat Nineveh.

Judge

Assyria's judgment was well deserved. She had exploited and cruelly treated other nations (cf. 3:1, 4), including God's own people (1:15). Although the Lord had used the Assyrians as an instrument to punish Judah (1:12–13), they had interpreted their success in a different light, proudly attributing it to their own power (cf. Isa. 10:5–19; 36:4–21). Viewing this arrogance as an evil plot against His sovereign authority (1:9, 11), the Lord announced He would destroy the rebellious Assyrians, avenging His oppressed covenant people in the process.

The Lord's punishment of Assyria would be appropriate. He would treat the Assyrians in the same way they had dealt with their victims. Several elements in Nahum's description of Assyria's judgment correspond to curses used by the Assyrians in treaties with their vassals. For example, curses in the treaties of Esarhaddon (ca. 680–669 B.C.) include the destruction of offspring (cf. 1:14), the heaping up of corpses (cf. 3:3), and an incurable wound (cf. 3:19).[18] In a treaty between Ashur-nirari V of Assyria (ca. 753–746) and Mati'ilu of Arpad one of the curses threatens, "If Mati'ilu sins against this treaty . . . may Mati'ilu become a prostitute, his soldiers women. . . ."[19] Ironically, according to 3:3, Assyria would suffer this same fate.

Other elements in Nahum's description of Assyria's judgment correspond to motifs that appear in Assyrian battle accounts. Assyrian kings frequently boasted of besieging, plundering, and destroying enemy cities (cf. 2:3–10). On occasion they compared their conquest to an overwhelming flood (cf. 2:6 and perhaps 1:8). For example, Sargon (ca. 721–705 B.C.) claimed to have overwhelmed a series of settlements "like a flood."[20] Assyrian kings delighted in describing the panic-stricken flight of the enemy (cf. 2:8; 3:11, 17) and their own superhuman pursuit (cf. 1:8). They also mentioned the enemy's being scattered over the mountains (cf. 3:18) and frequently drew attention to the numerous enemy corpses (cf. 3:3). For example, Ashurbanipal (ca. 668–627) recalled: "With the bodies of the warriors and people of Elam I dammed up the Ulai River. For three days I made that stream carry down, to its limit, their bodies instead of water."[21] Sennacherib (ca. 704–681) stated, "With the bodies of their warriors I filled the plain

---

[18]For these treaties, see Pritchard, *Texts*, pp. 533–41. Specifically, see sec. iv of Esarhaddon's treaty with Baal of Tyre and pars. 41, 45, 52, 66, and 67 of his "vassal treaties."

[19]Ibid., pp. 532–33.

[20]Luckenbill, *Ancient Records*, 2:16, par. 32.

[21]Ibid., 2:398, par. 1072.

like grass."[22] The physical response of the enemy to its defeat was sometimes highlighted (cf. 2:10). For example, Sennacherib boasted that his enemies "abandoned their tents and . . . trampled the bodies of their (fallen) soldiers, they fled like young pigeons that are pursued. They were beside themselves, they held back their urine, but let their dung go into their chariots."[23]

Israel's Protector

God's judgment of Nineveh would be an expression of His zealous devotion to His covenant people (cf. 1:2). Though God had used the Assyrians to chastise Judah, He announced through Nahum that the Assyrian oppression was about to end (1:13, 15). In delivering Judah from the Assyrian yoke, He would once again demonstrate His goodness to His people and prove that He does indeed take notice of those who are loyal to Him and trust Him for protection (1:7).

[22]Ibid., 2:127, par. 254.
[23]Ibid., 2:128, par. 254.

8

HABAKKUK

INTRODUCTION

Date

Though neither of the book's headings (1:1; 3:1) provides any chronological information, internal evidence points to the late seventh century B.C. as the most probable date of authorship. According to 1:6, the Lord was about to raise up the Chaldean (or neo-Babylonian) empire as an instrument of judgment against sinful Judah. Since the Babylonians first invaded Palestine in 605 (cf. Dan. 1:1–2), the prophecy appears to precede that event. However, the book also seems to assume that the Babylonians had already established a reputation as an imperialistic power (cf. 1:6–11, 15–17; 2:5–17). This portrayal of the Chaldeans best reflects the period following the battle of Carchemish, in 605. By defeating the Egyptians at Carchemish, the Babylonians established themselves as the leading power in the Near East. They quickly followed up their success by sweeping through southern Syria and Palestine and bringing the various states located there, including Judah, under their control. Thus Habakkuk's prophecy may have originated in 605 B.C., between the battle of Carchemish and the siege of Jerusalem.

However, if Habakkuk prophesied while the Babylonians were actually marching toward Judah, one wonders why the announcement of Judah's downfall at their hands would have been so unbelievable to his audience (1:5). Also, could the Babylonians have developed the reputation described in chapters 1–2 in such a short period of time? Perhaps the description of Babylonian imperialism is largely proleptic, anticipating, on the basis of tendencies already revealed, how the Chaldeans would treat others as they further expanded their empire. One should note that the series of woe oracles in 2:6–20, which include the most specific references to Babylonian imperialism in the book, are delivered primarily from the perspective of Babylon's future demise (note esp. 2:6a). In this case Habakkuk's prophecy may be dated anytime between 626 B.C., when Babylon began to assert its independence from the Assyrians, and 605.

Unity

Some have challenged the originality of chapter 3, attributing it instead to a later editor. Proponents of this view emphasize the chapter's musical notations (3:1, 3, 9, 13, 19) and hymnic style and draw attention to the Qumran commentary on Habakkuk, which omits discussion of chapter 3. However, the heading to the chapter attributes it specifically to Habakkuk (3:1). Several verbal, thematic, and structural parallels unite chapter 3 with chapters 1–2.[1] The pattern of divine revelation and prophetic response is consistent with the rest of the book. The presence of musical notations attests to the psalm's formal unity and sets it apart as a separate unit within the book as a whole but certainly does not necessitate the chapter's being divorced from the original prophecy. Finally, the Qumran evidence may point to the existence of an alternate recension of the book which omitted chapter 3. Then again, the absence of a commentary on chapter 3 may stem from sectarian motives.[2] Other early textual witnesses for the Book of Habakkuk include the third chapter.

Structure

The book contains two major sections (1:2–2:20 and 3:1–19). The first of these consists of a dialogue between the prophet

---

[1] Carl E. Armerding, "Habakkuk," in *The Expositor's Bible Commentary,* ed. Frank E. Gaebelein (Grand Rapids: Zondervan, 1985), 7:522.

[2] For fuller discussion, see Ralph L. Smith, *Micah–Malachi* (Waco: Word Books, 1984), p. 95.

and the Lord. After opening with a prophetic lament (1:2–4), the section oscillates between divine revelation and prophetic response:

Prophetic lament (1:2–4)
Divine revelation (1:5–11)
Prophetic response (1:12–2:1)
Divine revelation (2:2–20)

A heading and concluding musical notation (3:1, 19b) mark out chapter 3 as a separate unit. Classified as a prayer (3:1), it includes a petition (3:2), theophanic description (3:3–15), and statement of confidence (3:16–19a). Chapter 3 displays a pattern similar to that of chapters 1–2: prophetic initiative—divine revelation/response—prophetic response. Though God does not actually speak in chapter 3, the theophanic vision related by the prophet has a revelatory character and function, serving as the divine response to Habakkuk's petition.

ANALYSIS

God's Justice Revealed (1:2–2:20)

Habakkuk's Lament (1:2–4)

The book opens with the prophet's bitter lament over the injustice he saw all around him. Habakkuk lived in the final dark days of Judah. Despite Josiah's admirable attempts at reform (Jer. 22:15–16), society was infected by social injustice and violence (cf. Jer. 7:3–6; 22:3, 13–17).[3] To emphasize how bad the situation had become, Habakkuk used six different Hebrew words in referring to the violent acts of injustice he saw perpetrated: "violence," "injustice," "wrong," "destruction," "strife," and "conflict" (vv.2–3). God's law, which had been given to regulate covenant life, was paralyzed, in that it was no

[3] Some see the oppressor of 1:2–4 as the Babylonians or Assyrians. However, the language used in these verses (esp. "law") points to domestic strife. Prophets frequently lamented the injustice that permeated the society around them (cf. Mic. 7:1–6). Since the Babylonians are mentioned in 1:6 as the nation through whom the Lord would rectify the wrongs described in vv.2–4, they can hardly be the oppressor alluded to by the prophet. If the Assyrians are the oppressor, it is surprising that they are never specifically mentioned elsewhere in the book.

longer used as the standard of right and wrong. Justice was perverted (lit. "bent" or "twisted") in the courts as the wicked exploited the righteous (v.4). Despite Habakkuk's pleas for divine intervention, God had been silent (v.2).

God's Solution: The Chaldeans (1:5–11)

Suddenly the divine silence was broken. The Lord instructed Habakkuk's generation (the second-person verbal and pronominal forms in v.5 are plural in Heb.) to watch international developments very carefully, for He was about to intervene in an astonishing and shocking way (v.5). The Lord's solution to the problem of Judah's injustice was to raise up the Babylonians as an instrument of judgment against His people (v. 6a). The Lord's statement probably does not envision the Babyonians' appearance on the international scene for the first time but rather refers specifically to their being raised up as an instrument of judgment against the oppressors of 1:2–4.[4]

There is irony in the Lord's command in verse 5 to "look" ($r\bar{a}'\hat{a}$) and "watch" ($n\bar{a}\,\d{h}at$). These same Hebrew words are used in verse 3, where the prophet asked, "Why do you make me look [$r\bar{a}'\hat{a}$] at injustice? Why do you tolerate [$n\bar{a}\,\d{h}at$, lit. "watch"] wrong?" The prophet complained that the Lord had shown him nothing but wrongdoing. In response the Lord declared He would show Habakkuk the solution to his dilemma.

Verses 6b–11 contain a detailed description of the Babylonians. This hyperbolic portrayal emphasizes the effectiveness of the Lord's solution to the problem of injustice. No one would be able to resist this powerful instrument of divine judgment. The Babylonians were fierce conquerors (v.6b), feared and dreaded by all (v.7a). They were independent, submitting to no one's authority (v.7b). Their army moved swiftly, displaying extraordinary stamina, a carnivorous eagerness to attack, and a strong desire to enjoy the spoils of victory (v.8). Their prisoners were as numerous as grains of sand (v.9). The Babylonians had nothing but scorn for the royal authority and physical defenses of their victims. They erected siege works (cf. Jer. 32:24; Ezek. 4:2; 21:22; 26:8–9), captured cities, and then hurried on to conquer anew (vv.10–11a).

---

[4]See Armerding, "Habakkuk," p. 502; and Hobart E. Freeman, *An Introduction to the Old Testament Prophets* (Chicago: Moody Press, 1968), p. 257.

The rhetorical effect of Habakkuk's description is enhanced by allusion. The reference to the distant origins of the Babylonians, the comparison to a vulture, and the description of their siege techniques remind one of the covenant curses threatened in Deuteronomy 28:49–52 ("vulture" in Hab. 1:8 and "eagle" in Deut. 28:49 translate the same Heb. word).

Verses 6–11 repeat two key words from verses 2–4 in order to demonstrate the appropriate nature of God's judgment. Those who treated their fellow Judahites with "violence" (vv.2–3) would be subjected to the "violence" of the Babylonians (v.9). Those who suppressed and perverted God's standard of "justice" (*mišpāṭ,* v.4) would be overrun by an enemy that regarded justice in a similar fashion and followed their own standards of right and wrong (v.7, where "law" translates *mišpāṭ*). This correspondence between verses 4 and 7 is even more apparent when one translates the pertinent Hebrew phrases literally. Verse 4 states that "justice never goes out" and that "justice goes out perverted." Verse 7 declares, "his justice goes out from himself."

Though the Babylonians were God's instruments of judgment, He did not overlook their pride and self-reliance (v.11b). Rather than recognizing God as the source of their success, they attributed their victories to their own strength, thereby making them guilty in the sight of the sovereign Lord. This change in tone and perspective prepares the way for the prophecy of Babylon's demise in chapter 2.

Habakkuk's Response (1:12–2:1)

Habakkuk's response to the startling revelation of verses 5–11 consists of a declaration of confidence (1:12), a lament (1:13–17), and a determination to wait (2:1). Habakkuk was confident that Judah would not be entirely destroyed. He based this confidence on God's sovereignty and His commitment to His people. As the one "from everlasting," God controls history (cf. Isa. 45:21; 46:10). As the "Holy One," He transcends the affairs of people and nations. Though the fearsome Babylonians were coming, they were completely under the direction of the Lord. He would use them to punish, but they would not be able to overstep the bounds of God's sovereign will. Because God had promised through Moses and later prophets that Israel would ultimately experience His blessings, Habakkuk was certain that God would preserve His people through the coming judgment.[5]

In several ways the prophet drew attention to the Lord's relationship with His people. He addressed Him as "my God" and "my Holy One," revealing his assurance of a personal relationship with the sovereign God. He also called Him "Rock," a title that pictures God as a place of safety and protection for His people (cf. Ps. 18:2). The phrase "from everlasting" is a reminder of the Lord's great salvific deeds in Israel's history. Elsewhere this and related phrases refer to earlier periods of history when the Lord made promises to the patriarchs (cf. Mic. 7:20), delivered Israel from Egypt (Pss. 74:2; 77:11; Isa. 51:9), and led them in the conquest of Canaan (Ps. 44:1).

Though Habakkuk was confident of God's protective power and realized that the upcoming invasion would be an act of judgment upon the evil described in 1:2–4, a tension still existed in his mind. He was no longer willing to charge God with wrong (cf. 1:3 with v.13), yet the basic problem of the wicked exploiting the righteous was still not entirely resolved for him. If God was incapable of tolerating evil (v.13a), then why would He seemingly do just that by allowing the wicked Babylonians to swallow up those more righteous than themselves (v.13b)? Would not this plan of eliminating oppression in Judah actually backfire, resulting in violence being extended to the international sphere?

To support his point about the Babylonians' relative wickedness, Habakkuk drew the Lord's attention to the unjust nature of Babylonian imperialism (vv.14–17). The human society established by God was like fish and sea creatures—a teeming mass seemingly devoid of leadership and vulnerable to the wiles of the fisherman. The wicked Babylonians were like fishermen, who cheerfully gather in their catch with hooks and nets. Just as fish seem to exist merely to feed the fisherman, so the nations appeared to exist simply to gratify the Babylonians' greed for economic prosperity. To make matters worse, the Babylonians attributed their success to their own military might (symbolized here by the fishing implements), rather than the

[5]This interpretation follows the Masoretic text, which reads, "We will not die." An ancient scribal tradition, the value of which is debated, reads here, "You (God) will not die."

sovereign God. The injustice inherent in all this caused the prophet to ask, "Is he to keep on emptying his net, destroying nations without mercy?"

Despite his perplexity, Habakkuk was determined to wait patiently for further divine revelation (2:1). Like a watchman on a wall, he would look alertly for God's answer and ponder carefully what his own response would be.

God's Displeasure with Babylon (2:2–20)

The Lord's reply contained introductory instructions (vv. 2–3), a description of the wicked (vv.4a, 5), to which a parenthetical reminder to the faithful is attached (v.4b), and a lengthy announcment of the Babylonians' judgment in the form of a taunt song containing several woe oracles interspersed with praises to the Lord (vv.6–20).

The Lord instructed Habakkuk to record the revelation on tablets as an official and tangible reminder of the certainty of its fulfillment (vv.2–3). Though its fulfillment might seem to be delayed (might "linger"), it was certain to be realized at God's appointed time.

The revelation proper begins with an accusation against the Babylonians (vv.4a, 5), which serves as the basis for the judgment portrayed in verses 6–20. The Babylonians were proud and greedy. Because of their insatiable desire for a larger and larger empire, they are likened to a drunkard, who restlessly pursues wine, and to death, which always demands more and more corpses. This portrayal of personified death as having a voracious appetite (cf. also Prov. 30:15–16; Isa. 5:14) is also seen in Canaanite mythology, where deified Death is described as opening its huge mouth to devour its victims.[6]

In the midst of this description of Babylonian greed, the Lord included an encouraging word concerning the destiny of the righteous (v.4b), about whom Habakkuk had earlier expressed concern (cf. 1:4, 13). Even with the realities of Babylonian imperialism looming on the horizon, the truly righteous would be preserved through their faithfulness. The righteous are those oppressed by the wicked (cf. 1:4) because of their loyalty to the Lord (cf. Isa. 3:10; 57:1; Hos. 14:9; Mal. 3:18). In the immediate context "live" must refer to physical

---

[6]See J. C. L. Gibson, *Canaanite Myths and Legends,* 2d ed. (Edinburgh: T. & T. Clark, 1978), pp. 68–69.

preservation through the coming invasion. This promise is God's "amen" to Habakkuk's earlier affirmation, "We will not die" (1:12; cf. also 3:19). The promise takes on special significance in relation to the following verse, which compares the greedy Babylonians to death itself. The word translated "faith" is better rendered "faithfulness" here (NIV margin), in accordance with its Old Testament usage. The basic idea of the word is "firmness" or "steadiness" (cf. Exod. 17:12). When used of human character and conduct, it refers to reliability (Prov. 12:17, 22; Isa. 59:4; Jer. 5:3; 9:3) and honesty (2 Kings 12:15; 22:7; Jer. 5:1). In contrast to the wicked (cf. 1:2–4; 2:4a, 5), who would be swept away in judgment (cf. 1:5–11; 2:6–20), the righteous would be preserved because of their faithfulness to God and His standards.

The taunt song (vv.6–20) anticipates the coming judgment of Babylon. The nations who suffered under Babylonian imperialism (cf. v.5b) address their oppressor, pronouncing a series of five woes against him.

In typical fashion the first woe pronouncement (vv.6–8) contains accusatory elements and an announcement of judgment. Babylon accumulated wealth through violence, destroying weaker nations and plundering their storehouses. Appropriately the nations that remained would now plunder Babylon. These instruments of judgment are compared to terrifying "creditors" (NIV margin, NASB) who demand payment of all debts.

The second woe oracle (vv.9–11), which is strictly accusatory in tone, further develops the theme of the first. The Babylonians built their empire by robbing other nations. They sought to make themselves invulnerable to attack, like an eagle that builds its nest in an elevated, inaccessible spot. Ironically they used "unjust [$r\bar{a}$'] gain" in their attempt to prevent their own "ruin [$r\bar{a}$']."[7] In so doing, they brought only shame to their "house" (i.e., empire) and made their doom certain. Even the stones and beams of this house erected through unjust gain would cry out in protest. This vivid personification suggests that Babylon's very physical glory and strength, made possible by its oppression of others, testified loudly to its crimes of injustice.

---

[7] The wordplay involving repetition of the word $r\bar{a}$' uses its distinct senses of "moral evil" and "calamity."

The third woe oracle (vv.12–14) carries along the accusation of the preceding two, condemning the Babylonians for building their kingdom by violently destroying others. This oracle concludes with a statement of praise to the sovereign Lord, who brings the misplaced efforts of nations like Babylon to naught. The divine title "LORD Almighty" is appropriate here, since the Lord is viewed as a mighty warrior who destroys arrogant nations with the fire of judgment. Eventually the whole earth would recognize His glory (cf. Isa. 11:9), which in this context refers to His sovereignty, justice, and superiority to the gods of the nations (cf. vv.18–20).

The fourth oracle (vv.15–17), like the first, emphasizes the appropriate nature of Babylon's punishment. The imagery of drunkenness is used to describe Babylon's mistreatment of neighboring nations. The outpouring of Babylon's anger (in v.15 "anger," representing military destruction, is a better translation of the Heb. word than "wineskin"; cf. Isa. 51:17, 22; Jer. 25:15) is compared to enticing others to drink so much wine that they shamefully expose themselves (cf. Gen. 9:21–23; Lam. 4:21). Through such conquests the Babylonians sought to bring glory to themselves. However, the tables were about to be turned. Babylon would have to drink a cup of intoxicating wine served up by the Lord's "right hand," a symbol of His powerful judgment (cf. Ps. 21:8). Babylon's shame would then exceed that of its victims. NIV "be exposed" (v.16) literally reads, "show yourself uncircumcised." Not only would Babylon's nakedness be exposed, but its disgrace would be made even worse by its being uncircumcised. In Israelite eyes uncircumcision was especially shameful because of the association of circumcision with the covenant.[8]

The statement "disgrace will cover your glory" (v.16b) is a prime example of prophetic wordplay. The repetition of "glory" (cf. v.14) contrasts Babylon with the sovereign Lord. Knowledge of the Lord's glory would cover the earth; Babylon's glory would be covered by disgrace.

The reference to violence perpetrated against Lebanon and its animals (v.17a) may allude to Nebuchadnezzar's importation

---

[8]Another reading is "stagger" (NIV margin), which makes good sense contextually (cf. also Ps. 60:3; Isa. 51:17, 22; Zech. 12:2) and assumes a transposition of two letters in the Heb. text.

of cedars from Lebanon for his building projects.[9] At the same time, verse 17b suggests that Lebanon and its animals may represent the western Palestinian states and their inhabitants, whom Nebuchadnezzar conquered. Israel may even be specifically in view (cf. Jer. 22:23; Ezek. 17:3).

The warning "The violence you have done . . . will overwhelm you" is significant when compared to chapter 1. There the Babylonians' violence (1:9) is the Lord's instrument of judgment against the violent within Judah (1:2–3). However, here we learn that the Babylonians' violent ways would eventually prove to be self-destructive, for the Lord would call them into account for their misdeeds. While the Lord's glory would cover the earth "as the waters cover the sea," the Babylonians' glory would be overwhelmed by their own violence ("cover," v.14, and "overwhelm," v.17, translate the same verb).

The final woe oracle (vv.18–20) differs in several respects from the preceding four. It contains no specific allusion to Babylonian violence but instead introduces a polemic against idolatry. One must assume that the false gods of the Babylonians stand in the background here. Structurally this oracle opens with a rhetorical question, rather than the woe pronouncement, which is delayed until verse 19.

This final oracle is similar to the third in that it exalts the Lord as the sovereign King of the universe (v.20; cf. vv.13–14). By destroying the Babylonians (vv.6–17), the Lord would demonstrate His superiority to their gods and to all other supposed deities. Those who trust in man-made images for guidance are doomed for destruction. In contrast to the lifeless idols of the pagans, the Lord rules over the universe from His transcendent ("holy") heavenly temple. In His awesome, sovereign presence the proper response is fear (note "be silent").

Habakkuk's Theophanic Vision (3:1–19)

Habakkuk's Petition (3:1–2)

Habakkuk asked God to repeat His mighty saving works. The prophet was well aware of what the Lord had done for Israel in the past. Though he had not personally witnessed these

[9]Cf. Georges Roux, *Ancient Iraq* (Baltimore: Penguin Books, 1964), pp. 345–46, 359–60.

acts ("your fame" is lit. "the report about you"), he stood in awe of them. These deeds included the exodus from Egypt (Ps. 77:12–20) and the conquest of Canaan (Ps. 44:1–3). Habakkuk knew that judgment must come, but he prayed that God would also reveal His mercy as well as His wrath, just as He had done when Israel rebelled in the wilderness (cf. Exod. 32–34, esp. 34:6).

God the Warrior (3:3–15)

These verses should not be viewed as a mere rehearsal of the Lord's historical deeds (cf. v.2). Rather, they contain a visual revelation (note "I saw" in v.7) of the renewal (cf. v.2) of God's mighty acts and are a positive response to the prophet's petition for divine mercy.[10] This theophanic vision complements the verbal revelation of Babylon's downfall recorded in 2:2–20. In the theophany Babylon's Judge (cf. 3:13–14) comes as a mighty warrior to destroy His enemies and deliver His people. Of course, this coming intervention is described largely in terms of past events, the many allusions to Israel's salvation history demonstrating that the Lord was still the nation's active and powerful Deliverer.

The theophany may be divided into two parts.[11] Verses 3–7, which refer to the Lord in the third person, describe His glorious coming from the south (vv.3–5) and the cosmic disturbance it causes (vv.6–7). The geographical references in verses 3 and 7 form an inclusio for this first unit. In the second part, which begins with a question, the prophet addresses God. References to the sea and to horses in verses 8 and 15 form an inclusio for the unit.

The theophany opens with God coming from the south in radiant splendor (vv.3–4). The geographical sites named here point in the direction of Sinai. Teman was an Edomite city (Amos 1:12; Obad. 9). Mount Paran was probably located in the Sinai Peninsula among the mountains west of the Gulf of

---

[10] In light of the visionary character of the theophany, perhaps the verbs in vv.3–15 are best translated with the present tense. NIV's use of the past tense may be retained if one understands the events as being completed from the prophet's visionary perspective. Ps. 64:7–8 provides a parallel to Hab. 3:3–15. Using Heb. verbal forms that indicate completed action, the psalmist describes a future divine intervention in response to his petition (vv.1–2; cf. Hab. 3:2) and then expresses his confidence (Ps. 64:9–10; cf. Hab. 3:16–19).

[11] Armerding, "Habakkuk," p. 522.

Aqaba. Deuteronomy 33:2 also pictured the Lord coming from Mount Paran (Sinai and Seir are also mentioned) as He led His people to the borders of the Promised Land. According to Judges 5:4, He also came from the south-southeast (Seir and Edom being specifically mentioned) in the time of Deborah to renew Israel's conquest of the Canaanites. Habakkuk 3:3 appears to allude to these earlier poetic descriptions of the Lord's intervention. Just as God had marched on Israel's behalf in the days of Moses and Deborah, so He would do again. The God of Sinai was still alive and active.

The most striking feature of the divine theophany is its physical splendor, which is an outward manifestation of His majesty and power (v.4). Most translations, like NIV, suggest that God's radiance is compared here to bright rays of sunshine. It is more likely that the objects of comparison are bright flashes of lightning. The Hebrew word translated "sunrise" (lit. "light"), while sometimes used of sunlight, can also refer to lightning (Job 36:32; 37:3, 11, 15). The term translated "rays" (lit. "two horns") could just as easily refer to sharp, pointed forks of lightning. The weapon of "double lightning" appears often in Mesopotamian representations of warlike gods.[12] The immediate context suggests that lightning, not the sunlight, is in view. The allusion to Sinai (v.3a; cf. Deut. 33:2), where the Lord's theophany included lightning (Exod. 19:16; 20:18), and the cosmic disturbances described in verse 6a, which frequently appear in storm theophanies (cf. Judg. 5:4–5; Pss. 18:7, 13–14; 29:3–9; 77:17–18), favor this interpretation. References to the Lord's arrows (vv.9, 11), often associated with lightning (cf. Pss. 18:14; 77:17–18; 144:6; Zech. 9:14), also suggest that the "two horns" flashing from the Lord's hand (v.4) are lightning bolts.

Plague and pestilence accompany the Lord, overtaking and destroying His enemies (v.5).[13] The word translated "pestilence" refers elsewhere to fiery arrows (Deut. 32:24 [NIV

---

[12]Cf. E. D. van Buren, *Symbols of the Gods in Mesopotamian Art* (Rome: Pontifical Biblical Institute, 1945), pp. 70–73. A Ugaritic text appears to use "horn" for Baal's lightning flashes. See Gibson, *Myths,* p. 51.

[13]The personification of "pestilence" (*rešep*) in conjunction with the Lord's storm theophany has a close parallel in Canaanite mythology, where the deity Resheph aids the storm-god Baal in his fight against the chaotic sea. Cf. John Day, "New Light on the Mythological Background of the Allusion to Resheph in Habakkuk III 5," *Vetus Testamentum* 29 (1979): 353–55.

translates "pestilence" in Deut. 32:24, but v.23 refers to arrows]; Ps. 76:3, "flashing arrows"), bolts of lightning (Ps. 78:48), flames (Song 8:6, "mighty flame"), and sparks (Job 5:7). Therefore, a better translation in Habakkuk 3:5 might be "destructive firebolt."

The entire cosmos responds in fear (vv.6–7). The Lord frightens the nations, especially those, like Cushan and Midian, that lie in the path of His march. The language is reminiscent of Exodus 15:14, where nations respond in similar fashion to news of the Lord's approach. Even the ancient mountains, which are symbols of the earth's stability, shake before the Lord, just as Mount Sinai did. Though these mountains are "age-old" ('ôlām), they cannot resist the God whose "ways are eternal" (again 'ôlām). God's ways probably refer here to His saving acts, which characterized Israel's distant past and would be renewed.

Whether or not the questions of verse 8 expect an answer is uncertain. They may be designed merely to draw attention to the fact of God's anger and to raise the issue of the purpose for the coming judgment. If one seeks an answer from the following context, one finds only ambiguity. Verses 10–15 suggest that God is indeed angry with the waters (vv.10b, 15), but only insofar as they symbolize the nations that threaten His people (v.12). Despite this uncertainty concerning the function of the questions, the fact of God's anger is crystal clear. Three different Hebrew words are used to emphasize the degree of His wrath (NIV "angry," "wrath," and "rage").

As a victorious warrior, the Lord leads His chariots into battle (v.8b; cf. Isa. 66:15) and prepares to shoot arrows at His enemies (v.9a). The phrase "you called for many arrows" reads literally, "adjured are the arrows (with) a word." The Lord's personified arrows are viewed as receiving a divine commission under oath. In Jeremiah 47:6–7 the Lord's sword receives such a charge. In Ugaritic mythology the weapons of Baal are formally commissioned to smite Yam, the god of the sea.[14] In the same way, Habakkuk envisioned the Lord solemnly commissioning His weapons to destroy His enemies.

Verses 9b–11 describe more cosmic effects of the divine Warrior's appearance. Picking up the storm imagery of verses 4–6, the prophet pictured the mountains trembling in fear (cf.

[14]Gibson, *Myths*, pp. 43–44.

195

v.6), while a torrential downpour (cf. Isa. 28:2) causes flash flooding on the earth's surface. The raging waters of the sea lift their waves (lit. "hands"), as if crying out for mercy (cf. Ps. 28:2; Lam. 2:19). Even the sun and moon respond in fear, being paralyzed by the brilliance of the Lord's flashing arrows and spear.

The language and imagery of verses 9–11 contain allusions to the Red Sea crossing and the Lord's victory over the Amorites at Gibeon. The motifs of the torrential downpour, the fearful sea, and the Lord's rapidly flying arrows are combined as well in Psalm 77:16–18, a poetic description of the Lord's intervention for His people at the Red Sea. The reference to the sun's and moon's standing still is an allusion to Joshua 10:12–14, which records how the Lord miraculously prolonged the day so that Israel might pursue the Amorites. The God who revealed Himself so vividly in the days of Moses and Joshua would again burst on the historical scene to deliver His people and annihilate His enemies.

Verses 12–14 identify these enemies as the nations who threaten the Lord's people. In the context of Habakkuk's prophecy the judgment of Babylon is primarily in view. The "leader of the land [lit. 'house'] of wickedness" (v.13b) is probably the king of Babylon. The reference to a house of wickedness parallels 2:9–11, where the Babylonian empire is viewed as a house built by unjust gain. "Wickedness" may allude back to 1:13, where the Babylonians were characterized in this way. The enemy's desire to devour (v.14) God's people reminds one of the earlier comparison of the Babylonians to a devouring vulture (cf. 1:8).

In anger the Lord marches throughout the earth, threshing the nations. The verbs translated "strode" (v.12) and "came out" (v.13) probably allude to Judges 5:4 (NIV "marched" and "went out"), where they are used of God's theophanic march from the south-southeast to fight for the Israelite forces led by Deborah. Threshing imagery is frequently used of military conquest (e.g., 2 Kings 13:7; Isa. 41:15; Amos 1:3; Mic. 4:13).

The second half of this theophanic description ends as it began, with the Lord trampling the sea with His horses (v.15; cf. v.8). As elsewhere in hymnic literature, the sea and the great waters symbolize the Lord's enemies who seek to destroy His people (cf. Pss. 18:16–17; 32:6; 46:2–3; 74:13; 77:16–19; 114:3–

5; 144:7). In suppressing these forces, the Lord demonstrates He is the sovereign Ruler of the universe (cf. Pss. 29; 93).

Habakkuk's Confidence (3:16–19)

Having witnessed a panorama of the future, from Judah's judgment at the hands of the Babylonians (1:5–17) to the Lord's ultimate vindication of His people (2:4–20; 3:3–15), Habakkuk now had to face the historical realization of the prophesied events. As he considered the prospect of the immediate future, he shuddered with terror, for he had to wait patiently for the prophesied events to run their course (v.16).

The precise meaning of the last line of verse 16 is debated. NIV interprets the "day of calamity" to be the day of Babylon's judgment, described earlier in the book and in chapter 3. Others understand the "day of calamity" as the imminent invasion of Judah (NASB). In either case the prophet would have to wait, knowing that the dark night of judgment must precede the dawn of salvation.

Yet Habakkuk had received a positive answer to his prayer in 3:2. Through the theophanic vision he gained assurance that the God of the Exodus and Conquest would indeed renew His mighty acts. The Babylonians would invade the land as an instrument of divine punishment, but the Lord would ultimately vindicate the righteous among His people (cf. 2:4).

This assurance enabled Habakkuk to express unwavering confidence in God (vv.17–19). Though the coming invasion would actualize the covenant curses, including the destruction of crops and livestock (cf. Deut. 28:31–34, 49–51), Habakkuk would rejoice in the Lord, whom he recognized as his Savior (3:13) and source of strength. Using language very similar to Psalm 18:33, Habakkuk compared himself to a deer, which is capable of quickly and safely moving about in steep, rocky heights. Just as the deer travels through difficult terrain without stumbling or suffering injury, so Habakkuk would endure the hardships of the coming invasion, sustained by his trust in the sovereign Lord.

THEOLOGY

Summary

Habakkuk's theological message is quite similar to Nahum's. Like Nahum, he pictured the Lord in the roles of the sovereign King, mighty Warrior, just Judge, and Protector of Israel. The sovereign Lord would judge appropriately the injustice of Judah by raising up the Babylonians as His instruments of punishment. However, as the Protector of His people, He would sustain the faithful through the ordeal and eventually deliver Israel from foreign oppression. He would judge the proud, unjust Babylonians, demonstrating His absolute superiority to Babylon's gods. This renewal of His mighty acts would reveal Him to be the same powerful warrior who intervened so forcefully in Israel's early history.

Analysis

Sovereign King

Habakkuk pictured the Lord as sovereign over nature and nations. When the Lord appears in theophanic splendor, all of nature, including the mountains (3:6, 10), waters (3:10), and the sun and moon (3:11), responds in fear. The Lord controls the destinies of nations, including even the mighty Babylonians, whom He would raise up (1:6) and then judge (2:4–20; 3:3–15). Neither the nations (2:13) nor their lifeless gods (2:18–20) can resist His sovereign authority and will. The Lord is the "Holy One" (1:12), who sits enthroned over the earth (2:20), a fact that everyone will someday acknowledge (2:14).

Warrior

Habakkuk's vision of the Lord Almighty, or Lord of Armies (2:13), is one of the most vivid and detailed portrayals of God as warrior in all of Scripture. Armed with the elements of the storm and accompanied by pestilence (3:4–5), the Lord appears in anger and causes the entire world to shake with fright (3:6–7, 10–11). Like an ancient Near Eastern warrior-king, the Lord rides on a horse-drawn chariot (3:8, 15), employs arrows and spears (3:9, 11, 14), and pierces the head of his enemy (3:13–14).

Judge

Habakkuk affirmed that the Lord's "eyes are too pure to look on evil" (1:13). Consequently He would judge appropriately both Judah and Babylon for their sins of injustice against others. Since Judahite society was plagued by violence and a disregard for God's standards, the covenant curses would be implemented against the nation (cf. 1:5–11). Appropriately the Babylonians, a violent nation that followed no standard but its own, would invade the land as God's instrument of judgment. However, the Babylonians were a proud and unjust nation that greedily built its empire by exploiting and robbing other nations. Once He had used the Babylonians for His purposes, the Lord would judge them as well. Babylon would be plundered, just as it had plundered others (2:8). The Lord would give the Babylonians a dose of their own medicine, making them experience the shame they had brought on so many others (2:15–17).

Protector of His People

Even though the Babylonian invasion would devastate the land of Judah (3:17), the righteous, who had suffered under the oppression of the unjust (1:4), would be preserved because of their loyalty to God (2:4; 3:18–19). Through the righteous the Lord would preserve His covenant people (1:12), whom He would eventually deliver from their cruel and wicked foreign oppressors (3:13–14).

Habakkuk's vision presents this coming deliverance as a renewal of the deeds of salvation history. Knowing that God had often intervened in the past as Israel's protective Rock (cf. 1:12), Habakkuk prayed for a fresh exhibition of God's mighty acts. In response to this petition he saw the Lord coming to fight for Israel as He had in the days of Moses, Joshua, and Deborah. Several motifs in the theophany closely parallel earlier biblical accounts of the Lord's deeds as warrior, including the march from the south (3:3, 12; cf. Deut. 33:2; Judg. 5:4), God's appearance in the storm and its accompanying response (3:4–6; cf. the Sinai theophany, Judg. 5:4, and Ps. 18:7–15), the nations' fearful reaction to God's approach (3:7; cf. Exod. 15:14), the subduing of the sea (in conjunction with God's sending a torrential downpour and shooting His arrows, 3:8–10, 15; cf. Ps. 77:16–19), and the paralysis of the sun and moon (3:11; cf. Josh. 10:12–14). Habakkuk's application of this imagery to the Lord's future intervention emphasizes that the "everlasting" God (1:12), whose "ways are eternal" (3:6), controls history and never ceases to intervene in salvation for His people.

9

ZEPHANIAH

INTRODUCTION

Author and Date

The heading is unique in that it traces the prophet's ancestry through four generations. When genealogical information is provided, usually only the prophet's father is identified (cf. Isa. 1:1; Jer. 1:1; Ezek. 1:3; Hos. 1:1; Joel 1:1), although in the case of Zechariah (Zech. 1:1), two generations are included. Some have identified Zephaniah's great-great-grandfather Hezekiah with the famous king who ruled over Judah from 715 to 686 B.C. This connection would provide a reasonable explanation for the expanded heading, its purpose being to demonstrate Zephaniah's royal descent.

According to the heading, Zephaniah prophesied during the reign of Josiah (ca. 640–609 B.C.). The prophecy preceded the fall of Nineveh in 612, which it anticipated (cf. 2:13–15). Since the book presupposes the existence of pagan idolatry in Judah (cf. 1:4–6), many would date it prior to Josiah's cultic reforms (ca. 622–621), which to some extent eliminated such practices (cf. 2 Kings 22–23).

Structure

The book contains three major sections (1:2–18; 2:4–3:7; 3:10–20), which are linked by two hortatory hinges (2:1–3; 3:8–9). The first hinge, with its appeal to "seek" the Lord (2:3; cf. 1:6, where the same word is used) and its references to the

"Day of the Lord" (2:2–3; cf. 1:7–18), clearly concludes the preceding announcement of judgment (1:2–18). At the same time, this hinge leads into the following series of judgment speeches against the nations (2:4–15). The presence of the particle *kî,* "for" (NASB; untranslated in NIV), at the beginning of 2:4 indicates that verses 4–15 support the exhortation of verse 3. The judgment speeches against the nations, which also include brief notices of Judah's and the nations' eventual salvation (2:7, 11), culminate with a woe oracle against Judah that is purely accusatory in tone (3:1–7). After this accusation one expects a formal announcement of judgment to follow the introductory "therefore" of 3:8. Surprisingly, however, an exhortation to wait patiently appears instead (3:8a). This appeal is supported by the explanatory clauses in 3:8b–9 (*kî* precedes each of the three sentences in 3:8b–9 that follow "to testify"). While the first two (3:8b) announce the expected judgment, the third (3:9) pictures the future salvation of both the nations and God's people (3:10–20). The pivotal character of the exhortation and its supporting statements should be apparent. Verse 3:8b formally concludes the woe oracle, while 3:8a and 9 facilitate the transition to the salvation announcements that close the book. The book's conclusion fully develops the brief salvation notices in chapter 2 (cf. 2:7 with 3:13, 20; and 2:11 with 3:9).

The book's structure and movement may be outlined as follows:

A (1:2–18)	Guilt and judgment of Judah in the context of universal judgment	(= introduction of initial theme)
Hinge 1 (2:1–3)	Exhortation to seek the Lord in view of the coming judgment	(= conclusion to A and introduction to B)
B (2:4–3:7)	1. Guilt and judgment of Judah in the context of universal judgment	(= expansion of A)
	2. Notices of future salvation for the remnant and the nations	(= introduction of concluding theme)

Hinge 2 (3:8–9)	Exhortation to wait on the Lord in view of the coming judgment and salvation	(= conclusion to B1 and transition from B2 to C)
C (3:10–20)	Restoration of remnant in the context of universal salvation	(= expansion of B2)

ANALYSIS

The Destructive Day of the Lord (1:2–18)

This opening announcement of universal judgment has two parts (vv.2–6, 7–18), with the exhortation "Be silent" (v.7) marking the division between them. The first part contains a series of declarations in which the Lord expresses His intent to intervene in judgment, first against the whole earth (vv.2–3) and then against His covenant people (vv.4–6). In the second part the order is reversed, verses 7–13 focusing on the judgment of Judah/Jerusalem, with verses 14–18 once again stressing the universal nature of the impending catastrophe. Thus the overall structure of the chapter is chiastic.

A) Universal judgment (vv.2–3)

    B) Judgment on Judah (vv.4–6)

    B) Judgment on Judah (vv.7–13)

A) Universal judgment (vv.14–18)

Verse 7 provides a summary of the second part, affirming that "the Day of the LORD is near" (v.7a) and that the Lord has prepared a special sacrifice involving Judah's wealthy inhabitants (v.7b). Verses 8–13 then develop the sacrifice motif, while verses 14–18 elaborate on the nearness of the Day of the Lord. Once more a chiastic arrangement is discernible.

A) . . . the Day of the LORD is near. (v.7a)

    B) The LORD has prepared a sacrifice . . . (v.7b)

    B) On the Day of the LORD's sacrifice . . . (vv.8–13)

A) The great Day of the LORD is near . . . (vv.14–18)

The Lord's Intervention (1:2–6)

Using language reminiscent of the Noahic flood (Gen. 6:7; 7:4, 23), the Lord announced He would destroy all life from the face of the earth (vv.2–3). The totality of the destruction is specifically stated (cf. "I will sweep away *everything*") and then emphasized by the references to "men and animals," "the birds of the air," and "the fish of the sea." As in Hosea 4:3, human sin adversely affects all of nature.

God's own people would be the special objects of His judgment (vv.4–6). The people of Judah, while maintaining a semblance of loyalty to the Lord (v.5b), had, for all intents and purposes, rejected Him (v.6a). Rather than seeking His counsel and will (v.6b), they served other gods, including Baal and the starry host of heaven (vv.4b–5).

The word translated "Molech" (v.5) literally means "their king." Though the precise referent is uncertain, the most likely possibilities are Baal (already mentioned in v.4) or the Ammonite god Milcom. The cults of both gods were objects of Josiah's purge (2 Kings 23:4–5, 13), indicating that the people of Judah were heavily involved in the worship of these particular deities in Zephaniah's time. In either case, "their king" is a sarcastic allusion to the people's unfaithfulness. Despite their half-hearted attempt to give the Lord His proper due, they really regarded a pagan god as their sovereign ruler. If Milcom is in view, the reference is especially effective, since *malkām* ("their king") is a deliberate and telling alteration of the vowels of that god's name.

In the Day of Judgment the Lord would destroy those who worshiped these false gods. The destruction of Baal's followers would be especially thorough. "Every remnant of Baal" worship would be removed, including the priests of Baal, whose very memory (cf. "name") would be wiped out (v.4).

A Vivid Description of the Lord's Day (1:7–18)

These verses associate the judgment announced in verses 2–6 with "the Day of the LORD," the nearness of which is emphasized from the outset (v.7a). Zephaniah compared this day of harsh judgment to a specially prepared sacrifice (v.7b) because of the bloodshed involved in both (cf. Isa. 34:6; Jer. 46:10; Ezek. 39:17, 19). Within the figurative picture painted by

Zephaniah, the people of Judah correspond to the sacrificial animals. The invited guests (v.7b) are probably the enemy armies that would serve as the Lord's instruments of judgment.

In describing more specifically His judgment on the people of Judah, the Lord further exposed their guilt (vv.8–13). The influence of foreign customs was apparent in the royal palace, where the princes wore foreign clothing (v.8). A false sense of security had permeated Jerusalem. Many believed that the Lord was inactive, doing neither good nor bad (v.12). This amounted to a practical denial of God's sovereignty and His just character. The Lord satirically compared these individuals, in their ease and complacency, to wine that has not been separated from its dregs at the appropriate time (cf. Jer. 48:11). Such wine congeals and loses its strength and usefulness. Many in Jerusalem had also accumulated riches (v.13) at the expense of the poor, who were victims of the violent and treacherous deeds of the wealthy class (v.9).

The precise meaning of verse 9 is uncertain. The phrase "all who avoid stepping on the threshold" has been understood by some to refer to a pagan practice associated with the worship of the Philistine god Dagon (cf. 1 Sam. 5:5) or to a superstitious custom based on a belief that demons frequented the threshold of a house. Others, taking a nonreligious interpretation of the phrase, suggest that allusion is made to forceful and rapid entry into the homes of the poor. The phrase translated "temple of their gods" is also capable of various interpretations. Since the phrase literally reads, "the house of their lord(s)," it may refer to the human master(s) (NASB, KJV, RSV) of the thugs whose violent actions are described in the verse. In short, it is unclear whether verse 9 refers only to economic oppression or to a combination of false religion and social injustice.

What is transparently clear is that God's judgment would be severe, thorough, and appropriate. Verse 10 highlights its severity. Throughout Jerusalem cries of distress and lamentation would be heard, mingled with the horrible sounds of the city's destruction. The thoroughness of God's judgment is especially apparent in verse 12, which pictures the Lord searching every corner of the dark city with lamps in order that no evildoer might go unpunished. Appropriately, those who had profited economically from exploitation of the poor would be destroyed (vv.11, 13). Though they had acquired houses and vineyards at the expense of the poor, they would not enjoy their possessions (cf. Isa. 5:9–10; Amos 5:11).

In verse 14 the nearness of the Lord's Day again comes to the fore (cf. v.7a). Zephaniah characterized this day as one of warfare and distress (vv.14b–16). The repetition of "day" at the beginning of six consecutive lines and the heaping up of five pairs of (nearly) synonymous terms heighten the intensity of the description and emphasize the ominous and destructive nature of the coming judgment. Not even the strongest fortifications would be able to withstand the Lord's wrath (v.16b).

In verse 17a the Lord Himself announced He would bring distress on the sinful people, causing them, in their shock and confusion, to grope around helplessly as if blind. The violence of the battlefield is then portrayed in graphic detail (v.17b). Life would be cheap, a person's blood and internal organs being considered as worthless as dust or dung. Perhaps the imagery reflects the sacrifice motif of verses 7–8.

Developing further the theme of verses 11 and 13, the prophet affirmed that riches would bring no deliverance from the Lord's angry judgment (v.18a). In His fiery zeal He would destroy completely all the sinful rebels of the earth (v.18b). The references to "the whole world" and "all who live in the earth" indicate the cosmic proportions of the Lord's Day and, in combination with verses 2–3, form a frame around the entire chapter.

Prophetic Exhortations and Judgment Oracles (2:1–3:7)

Exhortations to God's People (2:1–3)

With the judgment of the Lord's Day just around the corner, Zephaniah exhorted the people of Judah to "gather together" (v.1). The force of this charge, directed to the "shameful nation," is uncertain. The verb translated "gather together" is used elsewhere of gathering straw for brickmaking (Exod. 5:12) and stubble or wood for making a fire (Num. 15:32–33; 1 Kings 17:10, 12). Zephaniah's command may be ironic, the nation being viewed as kindling for the fiery judgment of the Lord (cf. 1:18), which had been decreed (note "the appointed time" in v.2).

In a second exhortation (v.3) the prophet addressed the "humble of the land." Elsewhere in the prophets the humble are usually the poor (cf. Isa. 11:4) who suffer from the oppressive measures of the unjust (cf. Isa. 29:19; 32:7; Amos 2:7; 8:4). Perhaps this socioeconomic class, which would have been victims of the violence and deceit referred to in 1:9, is in view here. Regardless, emphasis is placed on the group's loyalty to the Lord (note "who do what he commands"; see also 3:12), not their poverty.

Zephaniah urged these individuals to "seek the LORD" by pursuing righteousness and humility. "Righteousness" refers here to justice; "humility" to obedient submission to the Lord's will (cf. Prov. 15:33; 18:12; 22:4). These qualities were sorely lacking in Judah (cf. 1:9; 3:1–4, 7).

As motivation for his appeal the prophet held out the possibility of protection on the Lord's Day. However, by prefacing his statement with "perhaps," he reminded his audience that such protection would not be automatic but solely depends on God's sovereign will and mercy. This qualification is immensely effective from a rhetorical standpoint. If even the righteous could not be certain about their preservation in the coming judgment, then the fate of the wicked was surely sealed.

Judgment Oracles Against the Nations (2:4–15)

This section contains judgment oracles against various foreign nations that, in relation to Judah, represent the four points of the compass: Philistia (west), Ammon and Moab (east), Ethiopia (south), and Assyria (north; cf. 2:13). References to Judah's and even the nations' eventual restoration are interspersed throughout this section (vv.7, 9b, 11b), serving as a reminder that God's ultimate purpose for His people and His world is a positive one.

The Philistines, who lived on the seacoast west of Judah, are the subject of the first oracle. The oracle singles out the Philistines' four major cities, emphasizing that the destruction would be complete. The phrase "at midday" (v.4) suggests that judgment would also be sudden and unexpected (cf. Jer. 15:8).

Wordplay is prominent in verse 4. The word translated "will be abandoned" ($^{a}z\hat{u}\underline{b}\hat{a}$) sounds like Gaza ($^{c}azz\hat{a}$). Ekron ($^{c}eqr\hat{o}n$) sounds like the word translated "uprooted" ($t\bar{e}^{c}\bar{a}q\bar{e}r$). This similarity between the cities' names and the words describing their downfall suggests that their fate was inherent in the very names given to them.

The Lord's personal involvement in Philistia's demise receives special stress. According to verse 5, "the word of the

LORD" was against the Philistines. This "word," the Lord's official decree that He would totally annihilate the Philistines, appears at the end of the verse ("I will destroy you, and none will be left"). Philistia would be destroyed, abandoned (v.4), and used as pasture land (v.6).

The remnant of Judah would benefit from Philistia's defeat (v.7a). Drawing on the pastoral imagery of verse 6, Zephaniah compared this remnant to sheep that would graze in Philistia (cf. 3:13). The ruins of Ashkelon (v.4) would again be occupied—by God's people!

The prophet characterized Judah's future restoration as a time of total reversal in their relationship to God (v.7b). The phrase "care for" translates the same Hebrew word rendered "punish" in 1:8–9 (pāqad, lit. "to visit [for good or evil]"). The repetition of this term in its two opposite senses draws attention to the reversal in the Lord's attitude toward His people. Because of their sin, He would visit them in punishment (1:8–9), but eventually He would visit them again, this time for good (2:7). At that time Judah's fortunes would be reversed, in fulfillment of Moses' ancient promise (Deut. 30:3).

In the second oracle of this section (vv.8–11), the Lord solemnly (note "as surely as I live") announced His judgment upon Moab and Ammon, two Transjordanian nations that had been hostile to God's people for some time (Num. 22–24; Judg. 3:12–30; 10:7–11:40; 2 Sam. 10–11; 2 Kings 3:4–27; Isa. 16:6; Jer. 48:27–29). Because they had arrogantly threatened and taunted Judah (vv.8, 10), the Lord would come as a mighty warrior ("the LORD Almighty") to vindicate His people (v.9a). He would totally annihilate Moab and Ammon, just as He had done to Sodom and Gomorrah (cf. Deut. 29:23; Amos 4:11). This comparison is especially ironic here, since the Moabites and Ammonites were the offspring from Lot's incestuous relationship with his two daughters following their escape from Sodom and Gomorrah (Gen. 19:36–38). Though these peoples had been a reminder of Lot's deliverance, the judgment of Sodom and Gomorrah would now catch up with them.

As with the Philistines, the remnant of Judah would benefit from Moab's and Ammon's destruction (v.9b). They would plunder any material goods that survived the judgment and would inherit their enemies' territory (cf. Isa. 11:14).

Verse 11 describes the universal effects of the Lord's judgment upon the nations. By defeating nations like Moab and

Ammon, the Lord would demonstrate His superiority to foreign gods. This in turn would prompt distant nations to worship Him as the one true God (cf. 3:9).

The oracle against the distant Cushites (or Ethiopians), which stands out because of its brevity, is proof of the universal scope of the Lord's judgment (v.12). Cush is later mentioned as a place from which God's exiled people would return to their homeland (3:10; see also Isa. 11:11).

The Assyrians, who had dominated the Near East for over a century, are the recipients of the fourth and final oracle (vv. 13–15). Because of their imperialistic success they had become arrogant and self-assured (v.15a). However, the Lord announced He would personally destroy the Assyrian empire, leaving its major city, Nineveh, a heap of ruins inhabited only by flocks and wild creatures. Once-proud Nineveh would become an object of derision.

Woe Oracle Against Judah (3:1–7)

Judah would not be spared, as this woe oracle against Jerusalem makes clear. The introductory address characterizes the city generally as oppressive, rebellious, and defiled (v.1). The word translated "defiled" is used in Isaiah 59:3 and Lamentations 4:14 of oppressors stained by the blood of their innocent victims. In this context (cf. v.3) social injustice is also in view.

Verses 2–5 expand the general accusation of the opening address, describing in greater detail the sins of the city. Jerusalem's inhabitants were disobedient, refusing to respond to the Lord's corrective instruction (v.2a). They did not trust in or draw near to their covenant Lord (v.2b). The city's leaders misused their position and failed to fulfill their responsibilities (vv.3–4). The administrative and civic leaders, rather than being shepherds who cared for the well-being of the Lord's flock (cf. Jer. 23:1–2), were like ravenous beasts in their greedy and violent exploitation of the poor (cf. Ezek. 22:27). The prophets, who were to be humble and honest in their position as divine spokesmen, were instead proud and unreliable (cf. Ezek. 22:28). The priests, who were responsible for maintaining cultic purity and teaching the Law, had instead "profaned the sanctuary" and failed to uphold the principles of the covenant (cf. Ezek. 22:25–26). These evildoers even had the audacity to perform their evil deeds in the sight of the Lord (who resided in the Jerusalem temple), whose absolutely just character should have been a deterrent to such activity (v.5).

In verses 2–5 word repetition draws attention to the evildoers' unabashed behavior and highlights the contrast between the just Lord and the city's unjust leaders. The phrase "within her" (i.e., the city) appears in verses 3 and 5. (The first line of v.3 is lit. "Her officials within her are roaring lions"; cf. NASB.) This indicates that the leaders carried out their oppressive measures in the Lord's very dwelling place. "Within her" (*qirbāh*) is also closely related to the verb translated "draw near" (*qārēḇâ*) in verse 2. Ironically, though the Lord was easily accessible within the city, His people refused to make the effort to draw near to Him. "Morning" appears in verses 3 and 5, contrasting the actions of the predatory leaders, who left none of the remains of the poor "for the morning," with those of the Lord, who "morning by morning . . . dispenses" justice.

The people's persistent rebellion was inexplicable (vv. 6–7). Throughout history the Lord had given them ample object lessons of the severity of His judgment by destroying numerous foreign nations (v.6). These illustrations should have prompted the people to obey the Lord and thereby avert disaster (v.7a). However, despite His efforts, they still eagerly sinned (v.7b). Their undeniable guilt made the destructive Day of the Lord inevitable.

Future Restoration (3:8–20)

An Exhortation to "Wait" on the Lord (3:8)

Verse 8 concludes the preceding judgment speech (note "therefore"), albeit in an unexpected fashion. Instead of delivering a straightforward announcement of judgment following the accusation of verses 1–7, the Lord gave an exhortation to wait. Apparently the humble, who were addressed in an earlier exhortation (cf. 2:3) and are identified with the remnant/exiles of Israel in 3:12, 20, are the recipients of this appeal. This rather surprising alteration of the usual judgment-speech pattern provides a ray of hope in the midst of an otherwise dismal picture. As elsewhere, "wait" has a positive connotation, being virtually synonymous with faith (cf. Ps. 33:20; Isa. 8:17; 30:18; 64:4; Hab. 2:3). Sinful Jerusalem would be severely punished when the Lord poured out His burning anger upon the entire world (v.8b; cf. 1:2–2:3), yet at least a small group of the faithful were told to trust in the Lord in anticipation of the coming judgment.

But why should the humble want to wait in faith for the Lord's judgment? The answer is given in the following verses, where the salvation of God's people and the nations, already hinted at in chapter 2, is described in detail. In short, the humble should wait patiently for the judgment because it would be the first stage in God's program of restoration.

The Purification of the Nations and of God's People (3:9–20)

The structure of these verses requires special attention. In stark contrast to verse 8, verses 9–10 portray a reversal in the nations' relationship to the the Lord. The return of Israel's exiles may also be in view. In verses 11–19 Jerusalem is addressed in a positive manner, in contrast to verses 1–7. In addition to the specific references to Jerusalem/Zion (cf. vv.11 ["this city"], 12 ["within you"], 14–16), the use of second-person singular feminine verbal and pronominal forms in the Hebrew text of verses 11–19 clearly indicates that God is here speaking to the personified city. ("Shout aloud" in v.14 is the lone exception, but note that it is addressed to Israel.) A switch to masculine plural forms in verse 20 signals a change in addressee, as the exiles are now in view.

Verses 8–10 and 20 correspond in several respects, forming a bracket around the address to Jerusalem. The use of masculine plural forms in verses 8 and 20 suggests the same group (the humble in v.8 and the exiles in v.20; cf. v.12) is being addressed. Verses 9–10 and 20 present the nations in a positive light. If the return of Israel's exiles is alluded to in verse 10, then another point of correspondence is apparent, for verse 20 clearly refers to this event.

Within the address to Jerusalem, key motifs and themes are arranged chiastically.

A) Jerusalem's shame removed (v.11a)

    B) Jerusalem purified and populated by a remnant (vv.11b–13)

        C) Jerusalem exhorted to rejoice over the Lord's salvation (vv.14–15)

C) Jerusalem exhorted to trust in the Lord's protection (vv.16–17)

B) Jerusalem restored and populated by a remnant (vv.18–19a)

A) The shame of Jerusalem's citizens reversed (v.19b)

Verse 9 describes the future restoration of the nations, an event already alluded to in 2:11. Though the nations followed false gods (cf. 2:11a), they would one day worship and serve the one true God.

Many have seen in the prophecy of verse 9 a reversal of the dispersion at Babel, recorded in Genesis 11. At Babel, God confused the language (lit. "lip" [Gen. 11:7, 9], the same Heb. word translated "lips" in Zeph. 3:9) of the whole world; in the eschaton He would purify the lips of the Gentiles. Even the words translated "confuse(d)" in Genesis 11:7, 9 (*bālal*) and "purify" in Zephaniah 3:9 (*bᵉrûrâ*, from *bārar*) are similar enough in sound and structure to suggest a contrast. At Babel proud men united in their effort to build the tower (Gen. 11:3–4); in the eschaton men would unite in their service to God (note "serve him shoulder to shoulder"). Though the precise identification of the worshipers mentioned in verse 10 is debated, the use of "scattered" there also appears to be an allusion to Genesis 11, where the same Hebrew word (*pûṣ*) appears three times (vv.4, 8–9).

As just noted, the precise meaning of verse 10 is uncertain. The text literally reads, "From beyond the rivers of Cush my worshipers, the daughter of my scattered ones, will bring my offering." The phrase "the daughter of my scattered ones" defies explanation and may reflect textual corruption. Whether the nations or exiled Israel are the worshipers is unclear. The use of the pronoun "my" with "scattered ones" suggests Israel is in view, especially in light of references in the immediate context to the exiles (cf. vv.19–20). Isaiah 11:11 pictures Israelite exiles returning from Cush, which is also mentioned here as the place of origin of these worshipers. However, other considerations suggest that the worshipers are foreigners. The word "scattered," when viewed in the light of the reversal-of-Babel motif in verse 9, seems to allude to the dispersion of the nations. The picture of the Cushites, whose judgment is announced in 2:12, coming to worship the Lord would provide a reversal consistent with the pattern already seen in 2:11 and 3:8–9. Finally, the words translated "bring" and "offerings" in verse 10 can refer to foreigners bringing tribute to the Lord (cf. Pss. 68:29; 72:10). Perhaps the language is general enough to include both exiled Israelites and purified Gentiles.

Through judgment the Lord would purify defiled and rebellious Jerusalem (vv.11–13). The city would soon experience the shame of judgment because of the sinful deeds of its proud inhabitants (v.11a). However, in the Day of Restoration it would suffer no more disgrace, for judgment would remove arrogant evildoers from God's holy presence (v.11b). In their place God would populate the city with the "meek and humble," who trust in Him (v.12) and follow His ethical standards (v.13a). This faithful and obedient remnant would in turn experience peace and prosperity under their divine Shepherd's protective care (v.13b; cf. 2:7).

Speaking from the standpoint of Jerusalem's future restoration, the prophet called the city to praise the Lord for His mighty deliverance (vv.14–15). The reasons for praise (v. 15), which follow the formal call to praise (v.14) in accordance with the usual hymnic pattern, deal with the past, present, and future. From the perspective of the future time of salvation, God had defeated Jerusalem's enemies and presently resided within the city as its King, guaranteeing its future safety.

In verses 16–17 restored Jerusalem hears a salvation oracle, which contains an exhortation "do not fear" (v.16), followed by reasons for a positive response (v.17). Like the preceding hymn, the oracle mentions the Lord's indwelling presence and power to deliver (v.17a). In addition, His great love for the city is highlighted (v.17b). The statement "he will take great delight in you" may picture the Lord as a happy bridegroom rejoicing over His bride Jerusalem (cf. Isa. 62:4). It certainly reminds one of the Mosaic promise that the Lord would again delight in His people after delivering them from exile (Deut. 30:9).

As noted above, the hymn and salvation oracle of verses 14–17 form the central elements in the chiastic structure of verses 11–19. Within verses 14–17 a chiastic arrangement of key words and themes is also apparent, with "sing" (v.14) and "singing" (v.17) forming an inclusio for the section.

A) *Sing* . . . be *glad* . . . O Daughter of Jerusalem (v.14)

B) The LORD . . . has *turned back your enemy* (v.15a)

   C) The LORD . . . is *with you* (v.15b)

      D) Never again will you *fear* any harm (v.15b)

         E) On that day . . . Jerusalem (v.16a)

      D) Do not *fear* . . . limp (v.16b)

   C) The LORD . . . is *with you* (v.17a)

B) He is *mighty to save* (v.17a)

A) He . . . will *rejoice* over you with *singing.* (v.17b)[1]

Word repetition draws attention to Jerusalem's reversal of fortunes in the eschaton. According to verse 11, Jerusalem in Zephaniah's day was populated by those who rejoiced in their pride ("those who rejoice" translates Heb. *'allîzê*).[2] However, the purified city of the eschaton would "rejoice" (*'olzî*, v.14) in God's strength (v.15), not their own. The phrase "with you" (*b⁰qirbēk*) in verses 15 and 17 is almost identical to "within her" (*b⁰qirbāh*) in verse 5. Verse 5 emphasizes the Lord's presence as righteous judge, implying that His concern for justice would necessitate judgment on the sinful city. However, verses 15 and 17 stress His presence as Jerusalem's Protector, drawing attention to the ethical change that would take place in the city.

Because of difficulties in the Hebrew text, the precise meaning of verse 18 is uncertain. NIV interprets the verse as a promise that the sorrow brought about by the cessation of Jerusalem's religious feasts would be removed. Another interpretation sees this verse as a direct promise of a return from exile for those who grieve over Jerusalem's destruction (NASB).

Verses 19–20 clearly refer to a restoration of the exiles. Drawing on the language of earlier promises made through Moses (Deut. 30:4), Isaiah (11:12), and Micah (4:6–7), the Lord

---

[1]This outline is based on and adapted from those of John W. Hilber, "A Biblical Theology of Zephaniah" (Th.M. thesis, Dallas Theological Seminary, 1984), p. 29; and Ivan J. Ball, Jr., "A Rhetorical Study of Zephaniah" (Ph.D. diss., Graduate Theological Union, 1972), pp. 263–70.

[2]Heb. *'allîz* is also used in 2:15 (NIV "carefree"), where it describes Nineveh's pride. Its use in 3:11 suggests that Jerusalem was no better than the pagan Assyrian city.

announced He would rescue Jerusalem's afflicted (cf. "the lame") and "scattered" exiles (v.19a). He would transform their shame into honor in the sight of the nations (vv.19b–20).

THEOLOGY

Summary

The "Day of the Lord" is the focal point of Zephaniah's prophecy. On this day, the nearness and severity of which are emphasized, the Lord would come as a mighty and just warrior-judge to punish the whole world, including Judah. Through this purifying judgment the nations would become genuine worshipers of the one true God. The judgment of the Lord's Day would also purge God's covenant people and their capital city, Jerusalem. A faithful remnant, the nucleus of the restored covenant community, would populate the purified city and rejoice in the Lord's deliverance and protection.

Analysis

God and the Nations

Zephaniah presented the Lord as the sovereign Judge of the nations. Throughout history He had destroyed nations as an object lesson to Israel of His sovereignty, power, and justice (3:6). In the near future He would unleash His might against the enemies of His people (2:4–15), repaying them for their mistreatment of Israel (2:8) and their arrogance (2:15). This judgment would eventually reach universal proportions (1:18; 3:8), with the destruction being as thorough as that of the Noahic flood (1:2–3).

Through this judgment the Lord would demonstrate the impotence of the pagan gods, prompting the nations to worship Him as the one true God (2:11). The Lord would give the Gentiles the capacity to worship and serve Him as faithful subjects (3:9–10). In so doing, He would completely reverse the effects of the judgment and dispersion that took place at Babel.

God and His People

Zephaniah singled out Judah and its capital city, Jerusalem, as special objects of judgment on the Lord's Day. He offered several examples of the nation's guilt as a basis for judgment.

The people exhibited a self-assured and arrogant attitude (1:12; 3:11), much like that of pagan Nineveh (cf. 2:15). They rejected the Lord's guidance, turning instead to pagan gods (1:4–6). The leaders in particular had rejected the Lord's standards and their God-given responsibilities (3:2–7). A denial of God's just character and involvement in their affairs (1:12) resulted in rampant socioeconomic oppression (1:9; 3:1, 3).

Contrary to Judah's misconception of God's character, the Lord was intensely concerned about justice (3:5). Consequently He would severely (1:7, 10, 14–17), thoroughly (1:12), and appropriately (1:13) judge His people, purging out the arrogant rebels among them (3:11).

In His sovereign mercy the Lord did not forget those who courageously followed His ways in the midst of a corrupt society. He urged this group to maintain its concern for justice and to continue to submit to His sovereign will (2:3) as it waited in faithful anticipation for His purifying judgment (3:8) to inaugurate His program of restoration and renewal. This faithful remnant, having been delivered from the shame of exile (3:19–20), would gain ascendency over its traditional enemies (2:7, 9) and assume a place of honor among the nations of the earth (3:19–20). Because of their devotion and obedience to the Lord (3:12–13a), these loyal ones would experience the protection of their divine Shepherd (2:7; 3:13b).

Through this remnant Jerusalem would experience a complete reversal in its relationship to the Lord. Populated by the Lord's loyal followers, the city would never again be overrun by enemies, for the Lord would take delight in it and restore pure worship to it (3:14–18). With His demand for justice now realized, the righteous Judge (3:5) would stand as the city's invincible Protector (3:17).

Excursus: The Day of the Lord in Zephaniah

Zephaniah's portrayal of the Lord's Day requires special attention. References to the nearness of this day (1:7, 14) and to Judah, Philistia, Moab, Ammon, Cush, and Assyria as participants in it suggest that Zephaniah anticipated the arrival of this day in the immediate future. Thus in its initial phase Zephaniah's day of the Lord should be associated with the Babylonian conquest of the Near East in the late sixth and early fifth centuries B.C. At the same time, the cosmic proportions of the judgment (1:2–3, 18; 3:8) and its ultimate outcome—nothing short of the salvation of Israel and the restoration of the nations—indicate that the prophecy cannot be limited to events in Zephaniah's day. The prophet presented a unified picture of the future, blending together events both near and far away.

10

HAGGAI

INTRODUCTION

Date

Haggai prophesied in 520 B.C., the second year of the reign of the Persian ruler Darius. The book provides precise dates for four of the messages contained within it (cf. 1:1; 2:1, 10, 20).[1]

Message	Date
1:1–11	6th month, 1st day (August 29, 520 B.C.)
2:1–9	7th month, 21st day (October 17, 520)
2:10–19	9th month, 24th day (December 18, 520)
2:20–23	9th month, 24th day (December 18, 520)

The brief message recorded in 1:13 cannot be dated with certainty. Since the other messages in the book can be dated, the chronological notation of 1:1 may apply to this message as well. However, since the people's positive response to the message came on September 21, 520 B.C. (the sixth month, twenty-fourth day; cf. 1:14–15), it could have been delivered any time between August 29 and that date.

[1] For these dates, see Joyce G. Baldwin, *Haggai, Zechariah, Malachi* (London: Inter-Varsity Press, 1972), p. 29.

Structure

Chapter 1 contains two prophetic messages, each of which is followed by a record of the people's response.

I. First message and response (vv.1–12)
   A. Message (concerning people's procrastination; vv.1–11)
   B. Response (v.12)

II. Second message and response (vv.13–15)
   A. Message (concerning people's obedience; v.13)
   B. Response (vv.14–15)

Chapter 2 includes three more messages (2:1–9, 10–19, 20–23).
   The book's main themes are arranged in parallel fashion. The first message (1:2–11) emphasizes agricultural matters. The second message (1:13) and the beginning of the third (2:1–5) focus on God's presence with His people (note "I am with you" in 1:13 and 2:4), while the latter part of the third message (2:6–9) deals with eschatological realities on a universal scale. The fourth message (2:10–19) returns to the theme of the first, once again focusing on agricultural concerns. The exhortation "give careful thought" (1:5; 2:15, 18) links the first and fourth messages. By-passing the theme of God's presence, the fifth message (2:20–23), like the third, pictures God's future universal judgment (cf. 2:6 with 2:21). However, in this final message the emphasis shifts from temple (2:7–9) to ruler (2:23). The following chart illustrates the thematic progression and parallelism of the book:

A	Agricultural matters (1:2–11)	Agriculture (2:10–19)
B¹	God's presence (1:13–15)	
B²	God's presence (2:1–5)	
C	Eschatology (2:6–9)	Eschatology (2:20–23)
	1 Judgment (2:6)	Judgment (2:20–22)
	2 Temple (2:7–9)	Ruler (2:23)

ANALYSIS

First Message and Response (1:1–12)

This message begins with an observation about the people's attitude toward the rebuilding of the temple (v.2). Though restoration of the temple had begun sixteen years before (cf. Ezra 3:8–13; 5:16), work had ceased because of the neighboring peoples' opposition (Ezra 4:1–5, 24). Discouraged by this hostility, the people had developed a spirit of procrastination, reasoning that it was not yet time for the temple to be finished.

The Lord viewed matters differently. From His perspective it was inappropriate for the people to be living in comfortable homes while the temple lay in virtual ruin (v.4). The Lord urged His people to consider carefully their behavior and its negative consequences (vv.5–11). Though they had worked hard, their economic needs had not been met. They had planted much (v. 6) with the expectation of an abundant harvest (v.9). However, because of their neglect of the temple (v.9) a divinely ordained drought had destroyed the anticipated harvest, leaving them short of food and impoverished (vv.6, 10–11). The word translated "drought" (*ḥōreb*, v.11) sounds like the word used in verses 4 and 9 to describe the unfinished temple—"a ruin" (*ḥārēb*). Through this wordplay the Lord drew attention to the appropriate nature of their punishment. The shortage of food had serious repercussions on society. As low supply, coupled with high demand, brought inflated prices, the people were unable to provide adequate food and clothing for themselves. Their money was used up so quickly it seemed as if their purses had holes in them (v.6).

The central theme of this message is a familiar one in the Old Testament. Through Moses the Lord made it clear that Israel's agricultural and economic success was contingent upon her faithfulness to God. Obedience would bring divine blessing (Deut. 28:1–14); disobedience would result in drought and eventual national ruin (Deut. 28:15–68). Much of the imagery of Haggai 1:5–11 reflects the curses of Deuteronomy 28 (cf. esp. vv.6, 10–11 with Deut. 28:18, 22–23, 38–40, 51). By drawing on this Deuteronomic background, God made it plain to the postexilic community that they, like their forefathers, were subject to the covenant demands of their sovereign Lord.

The Lord exhorted His people to respond favorably to His

rebuke by securing timber (probably from the nearby hills) and finishing the building of the temple (v.8). While provision had been made years before to acquire cedars from Lebanon (cf. Ezra 3:7), the suspension of the temple project for sixteen years made it necessary to secure timber once more.

Wordplay is employed to emphasize the need for a positive response to the Lord's exhortation. "Harvested" (v.6), "bring down" (v.8), and "brought home" (v.9) all translate the word *bô'*, used in all three instances in its causative form and meaning "bring." The Israelites had harvested (lit. "brought in") little (v.6). What they had brought in God had blown away (v.9). Why? Because they first needed to bring in wood for the temple (v.8).

Haggai's message fell on fertile soil (v.12). Zerubbabel (the governor of Judah), Joshua (the high priest), and the entire community, called here the "remnant of the people," responded in obedience. They "feared" the Lord in the sense that they now showed Him proper respect by submitting to His will. Since actual construction of the temple did not begin until approximately three weeks later (September 21; cf. v.14), verse 12 probably refers to the acquisition of the building materials (cf. v.8) in preparation for the project.

Second Message and Response (1:13–15)

Pleased by His people's favorable response, the Lord assured them of His protective presence (v.13). Going one step further, He "stirred up" the spirits of Zerubbabel, Joshua, and the people so that on September 21, 520 B.C., they entered into the rebuilding project with vigor (vv.14–15). In the same way the Lord had moved Cyrus sixteen years earlier to decree that the temple be rebuilt (cf. 2 Chron. 36:22–23, where "moved the heart" translates the same Heb. expression as "stirred up the spirit" in Hag. 1:14). Thus in its very inception this building project was proof of God's sovereign control over human will.

Third Message (2:1–9)

On October 17, 520 B.C., approximately one month after work on the temple was resumed (cf. 1:14–15), the Lord again delivered an encouraging message through Haggai. Many of the people, especially the elderly who had seen Solomon's temple in all its glory, were discouraged by the relative insignificance of the new structure (v.3). To counteract such sentiments the Lord exhorted the people to continue their efforts, assuring them that their labors would be richly rewarded. The threefold exhortation to "be strong" (v.4a) is motivated by the assurance that God would be present with the postexilic community (v.4b; cf. 1:13) in the same way He had been with Moses' generation (v.5a, cf. Exod. 29:42–46).

The exhortation "Do not fear" (v.5b), which provides a fitting conclusion to what precedes, is supported by a series of divine promises dealing with the place of the temple in God's future program (vv.6–9). In the Hebrew text the word *kî*, "for, because," appears at the beginning of verse 6, connecting "do not fear" with what follows. The Lord announced He would soon shake the universe and the nations (vv.6–7a). Through this disruption of the world order and its political structures, the Lord would bring the nations under His sovereign control. As His subjects, the nations would then bring their tribute to His temple (vv.7b–8), causing its splendor to surpass that of the Solomonic temple (v.9a). As the focal point of God's universal rule, the temple and the worshipers associated with it would experience prosperity and security (v.9b).

Some have interpreted the "desired of all nations" (v.7) as a messianic reference. This view is contextually improbable. The phrase is more naturally associated with the material wealth mentioned in verse 8, understood as the nations' tribute payments to the Lord (cf. Isa. 60:5–9; Zech. 14:14). In the Hebrew text "will come" is plural, suggesting that the singular form "desired" (*ḥemdat*) may have originally been "desirable things" (*ḥămudōt*). The plural reading involves only a change of the vowel pointing, not the consonants, of the Hebrew text.

Did the glory of the second temple ever surpass that of Solomon's temple (cf. v.9)? Some view Herod's impressive expansion of the second temple as the fulfillment of this prophecy (cf. Mark 13:1). However, the glorification of the temple predicted by Haggai is associated with universal judgment and the ingathering of the nations' tribute, not with the self-glorifying efforts of a godless ruler. Some understand Christ's physical presence in Herod's temple as fulfilling verse 9. However, this view is influenced by the questionable messianic interpretation of "desired" in verse 7 and fails to relate verse 9 adequately to its immediate context. As noted earlier, the glorification described in verse 9 comes in conjunction with the establishment of God's universal kingdom (vv.6–8). At best, Christ's appearance in the temple during his first advent was only a partial fulfillment of this prophecy, a foreshadowing of the eventual glory to come in the kingdom age. An examination of history shows that the events prophesied in verses 6–9 never were fulfilled, at least to the degree described, in conjunction with the second temple. As prophesied by Jesus (Matt. 24:1–2; Mark 13:2; Luke 21:6), the temple was destroyed in A.D. 70 without ever becoming the focal point of God's universal kingdom.

How then is one to explain this apparent failure of prophecy? It seems best to associate the prophecy of verses 6–9 with a future millennial temple, which should be viewed as an extension of, not as distinct from, the second temple. That the Lord should relate, rather than distinguish, the millennial and second temples should come as no surprise in light of verse 3 (*"this house* in *its former* glory"), which views the second temple as a continuation of the Solomonic temple. Apparently from God's perspective there is but one temple, despite its various historical forms. By associating the eschatological glory of the millennial temple with the work of Haggai's generation, the Lord assured this faithful remnant that the project that they obediently initiated would culminate in grand style, despite its seemingly meager beginnings.

Fourth Message (2:10–19)

On December 18, 520 B.C., approximately three months after work on the temple resumed (cf. 1:14–15), the Lord again spoke to the people through Haggai (v.10). He instructed Haggai to ask the priests some questions pertaining to ritual consecration and defilement (vv.11–13). His purpose in doing this was to illustrate a basic fact about the people's spiritual condition (v.14).

Haggai first asked the priests about ritual consecration. Though consecrated meat would make the garment in which it was carried holy (cf. Lev.6:27), that garment could not transmit holiness to objects that it subsequently contacted (v.12). However, ritual defilement operated differently. If a man touched a defiled object, such as a corpse, he would then transmit uncleanness to any object he touched (v.13; cf. Num.

19:22). Having elicited the proper responses from the priests, the Lord then applied the principle of ritual defilement to the people. Like the individual who touches a corpse, they too had been defiled in God's sight (v.14a). Like objects that come in contact with a defiled person, their deeds and sacrifices had been contaminated and were ineffectual (v.14b).

To demonstrate the truth of this assertion, the Lord urged the people to recall the state of affairs prior to the resumption of the temple project three months before.[2] The Lord had struck their crops "with blight, mildew and hail" (v.17; cf. 1:9–11), reducing the harvest to 40–50 percent of its anticipated yield (v.16). Surely this was proof of their uncleanness in His sight.

However, the people's obedient response to Haggai's earlier messages marked a turning point in their relationship to God. Starting on December 18 (the date this third message was delivered), they were to pay close attention (v.18a), for the Lord was about to bless them for their renewed devotion to Him and His dwelling place (v.19b). During the three months between the resumption of the temple project (dated September 21; cf. 1:14–15) and this latest prophetic message, the people had begun planting their fields once more, in conjunction with the early rains.[3] Though their empty barns gave testimony to past crop failures, this most recent planting would bring an abundant harvest and demonstrate that their obedience had cleansed them from their defilement.

The precise significance of the reference to the laying of the temple foundation (v.18b) is unclear. The Hebrew text of verse 18 literally reads, "Give careful thought from this day on, from the twenty-fourth day of the ninth month, from the day when the foundation of the temple of the Lord was/has been laid, give careful thought." Some interpret this to mean that the foundation of the second temple was laid on December 18, 520 B.C. (i.e., on the twenty-fourth day of the ninth month). This view is problematic in that Ezra 3:8–13 seems to date the laying of the foundation in 536, and Haggai 1:14–15 indicates that by December 18 renewed work on the temple had been underway for about three months. It is possible that two formal rededication ceremonies were held (in 536 and then again in 520), with

---

[2] Verses 15b–17 are best taken as parenthetical, with v.15a being resumed by v.18a.

[3] Baldwin, *Haggai, Zechariah, Malachi*, pp. 49–50.

both including the laying of a foundation stone.[4] Zechariah 8:9–10 may lend support to such a theory. Baldwin suggests that the word translated "laid" (*yāsad*) in verse 18 is not a technical term for laying a foundation (here or in Ezra 3:8–13, where it also appears). She proposes that it refers more generally to building or restoring.[5] If so, the apparent chronological tension between the two texts would be relieved. However, 2:18 would still need to be harmonized with 1:14–15, which indicates that work resumed on the temple in September, not December.

Others understand verses 18b–19a as a parenthesis in which the Lord urges the people to consider carefully the scarcity of crops that had characterized the sixteen years since the laying of the temple foundation in 536. In this case one might paraphrase verse 18b as follows: "Since the day when the foundation of the temple was laid, give careful thought to how badly things have gone."[6] In this view the promise of verse 19b ("from this day on I will bless you") resumes verse 18a. In this view, the structure may be outlined as follows:

2:18a: From this day on, from this twenty-fourth day of the ninth month, give careful thought.

2:18b–19a: (From the day the foundation of the Lord's temple was laid, give careful thought: Is there yet any seed left in the barn? Until now, the vine and the fig tree, the pomegranate and the olive tree have not borne fruit.)

2:19b: From this day on I will bless you.

Fifth Message (2:20–23)

The prophet followed up this promise of blessing with an address to Zerubbabel, Judah's governor (v.20). Utilizing the language of an earlier message (cf. v.6), the Lord reminded Zerubbabel that He was about to disrupt the world order (v.21)

[4]For discussion of this option, see Pieter A. Verhoef, *Haggai and Malachi* (Grand Rapids: Eerdmans, 1987), pp. 129–30.

[5]Baldwin, *Haggai, Zechariah, Malachi*, pp. 52–53.

[6]Herbert Wolf, *Haggai and Malachi* (Chicago: Moody Press, 1976), p. 49.

and overthrow kingdoms and powerful armies (v.22). In contrast to the kings of the earth, whose authority would be overturned, Zerubbabel would become God's official representative in the new eschatological order. In this role the Lord likened him to a signet ring, which contained the king's seal and was used to authorize royal documents and decrees (1 Kings 21:8; Est. 8:8, 10).

This prophecy was not fulfilled in Zerubbabel's day. The Lord did not overthrow gentile powers on the universal scale portrayed in verses 21–22, nor did Zerubbabel receive the honor promised in verse 23. How then can we explain this apparent failure of prophecy?

Understanding Zerubbabel's representative role as the chosen descendent of David is the key to interpreting this prophecy correctly. As a descendent of David (cf. 1 Chron. 3:1–19, esp. vv.18–19; Matt. 1:6–12, esp. v.12), Zerubbabel stood as the official representative of the Davidic dynasty in Haggai's day. As such he was called God's servant and chosen one, just as David had been (2 Sam. 3:18; 6:21; 7:5, 8, 26; 1 Kings 8:16). By comparing him to a signet ring, God reversed the judgment pronounced against Zerubbabel's grandfather Jehoiachin (Jer. 22:24–30) and guaranteed that the past failures of Davidic rulers did not invalidate the Davidic covenant. As promised by God, the Davidic throne would someday gain ascendancy over all the kings of the earth (Pss. 2:7–9; 89:19–29). Because of the promise given to Zerubbabel, messianic hopes may have been attached to his person by Haggai's generation. However, the progress of revelation makes it clear that the promise to Zerubbabel will be fulfilled through his descendent, Jesus Christ. As with the temple (cf. 2:6–9), the Lord attached ultimate eschatological realities to a historical representative visible to Haggai's contemporaries.

THEOLOGY

Summary

In response to the renewed efforts of the postexilic community to build the temple, the sovereign Lord promised to restore agricultural prosperity and assured His people that He would eventually overthrow the nations, glorify His temple, and bring honor to the Davidic dynasty.

Analysis

The Book of Haggai testifies to God's sovereignty over His world. The Lord speaks of His control of the natural elements and the agricultural cycle (1:5–11; 2:15–19). Because of the people's procrastination and misplaced priorities (1:2–4), He decreed a drought (1:11) and sent pestilence and hail (2:17) to destroy their crops. What they did manage to harvest He blew away (1:9). Yet He also promised that He would restore agricultural prosperity in response to their renewed obedience (2:19). The Lord Himself moved the people to follow through on their initial response of faith (1:14–15; cf. 1:12), demonstrating His sovereignty over human will. The Lord's sovereign control over the nations and His people's destiny is also apparent. He would disrupt the cosmos (2:6, 21), overthrowing powerful kingdoms and armies (2:7, 22). In that day His temple would become the focal point of His universal rule, its glory surpassing that of the Solomonic temple (2:7–9). He would also restore His chosen Davidic king to a position of prominence (2:23). Given the book's emphasis on divine sovereignty, it is quite appropriate that the title "LORD Almighty" appears fourteen times. This title depicts God as a mighty warrior who commands powerful armies.

The Book of Haggai also clarifies the position and responsibilities of the postexilic community. Three times the community is called "the remnant of the people" (1:12, 14; 2:2), emphasizing that it had survived God's purifying judgment. Though the Lord's impersonal references to "these/this people" (1:2; 2:14) and "this nation" (2:14) hint at His displeasure with the community, He clearly regarded it as the continuation of the nation established at the Exodus (2:5). Like earlier generations of Israelites, this commmunity was subject to the requirements of the Mosaic covenant. The people's response to the Lord's commands would determine whether they experienced blessing or curse. Their procrastination had brought economic disaster, yet God promised that their obedience in renewing the temple project would result in agricultural prosperity (2:19). However insignificant their rebuilt temple and their governor might seem, God guaranteed a glorious future. The temple would become the focal point of God's universal rule (2:7–9), with the Davidic dynasty serving as His earthly representative (2:23). With this assurance the postexilic community could move ahead in faith, confident that God had not abandoned His covenant people.

11

ZECHARIAH

INTRODUCTION

Authorship, Date, and Unity

Each of the three messages in chapters 1–8 begins with a heading that dates the message and identifies Zechariah as its author.[1]

Heading/Message	Date
1:1/1:2–6	October/November 520 B.C.
1:7/1:8–6:15	February 15, 519
7:1–3/7:4–8:23	December 7, 518

No such headings appear with the two "oracles" in chapters 9–14 (cf. 9:1; 12:1). Some suggest that Zechariah delivered these messages later in his ministry,[2] while many others regard them as anonymous appendixes to Zechariah's prophecies. Among this latter group, some attribute all or part of chapters 9–14 to a preexilic author (Jeremiah being a popular

---

[1] On the dates, see Joyce G. Baldwin, *Haggai, Zechariah, Malachi* (London: Inter-Varsity Press, 1972), p. 29.

[2] See, for example, C. Hassell Bullock, *An Introduction to the Old Testament Prophetic Books* (Chicago: Moody Press, 1986), pp. 316–17; and J. Carl Laney, *Zechariah* (Chicago: Moody Press, 1984), p. 13.

candidate), though most understand the section as originating after Zechariah's time.[3]

Scholars have denied the unity of Zechariah for various reasons. In the seventeenth century Joseph Mede assigned chapters 9–11 to Jeremiah on the basis of Matthew 27:9–10 (cf. Zech. 11:12–13), which he felt contradicts the canonical placement of the chapters with Zechariah's prophecies. Shortly thereafter others extended Mede's theory to include Zechariah 12–14. However, Matthew's quotation is probably a composite of Zechariah 11:12–13 and passages from Jeremiah (cf. 18:1–2; 32:6–9), perhaps being based on an early Christian testimonial collection.[4] Like Mark 1:2–3, which attributes a composite quotation (from Isa. 40:3 and Mal. 3:1) to Isaiah, the more prominent of the prophetic authors involved, so the quotation in Matthew 27:9–10 is ascribed to the well-known prophet Jeremiah, even though its wording is more dependent on Zechariah.

Proponents of both preexilic and post-Zecharian dates appeal to internal evidence for support. Alleged preexilic elements include references to Judah and Ephraim as separate political entities (9:13; 10:6–7) and to Assyria and Egypt as enemies of God's people (10:10–12). However, the prophet probably drew on earlier prophetic texts for his language, in which case these references should not be used for dating purposes. Long after the exile of the northern kingdom in 722 B.C., both Jeremiah (30:3–4; 31:6, 27, 31; 33:14) and Ezekiel (37:16), like Zechariah, envisioned the reconciliation of Israel/Ephraim and Judah.[5] In speaking of a return from Egypt and Assyria, Zechariah may have been alluding to the promises of Isaiah (11:11–16) and Hosea (11:11).

Those favoring a post-Zecharian date sometimes find support from 9:13, which refers to a military conflict between Israel and Greece ($y\bar{a}w\bar{a}n$, "Javan"). Some see in this an allusion to the Maccabean-Seleucid hostilities of the second century B.C. However, "Greece" may be used here to symbolize the distant

---

[3]On the history of interpretation, see Paul D. Hanson, *The Dawn of Apocalyptic,* rev.ed. (Philadelphia: Fortress Press, 1979), pp. 287–90; and Ralph L. Smith, *Micah–Malachi* (Waco: Word Books, 1984), pp. 169–73, 242–49.

[4]See Richard N. Longenecker, *Biblical Exegesis in the Apostolic Period* (Grand Rapids: Eerdmans, 1975), p. 150.

[5]Hobart E. Freeman, *An Introduction to the Old Testament Prophets* (Chicago: Moody Press, 1968), p. 343.

nations (cf. Isa. 66:19) who will resist the extension of the Lord's kingdom in the eschaton.[6] Even if the Maccabean wars are in view, one should note that the text prophesies a *future* event and therefore does not necessarily presuppose the existence of a Greek empire in the author's day. Even though Persia, not Greece, was the major power in Zechariah's time, a keen observer might have been able to foresee Greece's eventual rise to prominence.[7] If so, then certainly a divinely aided prophet could have looked beyond contemporary political realities and have foreseen future developments.

Those denying the original unity of the book also appeal to literary considerations, pointing to differences between chapters 1–8 and 9–14 in style, vocabulary, and themes.[8] Arguments of this type are often subjective. Others have presented lists of stylistic and thematic similarities between the two sections.[9] Any actual differences may be due to changes in subject matter and literary genre.[10]

Literary Genre

In many respects the book resembles the apocalyptic literary genre, of which the clearest biblical examples are Daniel and Revelation.[11] Symbolic visions, which make up a significant portion of Zechariah, are a prominent feature of apocalyptic literature. J. Collins observes that Zechariah's visions are "much less elaborate" than those of Daniel and

[6]Baldwin, *Haggai, Zechariah, Malachi*, pp. 168–69.

[7]Cf. R. K. Harrison, *Introduction to the Old Testament* (Grand Rapids: Eerdmans, 1969), pp. 952–53.

[8]See, for example, H. G. Mitchell, "A Critical and Exegetical Commentary on Haggai and Zechariah," in *A Critical and Exegetical Commentary on Haggai, Zechariah, Malachi, and Jonah* (New York: Charles Scribner's Sons, 1912), pp. 234–36.

[9]Edward J. Young, *An Introduction to the Old Testament*, rev.ed. (Grand Rapids: Eerdmans, 1960), pp. 280–81; Harrison, *Introduction*, p. 954; Baldwin, *Haggai, Zechariah, Malachi*, pp. 68–69; Freeman, *Introduction*, p. 344; Laney, *Zechariah*, pp. 11–12; Brevard S. Childs, *Introduction to the Old Testament as Scripture* (Philadelphia: Fortress Press, 1979), pp. 482–83.

[10]Freeman, *Introduction*, p. 344.

[11]For a discussion of how this genre should be defined, see Paul D. Hanson, "Apocalyptic Literature," in *The Hebrew Bible and Its Modern Interpreters*, ed. Douglas A. Knight and Gene M. Tucker (Philadelphia: Fortress Press; Chico, Calif.: Scholars Press, 1985), pp. 466–72.

Jewish apocalyptic literature. At the same time, Zechariah's visions are more developed than those of the earlier prophets Amos and Jeremiah.[12] According to Baldwin, other characteristics of apocalyptic appearing in Zechariah include animal symbolism (Zech. 1:8–21), symbolic numbers (two, four, and seven are prominent in the visions), the blending of history and eschatology (see chs. 7–8), the use of stereotypical imagery drawn from prophetic eschatology (see chs. 9–14), as well as several other motifs and images that are later taken up in Revelation.[13]

Structure

The book contains two major sections (chs. 1–8 and 9–14). The first of these consists of three distinct messages: (1) a call to repentance (1:1–6); (2) a series of eight visions (1:7–6:8), to which divine instructions concerning a symbolic act are appended (6:9–15); and (3) a series of four divine proclamations prompted by a question about fasting (7:1–8:23). The hortatory emphasis of the first and third (cf. 7:9–10; 8:16–17) messages provides a frame for chapters 1–8, the main theme of which is the restoration of Judah/Jerusalem (cf. 1:12–17; 2:1–13; 8:1–8, 15, 22). This theme is also the focal point of the two oracles that appear in chapters 9–14. Though the heading in 12:1 marks the division between the oracles, the theme of the Lord's ultimate vindication of Jerusalem, which appears in both chapters 9 and 14, frames the entire section and unifies it thematically with chapters 1–8.

ANALYSIS

Divine Messages and Visions (1:1–8:23)

An Opening Exhortation (1:1–6)

Zechariah delivered this opening call to repentance in October/November 520 B.C., shortly after the resumption of the temple project (September 21, 520; cf. Hag. 1:14–15) and Haggai's prophecy of the temple's future glory (October 17,

---

[12]See John J. Collins, *Daniel, with an Introduction to Apocalyptic Literature* (Grand Rapids: Eerdmans, 1984), pp. 6–7.

[13]Baldwin, *Haggai, Zechariah, Malachi*, pp. 72–73.

520; cf. Hag. 2:1–9). This exhortation balances Haggai's optimistic message by reminding the people that genuine repentance must accompany their efforts (v.3). Though the Lord did not specify here what true repentance entails, Zechariah's later messages suggest He had social justice in mind (cf. 7:8–10; 8:16–17, 19).[14]

In order to motivate a positive response to His appeal, the Lord promised, "Return to me, and I will return to you" (v.3), assuring the people of His willingness to seek reconciliation. He also urged them not to follow in the footsteps of their forefathers (v.4a). Though the forefathers and the earlier prophets had long since died (v.5), there was still something to learn from them. Because of the forefathers' refusal to obey the prophets' calls to repentance (v.4b), the prophets' warnings of God's angry judgment overtook them (vv.2, 6a).[15] Brought to their senses by the severity of God's judgment, the exilic generation repented, acknowledging that their sins had been justly punished (v.6b). The lesson for the postexilic community was clear. To avoid learning the hard way about God's punishment of the unrepentant, they must return to Him without delay.

Zechariah's Night Visions (1:7–6:15)

On February 15, 519 B.C. (cf. 1:7), Zechariah received a series of eight visions, the overriding theme of which is the restoration of Judah and its capital, Jerusalem. The following chart summarizes the theme(s) of each vision:

Vision	*Theme(s)*
1. A man among the myrtle trees (1:8–17)	1. God's devotion to Jerusalem (1:14)

---

[14]See Mitchell, "Haggai and Zechariah," pp. 110–11.

[15]The context suggests that "my words and my decrees" refers here to prophetic announcements of judgment (cf. the qualifying clause "which I commanded my servants the prophets" and the verb "overtake"). These prophetic messages of judgment were often based on the covenantal curses of Deut. 28, which God warned would "overtake" His disobedient people (cf. Deut. 28:15, 45, where the Heb. verb translated "overtake" in Zech. 1:6 also appears). For another example of judgment being "decreed" by the Lord, see Zeph. 2:2, where "appointed time" translates the same Heb. word as "decrees" in Zech. 1:6.

Vision	Theme(s)
	2. God's anger with the nations (1:15)
	3. Rebuilding of Jerusalem and temple (1:16)
	4. Judah's future prosperity (1:17)
	5. Consolation and election of Jerusalem (1:17)
2. Four horns and four craftsmen (1:18–21)	1. Judgment of Judah's oppressors
3. A man with a measuring line (2:1–13)	1. Jerusalem's future population growth (2:4)
	2. God's protection of Jerusalem (2:5a)
	3. God's glorious presence within Jerusalem (2:5b, 10, 11b)
	4. The return of the exiles (2:6–7)
	5. God's vengeance on Jerusalem's oppressors (2:8–9)
	6. God's kingdom encompasses nations (2:11a)
	7. God's election of Jerusalem (2:12)
4. Clean garments for the high priest (3:1–10)	1. God's election of Jerusalem (3:2)
	2. The cleansing and commissioning of the high priest (3:3–7)
	3. The prophecy of the Branch (3:8)
	4. The cleansing of the land (3:9)

Vision		*Theme(s)*
	5.	Future security and prosperity of the people (3:10)
5. The lampstand and olive trees (4:1–14)	1.	Rebuilding of the temple (4:6–10)
	2.	Leadership of Joshua and Zerubbabel (4:14)
6. The flying scroll (5:1–4)	1.	Purification of the land
7. A woman in a basket (5:5–11)	1.	Removal of evil to Babylon
8. Four chariots (6:1–8)	1.	God's conquest of the nations

This series of visions exhibits several recurring themes, including the judgment of the nations, God's election and future blessing of Jerusalem, the purification of the land, the rebuilding of the temple, and the centrality of Joshua and Zerubbabel in God's program. The fourth vision (3:1–10) is thematically pivotal. At its beginning (v.2) and conclusion (v. 10), themes from visions 1 and 3 appear, namely, God's election of Jerusalem (v.2; cf. 1:17; 2:12) and the future security and prosperity of the people (v.10; cf. 1:14, 17; 2:4–5). The themes of verses 3–9 are developed in more detail in the subsequent visions and appendix. The important role of the community's leaders (vv.3–8) is taken up again in the fifth vision and in the appendix. The cleansing of the land (v.8) becomes the theme of the sixth and seventh visions.

The concluding statement of this section (6:15b) suggests how the visions relate to the opening call to repentance (cf. 1:1–6). Zion would be restored *if* the people returned to the Lord (1:3) and diligently obeyed Him (6:15b). Thus the promises and visions appear within a framework that emphasizes the role of human responsibility in the realization of God's purposes.

1:8–17. This vision may be outlined as follows:

I. Vision proper (v.8)

II. Dialogue: Explanation of vision (vv.9–10)

III. Expansion of vision (vv.11–13)

IV. Divine oracle (vv.14–17)

Zechariah saw a man on a red horse standing among some myrtle trees in a ravine (v.8). According to verse 11, this "man" was the "angel of the LORD." Behind the man were red, brown, and white horses (v.8), the riders of which were scouts sent out by the Lord to reconnoiter the earth (v. 10).[16] This patrol reported to the angel of the Lord that they "found the whole world at rest and in peace" (v.11). Their statement probably refers to the relative peace that was restored to the Persian empire following the suppression of widespread revolts accompanying the accession of Darius I.[17]

This report prompted the angel of the Lord to cry out, "LORD Almighty, how long will you withhold mercy from Jerusalem and from the towns of Judah, which you have been angry with these seventy years?" "Seventy years" is a round figure, referring to the period between the destruction of Jerusalem in 586 B.C. and the date of the vision (519). This reference to seventy years should not be confused with Jeremiah's prediction of a seventy-year period of exile (25:11–12; 29:10). Jeremiah referred to the roughly seventy-year period between 605 and 538, as several texts make clear (cf. 2 Chron. 36:20–23; Ezra 1:1; Dan. 9:2).

In response to the angel's prayer the Lord delivered an encouraging message, predicting the judgment of the nations and promising the restoration of Judah (vv.13–17). This message did not come directly to the angel of the Lord, but to the angel serving as Zechariah's tour guide (v.13, cf. 1:9, 19; 2:3; 4:1, 4; 5:5, 10; 6:4). This angel in turn commissioned

---

[16] It is not certain if the details of the vision (the myrtle trees, the ravine, and the colors of the horses) are symbolic. Efforts to demonstrate symbolism here are often more ingenious than convincing. The context supplies little, if any, evidence for such speculation. The colors of the horses are probably included for the sake of vividness and realism. Perhaps the myrtle trees and ravine suggested to Zechariah a particular location, the identity and significance of which are lost to the modern reader.

[17] For a discussion of this rebellion, see John Bright, *A History of Israel,* 3d ed. (Philadelphia: Westminster Press, 1981), p. 369.

Zechariah to proclaim the message, presumably to the people of Judah (cf. v. 14b).

The message speaks of God's great jealousy (better, "zeal") for Jerusalem (v.14). His zeal is that of a warrior coming to protect his people from their enemies (cf. v.15; Isa. 42:13; 59:17). Verse 15 identifies these enemies as "the nations that feel secure." The phrase "feel secure" refers here to their arrogant complacency. (The Heb. word here translated "feel secure" in other places is rendered "the proud" [Ps. 123:4] and "complacent" [Isa. 32:4, 11; Amos 6:1].) Relatively speaking, the Lord had been "only a little angry" with His people. The nations, who were His instruments of punishment, "added to the calamity" by their excessive mistreatment of God's people. Consequently the Lord had transferred His anger to those nations (cf. v.15 with v.2).

The Lord also spoke of Jerusalem's glorious future (vv. 16–17). He would have mercy on Jerusalem (cf. the angel's prayer in v.12) and return to the city (cf. v.3). The temple and city would be rebuilt, the reconstruction being symbolized by the stretching out of the measuring line (cf. Jer. 31:39). The Lord would comfort Jerusalem (cf. Isa. 40:1–2; 51:3, 12) and once again choose it as His earthly dwelling place (cf. 1 Kings 8:48; 11:13, 36; 14:21; 2 Kings 21:7; 23:27; 2 Chron. 6:6; Ps. 132:13). All of the towns of Judah would overflow with prosperity as a result of the Lord's renewed blessing (cf. Isa. 40:9–10).

1:18–21. This second vision is arranged in two panels.

I. First panel (vv.18–19)
    A. Vision proper (v.18)
    B. Dialogue: Explanation of vision (v.19)

II. Second panel (vv.20–21)
    A. Expansion of vision (v.20)
    B. Dialogue: Explanation of expanded vision (v.21)

Zechariah first saw four horns (v.18), representing the nations that had scattered God's people into exile (vv.19, 21). The horn of a wild animal, which often symbolizes strength (Deut. 33:17; 1 Sam. 2:10; Pss. 75:10; 89:17, 24; 92:10; 112:9; Jer. 48:25; Lam. 2:17; Ezek. 29:21), makes an apt figure for the military power of these nations.

The significance of the number four is not clear. Some have identified the four horns with Assyria, Egypt, Babylon, and Medo-Persia or with the successive empires of Daniel's visions (Dan. 2:31–45; 7:1–27). However, the text specifically associates the horns with the nations responsible for the Exile, suggesting that the Babylonians and the peoples who collaborated with them in Judah's demise are in view. These would include Judah's immediate neighbors—the Ammonites, Moabites, Edomites, and Philistines (cf. 2 Kings 24:2; Ezek. 25:1–17; Obad. 8–21). In this case the number four probably stands for the points of the compass, indicating that Gentile hostility against God's people came from all directions. In support of this interpretation one may also point to the next vision, where the Lord speaks of His people being scattered in all directions as if by the "four winds of heaven" (2:6).

In this second vision Zechariah also saw four craftsmen (v.20) sent by God to terrify and throw down the four horns (v.21). Why craftsmen are introduced to combat the horns is not entirely clear. The imagery may be based on Ezekiel's prophecy of the "men skilled in [lit. "craftsmen of"] destruction," whom the Lord sends against Ammon (21:31). Possibly the craftsmen appear because they would forge the weapons used to destroy the nations (cf. Isa. 54:16–17). However, the vision seems to picture the craftsmen as having a more direct role in the downfall of the horns. Perhaps the entrance of the craftsmen brings the vision of the horns into sharper focus, suggesting that the horns are those of an altar (which would be constructed by craftsmen), rather than those of an animal (cf. Exod. 27:2).[18] Ironically the craftsmen here come to destroy the horns of the altar (cf. Amos 3:14). This ambiguity surrounding the figure of the horns may be intentional, drawing attention to the contrast between outward appearances and reality. The nations appear to be strong and dangerous, like the horns of a wild animal. In reality they are more like the stationary horns of an inanimate altar, which can be cut off by God's powerful smiths just as quickly as they were built. Since the horns of an altar were a place of refuge (cf. 1 Kings 1:50–51; 2:28), there

[18] Cf. David L. Petersen, *Haggai and Zechariah 1–8* (Philadelphia: Westminster Press, 1984), pp. 165–66.

may be another note of irony in that they are here associated with destruction, rather than safety.[19]

Whom do the craftsmen represent or symbolize? Those who identify the horns as successive empires see the craftsmen as the kingdoms that overthrew their respective predecessors. If the horns represent Babylon and the states surrounding Judah, then the craftsmen might be the nations responsible for their demise, including Persia. Others identify the craftsmen as supernatural spiritual agents, such as appear in the first (cf. 1:8–11) and perhaps the final (cf. 6:5) visions.

2:1–13. The third vision exhibits the following structure:

I. Vision proper (v.1)

II. Dialogue: Explanation of vision (v.2)

III. Expansion of vision: Divine oracle (to surveyor; vv.3–5)

IV. Divine oracle (vv.6–13)

Zechariah next saw a man with a measuring line (v.1). When questioned by the prophet, this surveyor explained that he was about to measure the dimensions of Jerusalem (v.2), apparently in preparation for the reconstruction of its protective walls (cf. vv.4–5).

As Zechariah's angelic guide began to leave the scene of this dialogue, he was met by another angel (v.3), who instructed him to run after the surveyor and tell him about Jerusalem's future dimensions (vv.4–5). In contrast to the past, Jerusalem would be an unwalled city, overflowing with men and livestock (v.4; cf. Isa. 49:19–20). No physical walls would be needed because the Lord Himself would be "a wall of fire around" the city, protecting it from invasion (v.5a). Once again His glory would reside in Jerusalem (v.5b; cf. Isa. 60:19).

In verses 6–7 the remaining exiles and personified Jerusalem become the recipients of God's message. Though He had scattered His people to the four corners of the earth (v. 6b; cf. Isa. 43:5–6), the Lord urged the former residents of Zion still exiled in Babylon to escape that city (vv.6a, 7). Babylon is

---

[19] Ibid., p. 166.

called "the land of the north" (v.6a) because the Babylonians had invaded Judah from the north (cf. Jer. 1:14; 4:6; 6:22; 10:22) and because the exiles would return to the land from that direction (cf. Jer. 3:18; 16:15; 23:8; 31:8).

Verses 8–9 present several interpretive problems, the chief of which concerns the identity of the speaker(s). According to NIV, the Lord Almighty is the speaker of all the words following the introductory quotation formula. However, the final statement of verse 9, in which the speaker says that the Lord Almighty had sent him (cf. also v.11), makes this interpretation extremely problematic.[20] It is more likely that there are two speakers in verses 8–9, the Lord Almighty and the servant He has commissioned.[21] This servant is probably Zechariah, since the prophet speaks of himself in the first person elsewhere in this vision (cf. vv.1–3; see also 2:11; 4:9; and 6:15, where identifying Zechariah as the one sent also makes good contextual sense). We may outline and paraphrase verses 8–9 as follows:

Zechariah: "For this is what the Lord Almighty says (for His own glory He sent me)[22] concerning[23] the nations

---

[20] Some try to resolve this difficulty of the Lord Almighty's sending the Lord Almighty by making the quotation indirect or by identifying the speaker as the Angel of the Lord or the Messiah, both of whom can be equated with God Himself. However, the Angel of the Lord is not specifically mentioned in this vision (cf. Laney, *Zechariah*, p. 47). In 2:3 only Zechariah's angelic guide and "another angel," both of whom are distinct from the Angel of the Lord, appear.

[21] Note the translation of Petersen, *Haggai and Zechariah 1–8*, pp. 172–73. Cf. also Carol L. Meyers and Eric M. Meyers, *Haggai, Zechariah 1–8* (Garden City, N.Y.: Doubleday, 1987), p. 162.

[22] The Heb. phrase is literally, "after glory [he?] sent me" (NIV "after he has honored me"). The meaning of "after glory" is uncertain. Proposals include, among others, "with heaviness" (i.e., "with insistence"; Baldwin, *Haggai, Zechariah, Malachi*, p. 109), "after (the) glory" (i.e., "after my prophetic vision[s]"; Mitchell, "Haggai and Zechariah," p. 141), "(to pursue) after (God's) glory" (Laney, *Zechariah*, p. 47; cf. Ezek. 39:21), and "after (his) Glory" (i.e., "after his divine presence"; Meyers and Meyers, *Haggai, Zechariah 1–8*, pp. 162, 165). My paraphrase follows the third of these.

[23] For this understanding of Heb. *'el*, see Mitchell, "Haggai and Zechariah," p. 146. Another possibility is to take the preposition with "sent," resulting in a translation, "For this is what the Lord Almighty says (for His own glory He sent me to the nations who plundered you). . . ." Cf. Petersen, *Haggai and Zechariah 1–8*, p. 172.

who plundered you (for whoever touches you touches the apple of His eye):[24]

Lord Almighty: 'I will surely raise my hand against them so that their slaves will plunder them.'

Zechariah: When He has done this you will know that the Lord Almighty has sent me."

The message of verses 8–9 supports the exhortations of verses 6–7. Those remaining in Babylon were to escape, for the Lord's judgment would fall on those who had plundered Jerusalem (cf. 1:15, 21). Appropriately these plunderers would get a taste of their own medicine by being plundered by those whom they had enslaved. At that point God's people would recognize Zechariah as the Lord's messenger.

Verse 8b gives the primary reason for the Lord's anger with Judah's oppressors (cf. 1:15). When the nations mistreated God's people, they touched the "apple [i.e., pupil] of His eye." To protect such a prized and irreplaceable possession, the Lord would react instinctively to the nations' hostility (cf. Deut. 32:10).

Another appeal to Zion follows this message of judgment against the nations (v.10). The Lord urged Zion to rejoice in anticipation of His return to the city. In that day foreign nations would turn to the Lord and become His people as well (v.11a; cf. 8:23).

Contrary to NIV, Zechariah, not the Lord, is the speaker of the final statement in verse 11 ("and you will know that the LORD Almighty has sent me to you"). Zechariah's words continue in verses 12–13 (note the third-person references to the Lord), where the prophet promises Judah and Jerusalem a renewed relationship to the Lord and exhorts all humankind to revere Him. The Lord would take possession of Judah, as if it were a prized inheritance (v.12a). The prophet may be drawing on the language of Exodus 34:9 (where Moses prayed, "take us as your inheritance") and Deuteronomy 32:9 ("For the LORD's

---

[24] Some textual witnesses have "my eye" here. If this reading is original, then the Lord's actual words begin in v.8b, rather than 9a. Verse 8b would then be translated, "Indeed whoever touches you touches the apple of My eye." Cf. ibid., p. 173.

portion is his people, Jacob his allotted inheritance"). The Lord would also choose Judah's capital, Jerusalem, as His earthly dwelling place (v.12b; cf. 1:17). In anticipation of the Lord's judgment on the nations (vv.8–9) and His restoration of His people (vv.10–12), all persons should stand in silent, fearful awe before Him (v.13; cf. Hab. 2:20; Zeph. 1:7). The stark contrast here between human inactivity ("be still") and God's activity ("he has roused himself") draws attention to His power and transcendence. When the sovereign Lord of the universe rouses Himself to action and emerges from His holy dwelling place, all humankind stands helpless before Him, totally subject to His will and might.

3:1–10. The structure of Zechariah's fourth vision is quite simple.

I. Vision proper (vv.1–5)

II. Divine oracle (to Joshua; vv.6–10)

This vision opens with Joshua, the high priest, standing before the angel of the Lord. Satan stood at Joshua's right hand and prepared to accuse him (v.1; cf. Ps. 109:6). The Hebrew word translated "Satan" is often used elsewhere of human enemies (e.g., 1 Kings 11:14, 23, 25). When the word has the article, as it does here and in Job 1–2, it refers to a particular angelic being who is hostile to God's servants. In the New Testament, where his character comes into clearer focus, his Old Testament epithet ("the adversary") becomes a proper name.

Before this adversary had a chance to accuse Joshua of sin (vv.3–4), the Lord rebuked him and affirmed His continuing devotion to Jerusalem (v.2). The Lord compared Joshua, in his role as representative of the postexilic community, to "a burning stick snatched from the fire." Because the words spoken to the adversary refer to the Lord in the third person ("The LORD said to Satan, 'The LORD rebuke you' "), many see the speaker as the angel of the Lord. Since this angel is the Lord's official representative and spokesman, the quotation can be introduced as the Lord's very own words.

The symbolic act described in verses 3–5 depicts the Lord's purification of His people. The angel of the Lord instructed the attendants to replace Joshua's filthy garments, symbolic of his and the nation's sins, with clean ones. He also told them to place a clean turban on Joshua's head.[25] "Filthy" ($ṣô'îm$) emphasizes the degree of the nation's sin. While the Hebrew adjective appears only here, related noun forms are translated "excrement" ($ṣē'â$, Deut. 23:13; Ezek. 4:12) and "urine" ($ṣô'â$, 2 Kings 18:27 [= Isa. 36:12]).

After Joshua's symbolic purification, the angel of the Lord solemnly charged him to obey the Lord's commandments (v. 7a). The Lord promised to reward Joshua's obedience by giving him administrative responsibility over the temple and its courts, as well as access to the divine council (v.7b), where he would represent his people before the Lord.

The Lord expanded this personal message to Joshua into a promise of the nation's future restoration (vv.8–10). Joshua's associates, who are not specifically identified, were "symbolic of things to come" (v.8a; lit. "men of a sign"). Though most identify them as Joshua's fellow priests, they might just as easily include the civil leaders of the postexilic community. In either case, as representatives of those who had been restored from exile, they were tangible reminders that God still had a positive plan for His people.[26] That plan included the restoration of the Davidic throne (v.8b), the purification of the land (v.9), and the establishment of peace and prosperity (v.10).

"The Branch" (v.8) is the ideal Davidic ruler prophesied by Jeremiah (23:5; 33:15). In Zechariah's day this promise was probably attached to the person of Zerubbabel, as a comparison of 4:9 and 6:12 suggests. According to the former passage, Zerubbabel's hands would complete the building of the temple, while 6:12 states the Branch would accomplish this task. In the progress of revelation the Branch prophecy, as well as the promises associated with it in Zechariah 3:8–10 and 6:12–13, are ultimately and completely fulfilled in and through Jesus Christ, whom Zerubbabel merely foreshadowed (cf. Hag. 2:23).

The significance of the stone and seven eyes (v.9) has puzzled scholars. Some identify the stone, like the Branch, with

---

[25] For the sake of consistency with v.4, I prefer to read in v.5a, "Then he [i.e., the angel] said." This reading has some support in ancient versions. The Masoretic text has a first-person verb form (cf. NIV, "Then I said"), the speaker apparently being Zechariah.

[26] See Petersen, *Haggai and Zechariah 1–8,* pp. 208–10.

Messiah, the seven eyes indicating his infinite knowledge.[27] E. Lipinski sees an allusion to the rock struck by Moses, from which water flowed (cf. Exod. 17:6).[28] In this interpretation the seven eyes are understood as springs ('ayin can mean either "eye" or "spring"), and the phrase rendered "I will engrave an inscription on it" is translated "I open its openings" (the Heb. words for "open" and "engrave" are virtually identical). According to this view, the water flowing from the stone cleanses the land of its iniquity (cf. v.9b). Others identify the stone as the cornerstone or capstone of the temple, on which the "seven eyes" of God, symbolizing His watchful care, are fixed. The engraving beautifies the stone, thereby preparing it for its prominent position.[29] D. L. Petersen sees the stone as the golden plate attached to the high priest's turban, on which were inscribed the words "Holy to the LORD" (Exod. 28:36).[30] This plate was associated with the symbolic removal of the people's guilt (Exod. 28:37–38). In this case the stone's seven "eyes" are its gleaming facets. This stone, because of its association with the removal of sin, would be a tangible symbol of the nation's purification, promised in verse 9b.

4:1–14. The fifth vision displays the following structure:

I.   Vision proper (vv.1–3)

II. Dialogue (vv.4–5)

III. Divine oracles (vv.6–10a)

IV. Resumption of dialogue: Explanation of vision (vv.10b–14)

After being roused from sleep by his angelic guide, Zechariah saw a golden lampstand with a bowl and seven lamps

[27] See, for example, Kenneth L. Barker, "Zechariah," in *The Expositor's Bible Commentary,* ed. Frank E. Gaebelein (Grand Rapids: Zondervan, 1985), 7:626.

[28] E. Lipinski, "Recherches sur le Livre de Zacharie," *Vetus Testamentum* 20 (1970): 25–29. Both Laney (*Zechariah,* p. 57) and Baldwin (*Haggai, Zechariah, Malachi,* pp. 117–18) are receptive to this view.

[29] See, for example, T. T. Perowne, *Haggai and Zechariah* (Cambridge: Cambridge University Press, 1897), p. 83.

[30] Petersen, *Haggai and Zechariah 1–8,* pp. 211–12.

on it (vv.1–2). According to some (e.g., NIV), channels or pipes connected the bowl containing the oil to the lamps. The construction in the Hebrew text suggests that each light had seven channels. However, the meaning of the Hebrew word translated "channels" is debated. It may refer to spouts or indentations on the rim of the lamp in which wicks were placed.[31] In this case, as Baldwin explains, there would be "seven small bowls, each with a place for seven wicks, arranged round the rim of the main bowl."[32] On either side of the bowl stood an olive tree (v.3). These trees apparently supplied the bowl with oil (cf. v.12).

The following dialogue and oracles elucidate the vision. Though the significance of the golden lampstand is not specifically explained, it probably symbolizes the rebuilt temple envisioned in verses 7–10. With one exception (2 Kings 4:10) the Hebrew word translated "lampstand" (cf. vv.2, 11) is used elsewhere of the golden lampstand of the tabernacle or the golden lampstands of Solomon's temple. According to verse 10b, the seven lamps (v.2) symbolize "the eyes of the LORD," which in turn represent His complete (symbolized by the number seven) awareness and control of all that happens on earth. The close association of the lamps with the lampstand points to the Lord's presence in the restored temple.

The interpretation of the two olive trees (cf. v.3) is complicated by verse 12. Before the angel had a chance to answer Zechariah's query about the identity of the trees (cf. v.11), the prophet rephrased his question (v.12). In so doing, he introduced a new element into the vision, namely, two olive branches[33] situated beside two golden pipes through which the olive oil pours (presumably into the bowl). Do the branches merely represent the trees as a whole, or is the reality behind the branches distinct from that which underlies the trees? The text provides no answer.

At any rate, the angel identified the two branches as "the

---

[31] Ibid., p. 221.

[32] Baldwin, *Haggai, Zechariah, Malachi,* p. 120.

[33] Elsewhere the Heb. word *šibbōlet* refers to "ears of grain." The usual suggestion is that the word is applied here to olive branches because they would resemble ears of grain in shape. However, there is a Heb. homonym *šibbōlet,* meaning "flowing stream," which Petersen finds more appropriate here (see *Haggai and Zechariah 1–8,* pp. 235–36). In this case the reference is to streams of olive oil flowing from the trees into the pipes.

two sons of fresh oil, who are standing by the Lord of the whole earth" (v.14, NASB margin). Because oil was used in anointing ceremonies, the NIV and others understand the phrase "sons of oil" as an idiomatic reference to "anointed" servants of the Lord. However, the word for oil used here (*yiṣhār*) never refers elsewhere to anointing oil (for which *šemen* is used) but usually refers instead to fresh oil as a symbol of a land's abundance and fertility.[34] Consequently the phrase "sons of oil" probably points to Joshua and Zerubbabel (cf. 3:6–8; 4:6–10; 6:9–15), the leaders of the postexilic community, as embodying the nation's renewed prosperity produced by God's blessing (cf. Hag. 2:19).

These branches apparently provide the oil that makes the lamps burn. Many commentators have been troubled by this interpretation because it seems to imply that God (symbolized by the lamps) is dependent on the nation's leaders (symbolized by the branches).[35] However, the vision need not "walk on all fours." According to verse 6, the accomplishments of the nation's leaders were made possible by God's power. The vision merely draws attention to the role these leaders play in the reestablishment of God's dwelling place and the formal worship conducted there. Zerubbabel would rebuild the temple (4:7–10), while Joshua would oversee its courts (3:7). At the same time, the sovereign God's presence within the temple (symbolized by the lamps on the lampstand) would ensure the continuing prosperity of His people.[36]

The divine oracles (vv.6–10a) focus on Zerubbabel's role in the restoration of the temple. The Lord reminded Zerubbabel that the successful completion of the temple depended on God's Spirit, not mere human strength (v.6; cf. Hag. 2:5). Energized by the Spirit, Zerubbabel would be able to overcome even the most formidable of obstacles, symbolized here by a "mighty mountain" (v.7a). The heap of ruins left from Solomon's temple may have suggested the mountain imagery, but the figure ultimately points to the opposition of the surrounding peoples (cf. Ezra 4:4–5, 24; 5:1–5). Though some thought

[34] Ibid., pp. 230–31.

[35] Note Baldwin's reservations (*Haggai, Zechariah, Malachi*, p. 123). Cf. Petersen's discussion of this problem (*Haggai and Zechariah 1–8*, pp. 236–37).

[36] On the "symbiosis" in the divine-human relationship that this vision suggests, see Petersen, *Haggai and Zechariah*, pp. 233–34.

lightly of the new temple (v.10a; cf. Hag. 2:3), its completion would cause many to shout for joy (vv.7b, 10b). Zerubbabel's hands, which had laid the foundation stone of the temple,[37] would also place the capstone on the completed temple (vv.7b, 9).[38]

5:1–4. The sixth vision in this series may be outlined as follows:

I. Vision proper (v.1)

II. Dialogue: Explanation of vision (vv.2–3)

III. Divine oracle (v.4)

Zechariah next saw a large scroll flying through the air (v.1). Since the prophet was able to give its dimensions (thirty feet by fifteen feet), the scroll was obviously unrolled (v.2). The words "every thief will be banished" were written on one side of the scroll. A similar statement ("everyone who swears falsely will be banished") appeared on the other side (v.3). Verse 4 indicates that oaths sworn falsely in the Lord's name are in view. Theft and false oaths were prohibited in the Ten Commandments (by the eighth and third commandments, respectively). These two sins may have been especially widespread in the postexilic community. Here they probably represent the two halves of the Decalogue. If so, then all

[37]The reference is either to the initiation of the temple project in 536 B.C. (cf. Ezra 3:8–13) or to its resumption in 520. For further discussion of the chronological issues involved, see the analyses here of Hag. 2:18 and Zech. 8:9–10.

[38]This capstone may also be referred to in v.10, where Heb. *hāʾeḇen habbᵉdîl* is translated by some as "stone of separation" (i.e., "chosen stone"). Cf. Baldwin, *Haggai, Zechariah, Malachi,* pp. 122–23. NIV's "plumb line" assumes the phrase means "stone of lead." In this case the plumb line would be a symbol of the temple's reconstruction. Some interpret vv.7 and 10 against the background of Mesopotamian temple-building ceremonies. Following this approach, Petersen understands *hāʾeḇen hārōʾšâ* (NIV "capstone") in v.7 as a stone from the former temple and *hāʾeḇen habbᵉdîl* in v.10 as a metal tablet deposited in the temple foundation (see *Haggai and Zechariah 1–8,* pp. 240–41, 243–44). However, Baldwin (*Haggai, Zechariah, Malachi,* pp. 121–23) and Laney (*Zechariah,* pp. 60–62) point out that the temple foundation had already been laid (cf. v.9) and argue that the completion of the temple, not its founding, is in view.

covenant violators, not just thieves and oath breakers, are in view.

Because of the words of judgment inscribed on the scroll, the angel identified it as a "curse" (v.3). The Hebrew word ('ālâ) often appears in covenantal contexts, referring to the oath taken by one or both of the parties to an agreement (e.g., Gen. 26:28; Ezek. 17:13). These oaths included curses, or threatened punishments, that would fall on the violators of the agreement (cf. 1 Sam. 14:24). Such curses were attached to Israel's covenant with God (cf. Deut. 28:15–68). In Deuteronomy 29, 'ālâ is used of both the oath of allegiance taken by Israel (vv.12, 14, 19) and the curses accompanying it (vv.20–21). If the commandments alluded to in the scroll of Zechariah's vision represent the entire Decalogue, which in turn encapsulated the demands of the covenant in general, then the scroll, with its threats against covenant violators, may represent the whole body of curses attached to the covenant.

Since the oaths were sworn in God's name, He was responsible for activating the curses against covenant violators. Because of the divine authority underlying the curse, it sometimes displays a dynamic character, as if possessing a power of its own (cf. Num. 5:23–28; Deut. 28:15, 45). One sees this factor in verse 4, where the scroll/curse, having been sent out by the Lord, enters the house of the sinner, settles down, and begins to eat away the stones and the timber. The destruction of the transgressor's house vividly depicts that one's elimination from the covenant community.

This vision makes it clear that the members of the community, like their forefathers, were subject to God's law. God intended to purge this community of covenant breakers, just as He had preexilic Israel. In addition to being a warning to evildoers, this vision also carried a positive message in the wider context of Zechariah's visions. God would indeed purify His people (cf. 3:9; 5:5–11) and their leaders (3:3–5) in order that He might again dwell in their midst and bless them (cf. 4:1–14).

5:5–11. The seventh vision exhibits a three-paneled structure.

    I. First panel (vv.5–6)
        A. Vision proper (vv.5–6a)
        B. Explanation of vision (v.6b)

II. Second panel (vv.7–8)
   A. Expansion of vision (v.7)
   B. Explanation of expanded vision (v.8)

III. Third panel (vv.9–11)
   A. Expansion of vision (v.9)
   B. Dialogue: Explanation of expanded vision (vv.10–11)

Zechariah's angelic guide drew the prophet's attention to a measuring basket (vv.5–6a). The angel identified the basket with the iniquity of the land (v.6b) because it contained a woman who symbolized the nation's wickedness (vv. 7–8a).[39] The angel pushed this woman down into the basket and closed its weighted lid so she might not escape (v.8b). Two women with wings like a stork then swept up the basket to carry it away to Babylon, where a special house was being prepared for it (vv.9–11). The women may be likened to storks because these birds, being unclean (Lev.11:19; Deut. 14:18), would be appropriate carriers of wickedness. The reference to the wind being in their wings suggests swift flight. Babylon (lit. "Shinar") would be a suitable dwelling place for wickedness. For centuries Shinar had symbolized human pride and rebellion against God (cf. Gen. 11:1–9). God had later exiled His sinful people to Shinar (Isa. 11:11; Dan. 1:2).

This vision is closely related thematically to the preceding one. God intended to purge the postexilic community of evildoers. He would judge the wicked, sending them swiftly into "Babylonian exile" (cf. 3:9). Rebels against God's covenant were not fit to dwell in His presence and experience His blessings.

6:1–8. The final vision may be outlined as follows:

I. First panel (vv.1–6)
   A. Vision proper (vv.1–3)
   B. Dialogue: Explanation of vision (vv.4–6)

---

[39]In v.6b the Masoretic text reads, "This is their eye [i.e., appearance] in all the land," which lacks suitable sense in the context. For a defense of this reading, see Meyers and Meyers, *Haggai, Zechariah 1–8*, pp. 297–98. NIV follows other ancient witnesses in reading "iniquity" for "eye." For a helpful discussion, see Barker, "Zechariah," p. 635.

II. Second panel (vv.7–8)
   A. Expansion of vision (v.7)
   B. Explanation of expanded vision (v.8)

In this eighth vision Zechariah saw four chariots emerge from between two bronze mountains (v.1). Each chariot's horses differed in color from those of the other three (vv. 2–3). Though some attempt to explain the horses' colors as symbolic (cf. Rev.6:1–8; 19:11–14), there is nothing in this context to support such interpretations. The variation in colors corresponds to the points of the compass (cf. v.6) and distinguishes the four units of the Lord's army. As in the first vision, the horses' colors are probably included merely for the sake of vividness and realism.

In verse 5 the chariots are identified as the "four winds of heaven" (NIV margin; note NIV's translation of the same Heb. phrase in 2:6). The association of these winds with chariots suggests that they represent the Lord's army (cf. 2 Kings 6:17; Ps. 68:17; Isa. 66:15; Hab. 3:8). Jeremiah 49:36 identifies these same winds as the Lord's agents of judgment. Since these winds go out from God's presence, the reality behind the imagery may be angelic beings, who swiftly carry out God's will (cf. Rev.7:1). If this vision is parallel to the first (cf. 1:7–17), then these winds/chariots would correspond to the angelic patrol of 1:8–11. However, the differences between the two visions far outweigh any superficial similarities.

Since the chariots came from before the divine throne (v.5), the two bronze mountains seem to form the gateway to the divine palace. Bronze symbolizes strength and impenetrability (cf. Isa. 45:2; Jer. 1:18). Perhaps the vision of a heavenly temple with bronze mountains as its gateposts mirrors the Solomonic temple, which had two bronze pillars located at its main entrance (1 Kings 7:15–22).

As the chariots emerged from God's presence, they headed in different directions (vv.6–7). Verse 6 omits any reference to the red horses or to a movement toward the east. Noting the syntactic awkwardness of the Hebrew text at the beginning of verse 6 (lit. "which in it"; NIV "the one with"), some suggest that a reference to the red horses moving toward the east has accidentally been lost from the text.[40] The phrase translated

---

[40] Baldwin, *Haggai, Zechariah, Malachi*, p. 131.

"toward the west" (lit. "after them"; cf. NIV margin) is also problematic. A more likely interpretation is that the white horses followed the black ones toward the north, with the dappled ones going in the opposite direction. In this case the red horses, rather than moving toward the east, may have been held back in reserve.

Verse 8 focuses on the horses sent to the north. As they proceeded to the "land of the north" (identified as Babylon in 2:6–7), they appeased the Lord's wrath (cf. 1:15), presumably by carrying out His judgment against that nation. In this context the phrase translated "have given my Spirit rest" (*hēnîḥû 'eṯrûḥî*) is better rendered "have appeased my wrath" (NASB). Examples of similar translations of Hebrew *rûaḥ* (more commonly "wind" or "spirit") are "resentment" (Judg. 8:3), "rage" (Job 15:13), "temper" (Prov. 16:32), and "anger" (Prov. 29:11; Eccl. 10:4).

6:9–15. Divine instructions concerning a symbolic act are appended to the visions. The Lord told Zechariah to collect silver and gold from three individuals who had returned from exile in Babylon (v.10). After taking the silver and gold to a certain Josiah's home, Zechariah was to make a crown and place it upon the high priest Joshua's head (v.11). This crown would eventually be placed in the temple as a memorial to the exiles who donated the precious metals from which it was made (v.14).[41]

In conjunction with the crowning of Joshua, Zechariah was to deliver a message to the high priest explaining the symbolic significance of the act (vv.12–13). The interpretation of this message is problematic. According to many commentators, Joshua is here identified as a type of the messianic Branch (cf. 3:8), who would build the temple and rule as a priest (hence Joshua's symbolic value). In this interpretation the statement "and there will be harmony between the two" (v.13b) points to

[41] Two of the four names appearing in vv.10–11 differ in the Heb. text of v.14. Helem (NIV margin) replaces Heldai (cf. v.10), while the son of Zephaniah's name is given as Hen, not Josiah (cf. v.10). Helem may be a textual corruption or an alternate name for Heldai. Cf. Meyers and Meyers, *Haggai, Zechariah 1–8*, p. 340. Hen may have been Josiah's nickname, although a recent proposal reinterprets the Heb. expression *lᵉḥēn*, "to Hen," as an official title of Josiah, meaning "temple steward." For discussion of the latter view, see Laney, *Zechariah*, pp. 76–77.

a fusing of the royal and priestly offices in the person of the Messiah.

Others prefer to see this statement as referring to two distinct individuals. In this view verses 12–13a contain a prophecy about the Branch, who would be a royal figure responsible for building the temple. In conjunction with this king's rule the high priest (typified by Joshua) would also exercise a rulership function within the covenant community (v. 13b). In this case the statement "and there will be harmony between the two" emphasizes the unity of purpose that would exist between the Davidic king and the high priest. In favor of this interpretation one may point to the preceding context, which predicts that Zerubbabel would complete the temple (4:9), a task accomplished by the Branch, according to 6:12. At the same time, the completion of the temple allows the priesthood to be fully restored (3:1–10). In this connection Joshua is promised a position of leadership in the temple (3:7) and is pictured as ruling with Zerubbabel over the restored community (4:11–14). Thus, according to this view, verses 12–13 do not directly prophesy the Davidic king's priestly role, though they do indicate that the high priest would lend his full support to the king's rule.

As noted earlier (in conjunction with Hag. 2:23 and Zech. 3:8), the ideal expressed in verses 12–13 was probably originally attached to the persons of Zerubbabel and Joshua (cf. 4:9 with 6:12). However, this ideal will be fully realized only in conjunction with the eschatological rule of Jesus the Messiah, who is also the High Priest appointed by God. Thus the royal and priestly ideals represented by Zerubbabel and Joshua are both ultimately fulfilled in Him.

The focal point of verses 9–15 is the restoration of the temple (v.13a), a major theme in the preceding visions (1:16; 4:6–10). The concluding statement (v.15) promises that "those who are far away will come and help to build the temple of the LORD." In the immediate historical setting the participation of returning exiles in the rebuilding project is probably envisioned. However, as in Haggai 2:7–9, the language probably supercedes the experiences of the postexilic community. In the ultimate fulfillment of this promise, Gentiles as well as Jews would take part in the glorification of God's temple (cf. 2:11; 8:22).

Divine Proclamations Concerning Justice and Future
Blessing (7:1–8:23)

On December 7, 518 B.C., almost two years after his night
visions, Zechariah received another message from the Lord.
The occasion for this message was an inquiry by the people of
Bethel, who asked the priests and prophets if they should
continue their annual custom of mourning and fasting for the
destruction of the temple. Since some of the exiles had returned
and the temple was being rebuilt, they wanted to know if the
time of lamentation was officially over. The Lord made it clear
that their preoccupation with cultic ceremonies was misplaced.
He demanded justice, not ritual. The people's obedience in this
regard was a prerequisite for full restoration (cf. 1:2–6; 6:15).
To motivate a positive response the Lord promised to dwell
again among His people and to bless them.

The phrase "the word of the LORD Almighty came to me"
(7:4, 8; 8:1, 18) divides the message into four parts. At the same
time the major themes of these chapters are arranged in a
chiasmus.

A) Messengers from Bethel entreat (*lᵉḥallôt*) the Lord
   (7:1–3)
   B) The Lord denounces ineffective fasts (7:4–7)
      C) An earlier generation rejected the Lord's
         demand for social justice (7:8–12)
         D) 1. The Lord sent His people into exile
               (7:13–14)
            2. The Lord promises to dwell again in
               Jerusalem and bless the remnant of
               His people (8:1–6)
         D) 1. The Lord will deliver His people from
               exile (8:7–8)
            2. The Lord exhorts the remnant of His
               people to rebuild His dwelling place,
               for He will again bless them (8:9–15)
      C) The Lord exhorts the postexilic community
         to promote social justice (8:16–17)
   B) Meaningful fasts will be restored (8:18–19)
A) All peoples will come to Jerusalem to entreat
   (*lᵉḥallôt*) the Lord (8:20–23)

7:1–7. Throughout the period of the Exile, God's people had fasted and mourned for the loss of their nation. During the fifth month the people and priests remembered the destruction of the temple, which occurred on either the seventh or tenth day of the fifth month in 586 B.C. (vv.3, 5; cf. 2 Kings 25:8; Jer. 52:12). A fast during the seventh month (cf. v.5) probably recalled the death of Gedaliah, whose assassination by Ishmael ben Nethaniah in the seventh month, 586, caused further humiliation for the people of Judah (cf. 2 Kings 25:25–26; Jer. 40:7–41:18).

The Lord questioned the motives of those who had been fasting and mourning. The rhetorical questions of verses 5–6 imply that these ceremonies had been motivated by self-interest, rather than a genuine desire to repent. The people should have realized that fasting was effective only if accompanied by a contrite heart (cf. Joel 2:12–13). This had been the consistent message of the preexilic prophets when Judah had enjoyed relative peace and prosperity (v.7).

7:8–14. The Lord exhorted the people to promote social justice (vv.9–10), reminding them that the preexilic generation's failure in this regard had resulted in the judgment of the Exile (vv.11–14). The juxtaposition of this appeal with the preceding denunciation of fasting suggests that the presence of social injustice within the community had negated its attempts to move the Lord through ceremonies of lamentation (cf. 8:10, 16–17; Isa. 58:1–7). In the same way the Lord rejected the cries for help of the preexilic generation because they had refused to listen to His call to repentance through the prophets (v.13).

Wordplay is prominent in verses 11–14. By making "their hearts as hard as flint" and refusing to listen to the Lord (v. 12), the people eventually made their own land desolate (v. 14). The repetition of Hebrew *śîm,* translated "made" in both verses 12 and 14, points to the self-destructive nature of their sinful deeds. Other wordplays point to the appropriate nature of their punishment. The phrases translated "made . . . hard as flint" (*śāmû šāmîr,* v.12) and "would not listen" (*miššeͨmôaͨ,* v.12) sound like the word "desolate" (*nāšammâ* and *šammâ,* v.14), while the word translated "stubbornly" (*sōrāret,* v.11) sounds like the verb rendered "scattered with a whirlwind" (*sāͨar,* v.14).

8:1–17. The subject suddenly shifts from exile to restoration. In the past the Lord had been very angry with His disobedient people (7:12), but now He was "very zealous" toward Jerusalem (8:2). The Lord would once more reside in the city (v.3), which would be called the City of Truth (better, "Faithfulness"), for it would be populated by those devoted to the Lord. The temple mount would be called the Holy Mountain, for it would be set apart as the center of true worship and never again be profaned by sinners and foreigners (cf. 14:20–21; Isa. 52:1; Joel 3:17).

Signs of the Lord's blessing would be readily apparent. God's people would live to a "ripe old age" and would enjoy seeing their descendants playing in the streets (vv.4–5; cf. Isa. 65:20, 23). Though the remnant of God's people might marvel over this swelling of its ranks, the sovereign and omnipotent Lord would not share their amazement, for nothing is beyond His capability (v.6; cf. Gen. 18:14; Jer. 32:17, 27). The Lord would deliver His scattered people (cf. 7:14) from distant nations (v.7), bring them back to Jerusalem, and reestablish a vibrant covenantal relationship with them (v.8).

Verses 5–6 appear to allude to the narrative of Isaac's birth and the divine promises associated with it. According to Genesis 18:12–15, Sarah laughed ($ṣāḥaq$) in disbelief at the announcement she would bear a son. The Lord rebuked Sarah, pointing out that nothing is "too hard" ($pālā'$) for Him (Gen. 18:14). When the promised child was born, he was named Isaac ($yiṣḥāq$, "he laughs") because, Sarah explained, "God has brought me laughter, and everyone who hears about this will laugh with me" (Gen. 21:6). Like the account of Isaac's birth, Zechariah 8:5–6 emphasizes the Lord's power to produce offspring against overwhelming odds. Verse 5 uses the key word from the Genesis account to describe how these children will play (lit. "laugh," $mᵉṣaḥᵃqîm$, from $ṣāḥaq$, an alternate form of $ṣāḥaq$), and verse 6, like Genesis 18:14, stresses that nothing is too "marvelous" ($pālā'$) for the Lord. The purpose of this literary allusion is to relate the future fertility of the remnant to the ancient Abrahamic promise of a seed, which found its initial expression in Isaac. Just as Isaac's birth brought laughter to his mother as it testified to God's power and faithfulness, so the laughing children of restored Jerusalem would be a reminder that the omnipotent God can overcome all obstacles, even the desolation of exile (cf. 7:14; 8:7–8), in fulfilling His promises to Abraham and his descendants.

The Lord would also restore peace and prosperity to the

covenant community (vv.9–17a). Before the temple foundation was laid, wages were low, and the land was plagued by social turmoil (vv.9–10; cf. Hag. 1:2–6, 10–11; 2:15–19). God's people had become a curse among the nations (v.13a). Yet the Lord intended to restore the land's fertility and bless His people again (vv.12, 13b). With this prospect in view, He urged them to continue their work on the temple (vv.9, 13) without fear (v.15) and to promote social justice as a prerequisite to restoration (vv.16–17).

It is unclear whether the phrase "when the foundation was laid for the house of the LORD Almighty" (v.9) refers to the initiation of the temple project in 536 B.C. (cf. Ezra 3:8–13) or to its resumption in 520. The situation described in verse 10 is similar to Haggai's description of the land prior to the resumption of the building project. If the "prophets who were there when the foundation was laid" (v.9) were Haggai and Zechariah, then this also points to 520, since they are mentioned only in conjunction with the resumption of the temple, not its initiation (cf. Ezra 5:1–2; 6:14). It is possible that a second foundation-laying ceremony was conducted in 520 or that the phrase "when the foundation was laid" should simply be translated "when work resumed."[42]

Verse 13 describes the transformation of God's people from an accursed nation to a paradigm of divine blessing. Though their name was used in formulas of cursing (for an example of a curse formula, see Jer. 29:22), it would someday appear in formal prayers of blessing (for examples of prayers of blessing, see Gen. 48:20 and Ruth 4:11).[43] The words "you will be a blessing" allude to the Lord's promise to Abraham (Gen. 12:2) and look forward to its fulfillment through his offspring.

8:18–23. In the day of Judah's restoration the fasts and ceremonies of lamentation would be transformed into joyous celebrations (v.19). In 7:3, 5, reference is made to fasts in the fifth and seventh months, commemorating the destruction of the temple and the murder of Gedaliah, respectively. In 8:19 two additional fasts are mentioned. The fast in the fourth month probably recalled the Babylonian invasion of Jerusalem during the fourth month in 586 B.C. (cf. 2 Kings 25:3–4; Jer. 39:2; 52:6–7). In the tenth month the people probably lamented

---

[42]On the latter option, see Baldwin, *Haggai, Zechariah, Malachi,* pp. 52–53.
[43]Cf. Petersen, *Haggai and Zechariah 1–8,* p. 308.

the beginning of the siege of Jerusalem in 588 (cf. 2 Kings 25:1–2; Jer. 39:1; 52:4; Ezek. 24:1–2).

In this day of celebration people from throughout the land would seek the Lord's favor (vv.20–21). Even foreigners would acknowledge Israel's God as their King and make the pilgrimage to His capital city, Jerusalem (v.22). Those who had considered God's people accursed (cf. v.13) would now recognize the Jews' privileged position (v.23).

Two Divine Oracles (9:1–14:21)

Chapters 9–14 may be summarized as follows: Chapter 9 foresees the Lord's judgment of hostile nations (vv.1–8), the establishment of His universal kingdom through a human ruler (vv.9–10), the deliverance of His people from exile (vv. 11–12), their victory over their enemies (vv.13–16a), and God's subsequent blessing on the land (vv.16b–17). Following an exhortation (10:1), oppressive leaders are denounced (10:2–3a). In contrast to these "shepherds," the Lord is a concerned shepherd-ruler (10:3b) who energizes His people for battle (10:3b–5, 7), delivers them from exile in a grand second exodus (10:6, 8–12), and judges hostile nations (10:11b; 11:1–3). Next, 11:4–17 expands on 10:2–3, alluding again to oppressive "shepherds" and describing the people's rejection of the good shepherd. The section 12:1–9 again foresees the Lord's intervention for His people. As in 9:1–17 and 10:3b–11:3, the Lord empowers them for battle and judges the nations. The focus is now on the deliverance of Jerusalem from military siege, rather than the restoration of the exiles. All Judah mourns for "the one they have pierced" (12:10–14), and the land is cleansed (13:1–6). Though the rejection of the good shepherd brings intense suffering (13:7–8), a remnant is refined and restored to covenantal relationship (13:9). The final chapter, like 12:1–9, describes the Lord's intervention on behalf of besieged Jerusalem (14:1–7). The Lord establishes His universal rule from Jerusalem, judging the nations and incorporating them into His kingdom (14:8–21)

From this summary it is apparent that the two oracles (chs. 9–11 and 12–14) are thematically and structurally related. These chapters focus on two major themes: the Lord's intervention for His people, and the people's relationship to its leaders ("shepherds"). These themes are developed in an alternating pattern.[44]

A1 The Lord's intervention: Deliverance from exile (9:1–17)
  B Oppressive leaders ("shepherds") denounced (10:1–3a)

A1 The Lord's intervention: Deliverance from exile (10:3b–11:3)
  B The good shepherd rejected (11:4–17)

A2 The Lord's intervention: Jerusalem delivered (12:1–9)
  B People mourn their rejection of the good shepherd and are cleansed (12:10–13:9)

A2 The Lord's intervention: Jerusalem delivered (14:1–21)

First Oracle (9:1–11:17)

9:1–17. Chapter 9, which takes the form of a divine warrior hymn,[45] opens with a judgment speech against several of Israel's traditional enemies, including the Arameans,[46] Phoenicians, and Philistines (vv.1–7). Many have labored to identify the historical situation to which the prophecy supposedly alludes. Though none of the proposals is entirely convincing, several details in verses 1–7 can be explained against the backdrop of Alexander's conquest of Syria and Palestine in the

[44] For an alternate proposal, which finds a chiastic structure in chs. 9–14, see Baldwin, *Haggai, Zechariah, Malachi,* pp. 75–81, who bases her work on that of P. Lamarche.

[45] Cf. Hanson, *Dawn of Apocalyptic,* pp. 315–16. According to Hanson, this hymnic pattern originated in ancient Near Eastern mythological texts. Ancient Israel utilized the form to celebrate the Lord's victories (cf. Exod. 15; Judg. 5). The pattern also appears in several psalms and in numerous passages in Isaiah. For Hanson's full discussion, see pp. 299–316.

[46] The land of Hadrach was located in Syria, north of Hamath, which in turn was north of the Aramean capital, Damascus. A further reference to Syria may have been present in the original text of v.1b. The phrase translated "the eyes of men" by NIV may be a corruption of an original "the people of Aram," in which case v.1b should be translated, "to the Lord belong the people of Aram and all the tribes of Israel." Cf. ibid., pp. 294–95, 297–98.

fourth century B.C.[47] Others argue that no specific historical events are in view but that the prophecy envisions the eschatological establishment of the Lord's kingdom over the nations, including in stereotypical fashion those traditionally hostile to His people.[48] By conquering these traditional enemies, the Lord extends Israel's borders to their ideal limits, as promised in the Pentateuch and approximated in the Davidic-Solomonic era.[49]

In verses 8–17 the focus shifts from the judgment of the nations to the Lord's relationship to His people. According to verse 8, the Lord would defend His "house" from foreign invaders and oppressors. The Lord's house is probably the temple, though it could refer more generally to the people as a whole.

Verse 9 pictures the arrival of Jerusalem's king. Since the Lord speaks in verses 6–8 and 10–13, the king referred to in verses 9 and 10b must be a human ruler who serves as the Lord's vice-regent. This king is described as "righteous" (better, "just") and as "having salvation." This latter expression (nôšāʿ) might be better rendered "victorious," or even "saved" (as the same Heb. form is translated in Deut. 33:29 and Ps. 33:16). This king is also depicted as "gentle [better, "humble"] and riding on a donkey, on a colt, the foal of a donkey" (v.9b). Riding a donkey is consistent with his royal status. In the Bible and in ancient Near Eastern literature, the donkey sometimes appears as the mount of princes or kings.[50] This king rides a donkey, rather than a war horse, in order to symbolize that peace will characterize his rule (cf. v.10). The significance of the additional description ("a colt, the foal of a donkey") is uncertain. Appealing to an ancient Near Eastern parallel from Mari, Baldwin suggests that the donkey's purebred status is in view, making it suitable for a king.[51] Verse 10 describes the king's peaceful rule. The Lord would remove the chariots, war horses, and weapons from the land, for they would no longer

[47] Cf. Barker, "Zechariah," pp. 657–61.
[48] See Hanson, *Dawn of Apocalyptic*, pp. 316–20; and Laney, *Zechariah*, pp. 93–95.
[49] Hanson, *Dawn of Apocalyptic*, p. 317.
[50] For a summary of the evidence, see Baldwin, *Haggai, Zechariah, Malachi*, pp. 165–66.
[51] Ibid., p. 166.

be needed. Through His vice-regent the Lord's rule would extend to all nations (cf. 14:9; Ps. 72:8).

Though verses 9–10 give the impression that the arrival of the king would immediately usher in God's universal kingdom, the New Testament indicates that the fulfillment of the prophecy comes in stages. According to Matthew and John, the prophecy of the king's arrival was fulfilled at Jesus' triumphal entry into Jerusalem just days before his crucifixion (Matt. 21:1–7; John 12:14–15). The events prophesied in verse 10 were not fulfilled in conjunction with Jesus' first advent, but rather will be realized in the eschaton.

Verses 11–17 elaborate on events that would accompany the establishment of the Lord's universal kingdom. Because of His covenantal promise the Lord would deliver those Israelites still in foreign lands (vv. 11–12). Though they were like prisoners trapped in a waterless pit, they were not without hope. The Lord would free them and restore to them blessings that would far surpass what they had lost through judgment (cf. Isa. 61:7). The degree of blessing is further emphasized in verses 16–17, where God's restored people are compared to a flock of sheep and to jewels in a crown. In that day the young men and women would thrive because of the abundance of grain and new wine, symbols here of the land's fertility (cf. 8:12; Deut. 33:28). This promise stands in stark contrast to those texts that describe the slaughter and exile of Israel's youth in conjunction with God's judgment (e.g., Deut. 32:25; 2 Chron. 36:17; Lam. 1:18; 2:21).

In the Day of Restoration the Lord would also energize His people for battle, enabling them to defeat their enemies (vv. 13–14). United once more, Judah and Ephraim (i.e., the northern kingdom) would be like weapons in the hands of the Lord (v. 13), who would burst forth in theophanic splendor to display His power as a warrior (v. 14). The imagery of verse 14 recalls the theophany of Sinai, where the Lord's appearance was accompanied by lightning and a trumpet blast (cf. Exod. 19:16, 19). As in Habakkuk's vision, the Lord marches through Teman (NIV "the south") as He comes from Sinai to lead His people to victory (cf. Hab. 3:3). The association of "storms" ($sa‘^a rôṯ$) with the Lord's salvation reverses the use of storm imagery in 7:14, where the Lord is said to scatter His people with a whirlwind ($’ēsā‘^a rēm$, from $sā‘ar$).

Greece (lit. "Javan") is mentioned as the specific enemy of

God's people (v.13b). Some understand this as a reference to the Maccabean wars with the Seleucids in the second century B.C. Others see Greece/Javan as representative of the distant nations to be incorporated into the Lord's kingdom.

Scholars have also debated the meaning of verse 15. Some understand the language in a militaristic sense. Following this line of interpretation, many relate the passage to Numbers 23:24 and see victorious Israel, under the figure of a lion, devouring the flesh of its enemies and drinking their blood. Others interpret verse 15 as a banquet scene celebrating Israel's victory.

10:1–3a. Having just described the agricultural prosperity that God would bestow on His people (9:17), Zechariah urged his contemporaries to look to the Lord alone as their source of blessing (v.1a). As the one who controls the storm, the Lord provides the rain necessary for a good crop (v.1b).

Unfortunately Israel had often trusted in substitutes, whose lies (i.e., unreliable advice and predictions) misled God's people and caused them to wander like sheep without a shepherd (v.2). The idols mentioned here are the *tᵉrāpîm,* which were consulted through divination (cf. Hos. 3:4). Though the Lord had given leaders to Israel, these "shepherds" had failed to care for the flock, bringing the Lord's angry punishment down on themselves (v.3a).

The precise identity of these shepherds is not certain. Because the background of verses 2–3a appears to be the Exile or the postexilic period, some contend that foreign rulers are in view. However, a comparison with earlier prophetic denunciations of such worthless shepherds suggests that Israelite civic leaders are the primary referent (cf. Isa. 56:10–11; Jer. 23:1–4; Ezek. 34:1–10). Since the postexilic leaders Zerubbabel and Joshua are considered in a positive light elsewhere in the book, they must be excluded from the denunciation. Perhaps these verses refer generally to the leaders of the exilic/postexilic community, reflect a later period in Zechariah's career, or anticipate developments in the intertestamental period.

10:3b–11:3. After removing these false shepherds, the Lord Himself would provide His people with the leadership they so desperately needed (10:3b; cf. 9:16). A wordplay in the Hebrew text contrasts the destinies of the shepherds and the sheep. Both "will punish" and "will care" translate the verb *pāqad,* which in its most basic sense means "to visit" (whether for good or bad). For the shepherds the Lord's visitation would mean punishment; for the sheep it would mean protection. In fact, the Lord would change His helpless sheep into strong war horses. Strengthened by the Lord and united once more with the northern kingdom (note "the house of Joseph" in v.6 and "the Ephraimites" in v.7), the house of Judah would destroy its enemies (vv.4–7).

Verse 4 presents interpretive problems. The verse reads literally, "From him a cornerstone, from him a tent peg, from him a battle bow; from him all ruler(s) come out together." NIV assumes that Judah is the antecedent of the pronoun "him" and that the verb "come (out)" is to be understood in the first three lines as well. However, some take the antecedent of "him" as the Lord or limit the verb "come out" to the last line. The meaning of the final line of the verse is also unclear. Some understand a prophecy of an unbroken line of kings (culminating in the Messiah) who would come from Judah. However, the word translated "ruler" (*nôgēś*) is used elsewhere in a negative sense, being applied often to those who oppress God's people (cf. 9:8, where NIV translates "oppressor"). Consequently some see here the elimination of all foreign oppressors, who would "go out from" (i.e., leave) Judah en masse.

The figures of a cornerstone and a tent peg used earlier in the verse may be royal titles, pointing to a future king who would emerge from Judah to provide stable leadership for the nation. Both terms are used of rulers elsewhere in the Old Testament, with the former translated "leaders" (Judg. 20:2; 1 Sam. 14:38), "capstone" (Ps. 118:22), and "cornerstones" (Isa. 19:13). On "tent peg," see Isaiah 22:23. If the imagery is royal, it likely refers to the king prophesied in 9:9–10.

The nation's rejuvenation, portrayed so vividly in 10:3–7, presupposes its deliverance from exile, which is described in 10:8–12. Though the Lord had scattered His disobedient people among the nations, He would bring them back in fulfillment of His promise through Moses (cf. Deut. 30:1–10). They would be so numerous that the Promised Land, even when expanded to include Gilead and Lebanon, would not be able to accommodate them (vv.8, 10). This deliverance is likened to a second exodus. As the Lord had done at the Red Sea, He would again remove all obstacles to His people's escape, destroying the nations that dare resist His purposes (v.11). These hostile nations are here represented by Assyria and Egypt and are symbolized by the "surging sea."

The section 11:1–3 depicts the Lord's victory over the nations in a highly figurative manner. His judgment, compared to a fire, would destroy the proud nations, symbolized by the stately trees of Lebanon and Bashan (vv.1–2). Such a fire, sweeping down from Lebanon through Bashan (a well-known pasture land; cf. Deut. 32:14; Ezek. 39:18; Amos 4:1; Mic. 7:14) and into the Jordan Valley (a habitat for lions; cf. Jer. 49:19; 50:44), would have caused the shepherds to wail and the lions to roar (v.3).

Because of the placement of the chapter division and the reference to shepherds, many understand 11:1–3 as the introduction to the following section, where shepherding imagery dominates. According to this view, these verses describe the punishment of Israel for its rejection of the good shepherd. However, verses 1–3 are better taken as a conclusion to the preceding message. Several key words link 11:1–3 with 10:10–11, including "Lebanon" (10:10; 11:1), "brought down/cut down" (*yārad*, 10:11; 11:2), and "pride" (10:11)/"thicket" (11:3) (*gā'ôn* in both cases). The trees of Lebanon and Bashan symbolize proud nations or kings elsewhere in the prophets (Isa. 2:13; 10:34; Ezek. 31:3). The imagery is appropriate here in conjunction with the symbolic references to Egypt and Assyria.

11:4–17. In the alternating thematic pattern of chapters 9–14, these verses expand on 10:2–3a, which introduced the subject of Israel's ineffective leaders. This passage, which Hanson calls a commissioning narrative,[52] may be outlined as follows:

I. Zechariah's first commission (vv.4–14)
   A. Zechariah commissioned as a good shepherd (v.4)
   B. Denunciation of bad shepherds (v.5) and judgment speech (v.6)
   C. Zechariah's obedience to his commission (vv.7–8a)
   D. Zechariah's rejection of his commission (vv.8b–14)

II. Zechariah's second commission (vv.15–17)

[52] Hanson, *Dawn of Apocalyptic*, p. 341. He observes that in 11:4–17 "the traditional genre is remolded in such a way as to give it an ironic twist which was alien to the original genre in question."

    A. Zechariah commissioned as a foolish shepherd
       (vv.15–16)
    B. Woe oracle against the foolish shepherd (v.17)

The actors and events referred to in these verses are symbolic in nature. Whether Zechariah performed these symbolic acts publicly or only in a vision is uncertain.

Zechariah's initial commission has an ironic and foreboding tone. Though the prophet was told to care for the sheep, they are described as "marked for slaughter" (v.4). Already other shepherds were selling the sheep to merchants, who in turn were slaughtering them (v.5). Verse 6 clarifies the symbolism of verse 5. The sheep were God's people, suggesting that the buyers were foreign kings and the sellers/shepherds Israelite rulers of the postexilic period.

On the basis of the preceding chapters, which portray the Lord as Israel's Shepherd (9:16; 10:3b) and Deliverer, one might expect a message of salvation to follow this description of the flock's exploitation (cf. 10:2–3). However, the Lord announced that He would hand the sheep over to oppressive foreigners, rather than rescue them (v.6).

The reason for this judgment becomes apparent in verses 7–9. Though he knew the sheep would eventually be destroyed, Zechariah obeyed his divine commission to care for the sheep. To accomplish this task he took two shepherd's staffs, called Favor and Union (v.7). The first symbolized God's favor to the people in the form of peaceful relations with foreign nations (v.10). The second symbolized the reunited northern and southern kingdoms (v.14). Zechariah also removed three shepherds (v.8a), presumably the negligent shepherds referred to in verse 5. Despite Zechariah's able attempts to care for the flock, the people rejected his leadership, causing him to renounce his commission (vv.8b–9). This rejection of the good shepherd explains why judgment would fall (cf. v.6). Between the period of oppression, described in 10:2 and 11:5, and the time of deliverance, prophesied in chapters 9–10, Israel must endure a time of suffering (11:6, 9, 15–17) caused by its rejection of God's leadership.

In order to renounce his commission officially and publicly, Zechariah broke his two shepherd's staffs (vv.10–11, 14) and announced the termination of his period of employment (v.12a). In exchange for his services he was paid the rather insignificant amount of thirty pieces of silver (v.12b), which he sarcastically referred to as "the handsome price at which they priced me" (v.13a). At the Lord's command Zechariah threw the money to the potter located in the temple (v.13). The significance of this action is uncertain.

Because God's people rejected His leadership, represented by the good shepherd, He would raise up a foolish and worthless shepherd who would oppress the people (v.16). To symbolize this ruler Zechariah also played the role of a shepherd (v.15). Though sent by the Lord as an instrument of punishment, this worthless shepherd was doomed to destruction for his mistreatment of the flock (v.17).

To whom do the good shepherd, the three bad shepherds, and the foolish shepherd specifically refer? In a general sense the good shepherd represents God's leadership as King of His people. Twice in the preceding context the Lord is portrayed as Israel's benevolent Shepherd (9:16; 10:3). Since the Lord's royal vice-regent is also mentioned in this context (cf. 9:9–10), some have identified the good shepherd with an ideal messianic ruler. In support of this view one may point to 13:7–8, where the Lord speaks of His shepherd, whose demise brings suffering to His sheep. If one follows through on this line of interpretation, Jesus Christ eventually emerges as this good shepherd (cf. Matt. 26:31).

Several attempts have been made to identify the three bad shepherds and the foolish shepherd, none of which are entirely convincing. Many have identified the three bad shepherds with particular Seleucid kings or Jewish high priests of the second century B.C.[53] The foolish shepherd has been identified with the high priest Alcimus, Herod the Great, Simon bar-Kochba, and the Antichrist, among others.

Despite uncertainty about particulars, the following scenario appears in verses 4–17. God's people, pictured as a flock of sheep, are being oppressed by their own Jewish leaders, who are in collaboration with foreign kings. God's leadership, perhaps offered in the person of a human ruler, is rejected by His people, bringing judgment upon the nation. The reuniting of Israel and Judah is postponed, and the people suffer even more intensely under an oppressive ruler. Though it may be too risky

---

[53] For a survey of interpretations along this line, see Baldwin, *Haggai, Zechariah, Malachi*, pp. 181–83.

to see specific events and persons referred to in these verses, the narrative does reflect in broad outline the experiences of the Jewish people during the intertestamental period and the first two centuries of the Christian era.

Second Oracle (12:1–14:21)

12:1–9. The second oracle begins on a positive note with an announcement of Jerusalem's and Judah's future deliverance and glory. The fulfillment of the prophecy cannot be in doubt, for it comes from the Lord, the sovereign Creator of the universe and of humankind (v.1).

The prophecy anticipates a day when the hostile nations of the earth would attack Judah and Jerusalem (vv.2b–3a). In this crisis the Lord would be with His people, energizing them for battle and annihilating their enemies. Jerusalem would be like an immovable rock, as the Lord directly intervenes against the attackers (v.3b) and causes them to stagger like drunken men (v.2a) in their panic and confusion (v.4).

Jerusalem's strength in the face of attack would inspire the leaders of Judah, who would move out like a destructive fire against the foreign invaders (vv.5–6). Judah would share the glory of Jerusalem and of the Davidic family (v.7). Under the Lord's protective hand, even the feeblest individual would be like the mighty warrior David, and the Davidic family would be like God Himself, the Warrior *par excellence* (v.8). (Note that verse 8 equates the "Angel of the LORD" with God.)

12:10–13:9. This section further develops themes introduced in 10:2–3a and 11:4–17. Though God's people suffered under oppressive leadership (10:2–3a; 11:5), they rejected His benevolent rule (11:8b), bringing judgment and more intense suffering on themselves (11:6, 9, 16). However, as 12:1–9 makes clear (cf. also 9:1–17; 10:3b–12), God would not abandon His people forever. He would lead them to repentance (12:10–14), cleanse them from sin (13:1–6), and restore to them a vibrant covenantal relationship (13:7–9).

By an act of sovereign grace (note "I will pour out"), the Lord would prompt His people to turn to Him in supplication (12:10a). Recognizing God as the one whom they had rejected (v.10b), the whole nation, led by the royal and priestly families (vv.12–14), would mourn bitterly (vv.10b–11). The houses of David and his son Nathan (cf. 2 Sam. 5:14) represent the nation's civil leaders, while the house of Levi and the clan of his grandson Shimei (cf. Num. 3:17–18, 21) represent the religious leaders.

The intensity of their mourning receives special emphasis, being compared to a parent's inconsolable grief over the loss of an only child or firstborn son. This mourning ceremony is also likened to the rites of lamentation performed in the plain of Megiddo, which were apparently well known to Zechariah's contemporaries. Some interpret Hadad Rimmon as a place-name and associate this ceremony with the lamentations over King Josiah, who was fatally wounded while fighting on the plain of Megiddo (2 Chron. 35:22–25). Others identify Hadad Rimmon as the Canaanite storm-god whose death was periodically mourned by his devotees.

The meaning of 12:10b has occasioned much debate. The pronoun "me" most naturally refers to God, who speaks throughout this chapter (cf. vv.2–4, 6, 9, 10a). The phrase "the one they have pierced" refers to God as the object of the people's rejection.[54] "Pierced," which elsewhere refers to a violent physical act (cf. 13:3, where the Heb. word is translated "stab"), is here employed anthropomorphically, the people's rejection of God being compared to a physical wound. While this interpretation may seem rather obvious and straightforward, the context suggests something more is involved. In 13:7–8 the Lord's shepherd, apparently a divinely appointed leader, would be struck with a sword. If this shepherd is equated with the good shepherd of 11:4–14, then the people's rejection of God's leadership (cf. 11:8; 12:10) is given tangible expression in their rejection of His shepherd. The apostle John seems to follow this line of interpretation in applying verse 10 to Jesus' being literally pierced by a spear while on the cross (John 19:37).

The Lord would cleanse the repentant royal family and the

[54] In the Heb. text "the one they have pierced" is a relative clause. It is preceded by the particle 'ēṯ, which here has a specifying function in relation to the preceding pronominal suffix attached to the preposition 'el. Note that 'ēṯ is used in the same way in Jer. 38:9b ("to Jeremiah the prophet whom they have cast into the cistern" NASB), where it precedes the relative pronoun modifying the object ("Jeremiah the prophet") of the preceding preposition ("to"). See also Ezek. 14:22b and 37:19b for this same use of 'ēṯ. The use of the third-person pronoun in the phrase "they will mourn for him" has caused some to see this "pierced" individual as distinct from the speaker (God). However, such shifts in person are not uncommon in Heb. poetry, and this particular change in person is understandable following the relative pronoun.

inhabitants of Jerusalem from their sin (13:1). This cleansing would include the elimination of idolatry (v.2) and false prophets (vv.3–6; cf. 10:2). In obedience to the Mosaic Law (Deut. 13:6–9) parents would execute a child who dares to prophesy falsely (v.3). False prophets would keep their occupation a secret, discarding the characteristic clothing of a prophet and claiming to be farmers instead (vv.4–5).

The meaning of verse 6 is unclear. One interpretation understands the wounds to be self-inflicted as part of rites performed by false prophets (cf. 1 Kings 18:28). In order to cover up the truth, these false prophets would claim they received the wounds from "friends" (*m^e'ahăbîm*). The use of this Hebrew word militates against this view, for elsewhere this word is used exclusively of false gods or political allies viewed figuratively as illicit lovers (Jer. 22:20, 22; 30:14; Lam. 1:19; Ezek. 23:5, 9, 22; Hos. 2:5, 7, 10, 12–13). Consequently some understand verse 6b as a straightforward confession of idolatrous practices (but note the earlier reference to their deception) or as an intentionally ambiguous answer.

The Lord would restore His repentant and cleansed people to a vital covenantal relationship (vv.7–9). Though the violent treatment of God's shepherd would bring confusion and suffering to God's flock (the people of Judah; cf. 9:16 and 10:3), a remnant would be preserved. Once it passed through the fire of judgment, this remnant would emerge spiritually pure. The people would look to God for guidance, not to idols or false prophets, and He would direct them. God would affirm that they are His people, and they would swear allegiance to Him alone. At last the covenant ideal revealed to Israel through Moses would be realized (cf. Exod. 6:7; Lev.26:12).

14:1–21. The final chapter of the prophecy expands on 12:1–9. The Lord's intervention on behalf of besieged Jerusalem is described in even further detail, and additional information concerning the city's future is provided.

According to verses 1–2, Jerusalem would initially experience defeat, a fact that is omitted in 12:1–9. Enemy soldiers would loot the city, rape its women, and carry off half the population as prisoners. When all seemed lost and hopeless, the Lord would intervene with His angelic armies to do battle against the hostile nations (vv.3, 5b). His arrival on the Mount of Olives, located east of the city, would produce a great fissure (v.4), through which the remaining half of the city's inhabitants (cf. v.2) would run for safety (v.5a). Comparison is made to "the earthquake in the days of Uzziah" (cf. also Amos 1:1).

Verses 6–7 emphasize the unique character of the Lord's day of intervention. In a manner typical of apocalyptic literature, extreme cosmic disturbances are anticipated. During the time when the sun normally shines, there would be no light (v.6). Yet this gloomy, dusky condition is classified as neither daytime nor nighttime (v.7a). Finally, at the time when evening usually begins, light would burst forth (v.7b).

The meaning of verse 6b is unclear. The Masoretic text reads literally, "the precious ones will thicken" (cf. NASB margin, "glorious ones will congeal"). Those who favor this reading understand the "precious ones" as the luminaries of heaven and take the verb in the sense of "dwindle" (NASB). Taken in this way, this statement reiterates the one that precedes. Others, following the Septuagint, read "no cold or frost" in verse 6b (NIV). This reading makes good sense in relation to verse 7. On the one hand, the absence of light (v.6a) prohibits one from using the label "daytime." On the other hand, the cold and frost characteristic of nighttime would be absent as well.

Before describing the Lord's destruction of His enemies (vv.12–15), the prophet jumps ahead to a time after the battle (vv.8–11). The Lord would make Jerusalem the capital of His worldwide kingdom (v.9). Flowing from Jerusalem toward the west and east would be two perennial streams of "living [i.e., running] water," symbolic of the land's renewed fertility, which finds its source in the divine King's blessing (v.8; cf. Ezek. 47:1–12; Joel 3:18). With the exception of Jerusalem, the entire land of Judah, from Geba in the north to Rimmon in the south, would become level like the Arabah, thereby drawing attention to the elevated status of the capital city (v.10). The Lord's presence in Jerusalem would make it inviolable (v.11).

In verses 12–15 the prophet returns to the battle scene that follows the Lord's arrival on the Mount of Olives (cf. vv.3–5) and precedes the establishment of His kingdom (vv. 8–11). The picture is not a pretty one. The Lord would send a plague on the attacking armies and their animals, causing their flesh, eyes, and tongues to rot while they are still alive (vv. 12, 15). Overcome by panic, the enemy armies would destroy one another (v.13). Judah would share the spoils of victory with the people of Jerusalem (v.14).

Several of these motifs recall elements of Israel's salvation history and the Lord's holy wars. The reference to a plague (v.12) reminds one of the Egyptian plagues, as well as the plague that came on the Philistines when they captured the ark (1 Sam. 6:4). The word translated "panic" appears in 1 Samuel 14:20 (there translated "confusion"), which describes how the Lord confused the Philistine soldiers, causing them to kill one another (cf. Zech. 14:13). On other occasions in Israel's history the Lord also caused enemy armies to destroy themselves (Judg. 7:22; 2 Chron. 20:23).

Following the nations' defeat, their survivors would become subjects of the Lord (vv.16–19). They would make annual pilgrimages to Jerusalem to worship the Lord and to observe the Feast of Tabernacles (v.16). Because this feast celebrated the fruit harvest, it was a testimony to the Lord's power over fertility (cf. Deut. 16:13–15). Consequently if any of the nations refused to observe this festival, they would be deprived of the rain needed for good crops (v.17).

Since Egypt is dependent on the flooding of the Nile, not rainfall, verse 18 has puzzled commentators. The Masoretic text reads literally, "And if the Egyptian people do not go up and do not take part, then not upon them. There will be the plague with which the Lord will smite the nations who do not go up to celebrate the Feast of Tabernacles." Noting that verse 17 ends with the words "then not upon them shall be rain," some (e.g., NIV, NASB) supply a reference to the rain in verse 18 as well (after "then not upon them"). Proponents of this view point out that the Nile is dependent on rainfall at its source for its water supply. Others, following the Septuagint and a few Hebrew manuscripts, eliminate the negative particle in the phrase "then not upon them" and read instead, "And if the Egyptian people do not go up and do not take part, then upon them there will be the plague with which the Lord will smite. . . ." In this case the plague is drought, no matter what the specific cause might be.

In the day the Lord establishes His rule in Jerusalem, even the most common things, including the horses' bells and the people's cooking utensils, would be set apart for the Lord (vv.20–21). Though the inscription "Holy to the LORD" had been reserved in the past for the most sacred of items (cf. Exod. 28:36; 39:30), holiness would now characterize the entire nation, in fulfillment of the covenant ideal (Exod. 19:6; Jer. 2:3). No longer would the Lord's temple be profaned by the presence of pagans.

THEOLOGY

Summary

The Lord would completely restore His covenant people, delivering the rest of the exiles and bringing them back to their homeland. He would make the rebuilt temple in Jerusalem the center for His worldwide rule and restore the Davidic throne and the priesthood to their former positions of leadership and prominence. Though the realization of these promises would be delayed and seemingly jeopardized by the postexilic community's rejection of God's leadership, the Lord would eventually deliver His people from renewed Gentile oppression, move them to genuine repentance, and restore them to a vibrant covenant relationship with Himself. In that day He would also bring the nations into His kingdom.

Analysis

God and His People

Zechariah prophesied at a time when God had begun to restore His people from exile. Some of the exiles had returned to Judah, and the rebuilding of the temple was underway. Zechariah made it clear that this new beginning, no matter how meager it might seem, would culminate in the complete restoration of God's covenant people. The Lord promised to bring all of the exiles back from Babylon and the other regions to which they had been scattered (2:6–7; 8:7–8; 9:11–12; 10:8–9). By comparing this deliverance to a second exodus, the Lord emphasized that He was still active and sovereign over hostile Gentile nations (10:10–11).

While the restoration of both Judah and the northern tribes is prophesied (1:17; 2:12; 10:6–7; 12:7), the focal point of God's program for the future would be Jerusalem and the rebuilt temple (1:14–17). Once again the Lord would take up residence in the city (1:16; 8:3), defending it (2:5; 14:11) and making it the center of His worldwide rule (14:9, 16–19). The Lord's presence in the temple would ensure the prosperity of the entire land (4:1–14; 14:8).

Accompanying the restoration of Jerusalem and the temple would be the elevation of the Davidic throne to its former status and glory. As a representative of the Davidic dynasty, Zerubbabel, the governor of the postexilic community, was associated with the messianic Branch prophesied by Jeremiah. In this capacity he would participate in the completion of the temple (4:6–10; 6:12–13). While Zechariah's generation may have viewed Zerubbabel as the Branch, he actually foreshadowed or typified Jesus Christ, the messianic ruler through whom the Lord would establish His universal kingdom (cf. 9:9–10).

The priesthood also plays a prominent role in Zechariah's vision of the future. Joshua the high priest was given clean garments, symbolizing the purification of the priesthood (3:3–7), and had a crown placed on his head, signifying the future leadership role of the priesthood in the covenant community (6:11–13). Through the harmonious coleadership of king and priest, the land would be purified and would prosper (3:8–10; 4:1–14; 6:10–15). Later revelation makes it clear that this ideal would be fully realized in one person, the King-Priest Jesus Christ.

Despite these prospects for a glorious future, the postexilic community was not to be spiritually complacent. In order to experience God's blessings they were to exhibit genuine repentance (1:3–6; 7:4–7) and obedience (6:15). More specifically, they were to promote social justice (7:8–10; 8:16–17). Only then would their religious rituals carry any significance in the sight of God (7:1–10; 8:16–19).

Chapters 9–14 anticipate the postexilic community's failure to live up to God's requirements. The people, compared to a flock of sheep, would reject the leadership of its true shepherds—God (9:16; 10:3) and His appointed ruler (13:7)—bringing disaster and suffering on themselves (11:4–17; 12:10; 13:7–8). Even Jerusalem would suffer invasion and humiliation (14:1–2).

At the last moment the Lord would come as a mighty warrior and deliver His people from their enemies (12:1–9; 14:3–5, 12–15). He would move His people to repentance (12:10). Led by the royal and priestly families, they would grieve over their sin (12:11–14). The Lord would cleanse the land from idols, false prophets, and covenant breakers (5:1–4; 13:1–6). He would renew His covenant with the remnant of the people (8:6, 11–12; 13:8–9) and grant them fertility and prosperity as signs of His blessing (8:4–5, 12; 9:16–17). In fulfillment of God's promise to Abraham, they would become a blessing to the nations (8:13).

God and the Nations

God's relationship to the Gentile nations is also a prominent theme in Zechariah's prophecies. As God's instruments of judgment the nations were responsible for the exile of God's people. Because the nations had overstepped their bounds, God was angry with them (1:15) and would bring judgment on them (1:18–21; 2:8–9; 6:1–8; 9:1–7). God would subdue powerful nations in delivering His people from exile (10:11). Though hostile nations would be allowed to plunder rebellious Jerusalem one last time (14:1–2), eventually the Lord would intervene and destroy the nations' armies completely and finally (12:1–9; 14:3–5, 12–15). At that time God would incorporate the nations into His universal kingdom (2:11). Recognizing the Lord as the source of blessing, the nations would join Israel in worshiping Him at Jerusalem (8:20–23; 14:16–19).

12

MALACHI

INTRODUCTION

Authorship and Unity

Interpreters have traditionally understood "Malachi" as the author's name. Analogy with other prophetic books, all of which identify their author in the introductory heading, strongly favors this interpretation. The meaning of the name is uncertain. Possibilities include "my messenger," "messenger of the Lord," and "the Lord is messenger."[1]

In modern times many have taken "Malachi" as a title, not a proper name. Some have understood Zechariah 9–11, 12–14, and Malachi as originally anonymous works appended to the Minor Prophets.[2] For support, appeal is made to the similar headings in Zechariah 9:1, 12:1, and Malachi 1:1. Upon closer examination the alleged similarity between the headings is superficial[3] and cannot sustain the theory of anonymous authorship for Malachi. Other arguments in support of taking "Malachi" as a title (e.g., the alleged inappropriate nature of such a name, the absence of the name elsewhere in the Old Testament, the omission of background material about the

[1] Beth Glazier-McDonald, *Malachi* (Atlanta: Scholars Press, 1987), p. 28.
[2] See, for example, J. M. P. Smith, "A Critical and Exegetical Commentary on the Book of Malachi," in *A Critical and Exegetical Commentary on Haggai, Zechariah, Malachi, and Jonah* (New York: Charles Scribner's Sons, 1912), p. 4.
[3] Cf. Glazier-McDonald, *Malachi*, pp. 26–27.

prophet) are equally inconclusive and have received well-reasoned responses from various writers.[4]

From time to time scholars have questioned the authenticity of certain passages in the book. In particular, some regard the final three verses (4:4–6) as a later appendix to the book or perhaps even to the Minor Prophets as a whole.[5] However, others have demonstrated the close relationship between these verses and the rest of the book, making redactional theories of their origin unlikely.[6]

Date

Internal evidence indicates the book was written in the postexilic period. The reference to a governor (*peḥâ*, 1:8) points to the Persian period. This title is used frequently in Nehemiah for Persian governors. Earlier Haggai applied the title to Zerubbabel (Hag. 1:1, 14; 2:2, 21). Various parallels between Ezra-Nehemiah and Malachi suggest that the latter dates to the mid-fifth century B.C. Both Ezra-Nehemiah and Malachi refer to intermarriage with foreign wives (Ezra 9–10; Neh. 13:23–27; Mal. 2:11), failure to pay tithes (Neh. 13:10–14; Mal. 3:8–10), and social injustice (Neh. 5:1–13; Mal. 3:5). The precise date of Malachi is impossible to ascertain.[7] A comparison of Malachi 1:8, which seems to assume the governor accepted offerings from the people, with Nehemiah 5:14, 18, where Nehemiah refuses such offerings, suggests Nehemiah is not the governor referred to in Malachi.

---

[4]See ibid., pp. 28–29; Pieter A. Verhoef, *The Books of Haggai and Malachi* (Grand Rapids: Eerdmans, 1987), p. 155; Joyce G. Baldwin, *Haggai, Zechariah, Malachi* (London: Inter-Varsity Press, 1972), p. 212; Hobart E. Freeman, *An Introduction to the Old Testament Prophets* (Chicago: Moody Press, 1968), pp. 350–51.

[5]See, for example, Georg Fohrer, *Introduction to the Old Testament*, trans. David E. Green (Nashville: Abingdon, 1968), p. 470; and Brevard S. Childs, *Introduction to the Old Testament as Scripture* (Philadelphia: Fortress Press, 1979), pp. 495–96.

[6]Baldwin, *Haggai, Zechariah, Malachi*, p. 214; Glazier-McDonald, *Malachi*, pp. 267–68; Rolf Rendtorff, *The Old Testament: An Introduction*, trans. John Bowden (Philadelphia: Fortress Press, 1986), pp. 242–43.

[7]For a discussion of various views, see C. Hassell Bullock, *An Introduction to the Old Testament Prophetic Books* (Chicago: Moody Press, 1986), p. 338; Freeman, *Introduction*, pp. 349–50; Verhoef, *Haggai and Malachi*, pp. 157–60; Baldwin, *Haggai, Zechariah, Malachi*, p. 213.

Structure

Malachi contains six major units, all of which follow the disputational pattern outlined below:

Unit	Introduction	People's Question(s)	Conclusion
1. 1:2–5	1:2a	1:2b	1:2c–5
2. 1:6–2:9	1:6a, 7a	1:6b, 7b	1:7c–2:9
3. 2:10–16	2:10–13	2:14a	2:14b–16
4. 2:17–3:5	2:17a	2:17b	2:17c–3:5
5. 3:6–12	3:6–7b, 8a	3:7c, 8b	3:8c–12
6. 3:13–4:3	3:13a	3:13b	3:14–4:3

More detailed outlines of each oracle appear below. A brief conclusion to the book (4:4–6) includes a general exhortation (v.4), followed by a motivating prophecy (vv.5–6).

ANALYSIS

First Disputation: God Affirms His Love (1:2–5)

This oracle may be outlined as follows:

I. Introductory statement (affirmation; v.2a)

II. The people's question (v.2b)

III. Concluding statement (vv.2c–5)
    A. Explanation of affirmation (vv.2c–3)
    B. Expansion (prophecy; vv.4–5)

The prophecy begins on a positive note as the Lord affirms His love for His people (v.2a). Surprisingly Israel's response (v.2b) expresses doubt about the truth of the Lord's affirmation. Apparently the humiliation of the Exile and the seemingly relative insignificance of postexilic developments had produced cynicism within the community.[8]

As proof of His love for His people, the Lord contrasted their experience and destiny with Edom's (vv.2c–5). Despite the fact that Jacob and Esau (the father of the Edomites) were brothers, God chose Jacob and his descendents as his special covenantal people. This covenantal relationship, based on God's unconditional promise to Abraham, assured Jacob's offspring eternal possession of the Promised Land (cf. Gen. 28:3–4, 13–15). On the basis of this promise God had delivered them from exile and restored them to their land. By contrast, the Edomite kingdom, which by this time had experienced to some degree the divine judgment prophesied by Obadiah and others, would not be revived. Though they might attempt to rebuild their ruined cities, the Lord would violently oppose their efforts. Edom would be called "Wicked Land," for it would continually experience the Lord's angry judgment. As restored Israel watched all of this, they should have praised the Lord and recognized their favored status as His people.

Some have explained the love/hate language of these verses as a Hebrew idiom, according to which "love" means "love more" and "hate" means "love less." Though this particular idiomatic use is attested elsewhere (e.g., Gen. 29:31, where "not loved" is literally "hated," and Deut. 21:17, where "unloved wife" is literally "hated wife"), an interpretation along these lines fails to do justice to Malachi 1:2–5, where the sharp contrast between Jacob and Esau must not be overlooked. There is no indication here (comparable to the marriage relationship referred to in Gen. 29 and Deut. 21) that God loved both Jacob and Esau, only to varying degrees. Rather He treated the two in opposite ways. He chose (i.e., "loved") Jacob, but He actively opposed and destroyed (i.e., "hated") Esau.[9]

Second Disputation: The Priests Denounced (1:6–2:9)

The structure of this second disputation, though following the basic pattern outlined above, is more complex than most of the others in the book. It may be outlined as follows:

[8]Cf. Smith, "Malachi," p. 20; and Verhoef, *Haggai and Malachi*, p. 198.
[9]For a helpful discussion, see Verhoef, *Haggai and Malachi*, pp. 200–201.

I. Introductory statement (analogy and affirmation; 1:6a)

II. The people's question (1:6b)

III. The affirmation restated (1:7a)

IV. The question restated (1:7b)

V. Concluding statement (1:7c–2:9)
   A. Explanation of affirmation (1:7c–14)
   B. Warning (2:1–9)

This oracle begins with an analogy (1:6). It is normal for a son to honor his father and for a servant to respect his master. Since the Lord was Israel's father and master, as it were, He expected to receive similar honor. Yet the priests (of all people!) treated Him with contempt by offering defiled food on His altar (1:7). In direct violation of the Mosaic Law, they sacrificed blind, crippled, and diseased animals (1:8a, 13b; cf. Lev.22:17–25; Deut. 15:21), even though they possessed and had promised to bring to God acceptable offerings (1:14a).

The absurdity of all this should have been self-evident. If a mere human governor would consider such blemished animals inappropriate tribute (1:8b), then how much more would God regard them as unacceptable (1:9, 10b). The Lord reminded the priests that someday He would receive universal worship (1:11). How then could He, the sovereign, awe-inpiring King of the world (1:11, 14b), accept their polluted sacrifices? It would be better for one of the priests to slam the temple doors shut and put an end to the entire sham (1:10a), for those who demonstrated such contempt (1:12–13a) and deceit[10] were under the curse of God (1:14a) and had no business imploring His favor (cf. 1:9a).[11]

Verse 11 requires special attention. NIV understands a

[10] The word translated "cheat" in 1:14a is used elsewhere of Joseph's brothers' devious plan to kill him (Gen. 37:18, translated "plotted"), of the Egyptians' attempts to wipe out Israel (Ps. 105:25, "conspire"), and of the Midianites' plot to seduce Israel with idols (Num. 25:18, "deceived").

[11] In v.9a the prophet sarcastically challenges the priests to seek God's favor. The Lord's rhetorical question and statement (vv.9b–10) make it clear that such a petition would be completely ineffective.

reference to a future time when the Lord would receive universal worship. The Hebrew text includes no time indicators. One could just as easily translate, "My name is great . . . offerings are brought . . . my name is great" (cf. RSV). Some modern commentators prefer this interpretation, understanding a reference to the worship of the pagan nations, Jewish proselytes, or exiled Jews dispersed throughout the world.[12] However, this line of approach does not adequately explain the language of the text or accurately reflect conditions in Malachi's day (even if allowance is made for a measure of hyperbole). Malachi's obvious concern for cultic propriety, his negative attitude toward foreigners and their gods (1:2–5; 2:11), and his reference to offerings being made to the Lord's name preclude any possibility of his viewing pagan worship as a legitimate form of worship to the one true God.[13] The text's universalistic language, coupled with the lack of evidence for widespread proselytism or cultic activity among exiles in Malachi's day, militates against the view that allusion is made to Jewish worship outside Judah's borders. The language of the text is best interpreted as referring to future developments. Elsewhere the prophets anticipate universal worship as an ideal to be realized in the future (Isa. 2:2–4; 19:19–21; 24:14–16; 42:6; 45:22–24; 66:18–21; Mic. 4:1–3; Zeph. 3:8–9; Zech. 8:20–23; 14:16).[14]

After explaining exactly how the priests had treated Him with contempt (1:6–14), the Lord warned them of the dire consequences of continued sin (2:1–3). If they failed to change their ways, the Lord would send a curse on them and eliminate their blessings (vv.1–2). The priests' "blessings" refer either to blessings bestowed by God on the priests or to words of blessing pronounced by the priests over the people (cf. Lev.9:22–23; Num. 6:23–26; 2 Chron. 30:27). According to verse 3, the Lord's curse would extend to the priests' descendents (cf. Hos. 4:6) and would result in humiliation and loss of office for the priests themselves. The word translated "rebuke" is here a virtual synonym for "curse," in the sense of "suppress

---

[12]For a discussion of these views, see Smith, "Malachi," pp. 30–31.

[13]For a more detailed refutation of this view, see Verhoef, *Haggai and Malachi*, pp. 227–28.

[14]For a more detailed defense of this position, see Glazier-McDonald, *Malachi*, pp. 60–61; and Baldwin, *Haggai, Zechariah, Malachi*, p. 230.

an object's vitality or effectiveness."[15] It may point to the ineffectiveness of the priests' descendents in their priestly role or even may indicate they would not inherit their fathers' office. The description of the priests' own humiliation and rejection is particularly vivid. The Lord threatened to spread the offal of their unacceptable sacrifices on their faces and take them outside the camp where the offal was burned (cf. Exod. 29:14; Lev.4:11–12; 8:17; 16:27).

The Lord's purpose in warning the priests was the preservation of His covenant with Levi (v.4). By shaking them out of their complacency, He hoped to restore the vitality that once characterized His relationship with the priests (vv.5b, 6).

It is uncertain when this covenant, which is also mentioned in Jeremiah 33:21 and Nehemiah 13:29, was established. The "covenant of salt" made with the Levites in Aaron's time (Num. 18:19) was more limited in scope than the covenant alluded to by Malachi. Because of verbal parallels with Numbers 25:12–13, some associate the covenant of Malachi 2:4 with the one made with Phinehas.[16] However, this covenant with Phinehas (not Levi as a whole) involved an unconditional promise given as a reward for faithful behavior. No mention is made of stipulations governing continuance of the relationship, such as are implied in Malachi 2:5–8.

Though the precise origin of this covenant is not certain (and perhaps not recorded in the Old Testament), it is clear that Malachi 2:4–9 views God's relationship to the priesthood as a bilateral agreement involving mutual responsibility. God promised the priests "life and peace" in exchange for reverence and devotion (v.5). Earlier Levites had demonstrated such loyalty to the Lord (Exod. 32:26–29; Num. 25:11–13; Ezek. 44:15). As messengers of the Lord, the priests were responsible to instruct the people concerning righteous behavior and turn them from their sins (vv.6–7). In contrast to this ideal the priests in Malachi's day misled the people (v.8) and showed partiality in their legal decisions (v.9a). Consequently the Lord made them "despised and humiliated" before the people. The use of "despised" is particularly appropriate here, since the same

---

[15]For this sense of *gāʿar*, "rebuke," elsewhere, see Ps. 106:9; Isa. 17:13; Nah. 1:4; Zech. 3:2; Mal. 3:11. Cf. also the discussion of Glazier-McDonald, *Malachi*, pp. 66–67.

[16]Ibid., pp. 79–80.

Hebrew word is employed in 1:6–7 of the priests' "contempt" for the Lord.

Third Disputation: Unfaithful Behavior Denounced (2:10–16)

This disputation may be outlined as follows:

I. Introductory statement (vv.10–13)
   A. Questions (v.10)
   B. Affirmation (vv.11–13)

II. The people's question (v.14a)

III. Concluding statement (vv.14b–16)
   A. Explanation (vv.14b–15a) and exhortation (v.15b)
   B. Explanation (v.16a) and exhortation (v.16b)

In this disputation the Lord accused the people of faithless behavior that violated the basic demands of covenantal life. As members of the covenant community, God's people were like a family, with God as their Father (v.10a; cf. Deut. 32:6; Isa. 63:16; 64:8; Mal. 1:6). Within this covenantal framework each member of the community was to be faithful to God and to others (v.10b).

Many in Judah (so many that God simply generalizes, "Judah has broken faith . . . Judah has desecrated," v.11) had married foreign women (v.11; cf. Ezra 9–10).[17] Unless these women became proselytes (and the language of the text, "daughter of a foreign god," strongly indicates they did not), they would inevitably lead their husbands into idolatry and contaminate Israelite worship (cf. Exod. 34:15–16; Deut. 7:3–4; Judg. 3:6–7; 1 Kings 11:1–6). The Lord regarded such marriages as detestable. Those who married foreign women desecrated His sanctuary (either the temple or the community as

---

[17] The debate over the referent of "the daughter of a foreign god" has focused on two options: a literal woman and a pagan goddess. As Glazier-McDonald points out, the two options are probably not as mutually exclusive as they might seem. The referent is probably to a literal wife, but by seducing her husband to worship her gods, she became, as it were, a "goddess" as well. See ibid., pp. 91–93, 113–20.

a whole) and disqualified themselves from further participation in the community (vv.11–12). Some of these individuals made their crime worse by divorcing their wives prior to marrying foreigners (v.14). This act violated the covenantal nature of marriage, whereby the marriage partners were united by a binding, legal agreement.

The Lord's reaction to this widespread unfaithfulness was threefold. First, He refused to accept the sinners' offerings, even when they wailed and lamented over His displeasure (v.13). Second, He urged them to come to their senses and return to their wives (vv.15b, 16b). Third, He declared His hatred of divorce, which He characterized as a violent deed (v.16a).[18]

Fourth Disputation: God Affirms His Justice (2:17–3:5)

This disputation displays the following structure:

[18]The Heb. text of vv.15–16 is extremely rough in places. Verse 15a has stubbornly resisted attempts at interpretation. It is beyond our scope to interact with the various proposals that have been offered. For helpful summaries of options, see ibid., pp. 103–8; and Verhoef, *Haggai and Malachi*, pp. 275–77. Verse 16a also presents difficulties. The Heb. text literally reads, "For he hates [*śānē'*, a third-person verbal form] divorce [*šallaḥ*, "sending away," an infinitival form]." Since God is speaking here, the third-person verbal form is problematic. Perhaps God here refers to himself in the third person, as He apparently does in 1:9. To achieve a first-person reading (i.e., "*I* hate divorce"), one must alter the Heb. text in one of the following ways:

1. Emend the third-person verb to the first-person form (*śānē'tî*; see Ralph L. Smith, *Micah–Malachi* [Waco: Word Books, 1984], p. 320).
2. Emend the third-person verb to a masculine singular active participle (*śōnē'*) and understand the pronominal subject to be omitted by ellipsis (cf. Verhoef, *Haggai and Malachi*, p. 278).
3. Emend the third-person verb to an infinitive absolute (*śānō'*) and understand the infinitive as functionally equivalent to a first-person verb.

Some prefer to see a human being, rather than God, as the subject in this sentence. For example J. M. P. Smith repoints *šallaḥ*, "sending away," as a third-person verbal form (*šilleaḥ*) and reads, "For one who hates and sends away covers his clothing with violence" ("Malachi," p. 60). Glazier-McDonald repoints the third-person verbal form as an active participle and reads, "For one who divorces because of aversion . . . thereby covers his garment with violence" (*Malachi*, pp. 82, 110–11). Finally, NIV's "a man's covering himself with violence" is better translated "(the one who) covers himself [lit. "his garment"] with violence" (cf. NASB). "Covers" is a third-person verbal form in Heb., not an infinitive, suggesting that the individual, not merely his action, is in view.

I. Introductory statement (2:17a)

II. The people's question (2:17b)

III. Concluding statement (2:17c–3:5)
   A. Explanation of introductory statement (2:17c)
   B. Expansion (prophecy; 3:1–5)

In this oracle the Lord disputed with those who questioned His justice. Some had wearied the Lord by claiming He approved of evildoers and was unconcerned about justice (2:17). In refuting this charge, the Lord announced He would come in judgment to purify His people (3:1–5). Only those who genuinely feared the Lord (cf. 3:16–18; 4:2–3) would be able to withstand this righteous judgment (v.2a). Like a refiner's fire, which burns away the dross from precious metals, or a launderer's soap, which removes the stains from clothing, the Lord would purify the Levites (cf. 1:6–2:9) so that they might once again bring Him acceptable offerings (vv.2b–4). He would also take decisive action against all covenant breakers, whose faithless and oppressive deeds demonstrated their lack of respect for the Lord of the covenant (v.5).

Verse 1 raises several interpretive questions, the most important of which concerns the identity of the individual(s) referred to as "my messenger," "the Lord," and "the messenger of the covenant." The Lord's "messenger" is clearly distinguished from the Lord Himself (v.1a). The function of the former is to prepare the way for the Lord. In light of 4:5–6 this messenger is best identified with Elijah. (Note that the phrase "See, I will send" appears in both 3:1a and 4:5 and that Elijah's function [4:6] is preparatory in nature [cf. 3:1a].) The identity of the "the Lord" and "the messenger of the covenant" (v.1b) is more problematic. The structure of verse 1b, which is chiastic in the Hebrew text, suggests that the titles refer to one individual.[19] The text reads:

> And suddenly he will come to his temple/the Lord
>   whom you seek;
> the messenger of the covenant (in) whom you
>   delight/behold he will come.

[19] Verhoef, *Haggai and Malachi*, pp. 288–89.

The precise form "the Lord" (*hā'ādôn*)and the phrase "messenger of the covenant" occur only here in the Old Testament, so one is unable to appeal to parallel usage.[20] Since the word "messenger" (referring to Elijah) appears earlier in the verse, it is tempting to equate the "messenger of the covenant" with Elijah as well. However, because "the Lord/messenger of the covenant" comes to "his *temple*" (cf. Ezek. 43:1–9), this seems unlikely. It is more probable that the reference is to the Lord Himself.

In what sense can the Lord be called "the messenger of the covenant"? The phrase probably refers to His role as enforcer of the covenant, whereby He has the authority to reward or judge His people on the basis of their loyalty (or lack thereof) to His demands.[21] The title may even recall earlier Old Testament texts that virtually identify God with His angel (lit. "messenger") in His role as covenant Lord (cf. Exod. 3:1–22; 23:20–23; 32:34; Isa. 63:9).[22]

Fifth Disputation: Neglect of Offerings Denounced (3:6–12)

Like the second disputation (cf. 1:6–2:9), this oracle's structure is more complex than most others in the book. It may be outlined as follows:

  I. Introductory statement (vv.6–7b)[23]
     A. Affirmation (vv.6–7a)
     B. Exhortation and promise (v.7b)

  II. The people's first question (v.7c)

  III. The exhortation clarified (v.8a)

---

[20] Though *hā'ādôn* occurs in seven other passages, only here does it appear without being followed by "Yahweh" ("the LORD").

[21] See Glazier-McDonald, *Malachi*, pp. 131–32; and Verhoef, *Haggai and Malachi*, p. 289.

[22] See Glazier-McDonald, *Malachi*, pp. 130–31; and Verhoef, *Haggai and Malachi*, p. 289.

[23] I understand Heb. *kî*, "for," at the beginning of v.6 (untranslated in NIV) as assertive, "surely, indeed."

IV. The people's second question (v.8b)

V. Concluding statement (vv.8c–12)
   A. Affirmation (vv.8c–9)
   B. Exhortation and promise (vv.10–12)

The Lord affirmed that He remains faithful to His covenant promises ("I the LORD do not change," v.6a). Because of His covenantal fidelity, He had preserved His people (v.6b), despite their history of rebellion (v.7a). His faithfulness was also evident in His gracious call to repentance, accompanied by the promise of a restored relationship (v.7b).

The people's questions, like the others in the book, testify to their spiritual insensitivity (vv.7c, 8b). They were unaware of any improprieties on their part for which repentance was necessary. As specific evidence of their guilt, the Lord pointed to their failure to bring the required tithes and offerings to His temple (vv.8c–9). The tithes and offerings referred to here are probably those used to sustain the Levites (Num. 18:8, 11, 19, 21–24; cf. Neh. 13:10).

The Lord challenged the people to test His word. If they would bring the full tithe to Him, He promised to shower agricultural blessings on them (v.10). No longer would they be cursed (cf. v.9) with crop-destroying insects and ruined harvests (v.11). As a result, even surrounding nations would recognize their special status (v.12).

Sixth Disputation: The Lord Again Affirms His Justice (3:13–4:3)

The disputation exhibits the following elements:

I. Introductory statement (affirmation; 3:13a)

II. The people's question (3:13b)

III. Concluding statement (3:14–4:3)
    A. Explanation of affirmation (3:14–15)
    B. Promise to the righteous (prophecy; 3:16–4:3)

In this final oracle the Lord once again dealt with the people's wrong perceptions of His justice (cf. 2:17). They complained that obedience to God's law brought no rewards or benefits (3:14). Proud people and evildoers, not the righteous, prospered. Those who challenged God's authority went unpunished (3:15).

Despite outward appearances, this accusation of divine injustice was unfounded. The Lord was taking careful note of those who genuinely feared Him. The prophet pictured a scroll in God's presence, upon which were recorded the names of His loyal servants (3:16). The Lord called this group His "treasured possession," to whom He would extend His fatherly compassion (3:17). The word translated "treasured possession" is the same one used of the nation Israel in Exodus 19:5, where the Lord promised, "Now if you obey me fully and keep my covenant, then out of all nations you will be my treasured possession. Although the whole earth is mine, you will be for me a kingdom of priests and a holy nation" (cf. also Deut. 7:6; 14:2; 26:18; Ps. 135:4). Throughout its history the nation never lived up to this high calling. However, the Lord promised the righteous remnant of Malachi's day that the ideal would be realized. Rather than overlooking them (cf. 3:14), God intended to establish them as His true covenant people.

In that day God's justice, evidenced by His careful discrimination between the righteous and the wicked, would be obvious to His followers (3:18). The Lord's fiery judgment would destroy all evildoers, just as fire burns up stubble (4:1). He would vindicate those who fear Him, removing their suffering and filling them with joy (4:2). To symbolize their vindication, they are pictured trampling on the ashes (cf. 4:1) of the wicked (4:3).

The imagery of verse 2 needs comment. Righteousness is here pictured as the rising sun, which bursts on the scene and dispels darkness. Its "wings," probably a reference to the sun's rays, bring healing to those they touch. In this context "righteousness" refers to the vindication that divine judgment brings to the God-fearers and to the restoration of just order in society.[24] "Healing" refers to the reversal of the harm done by the wicked (cf. 3:5). Released from the bondage of oppression, the righteous would be filled with energy and joy, like a calf released from its stall (cf. Jer. 50:11).

---

[24]Smith, "Malachi," p. 80; Glazier-McDonald, *Malachi,* p. 236.

Concluding Exhortation and Prophecy (4:4–6)

The book concludes with an exhortation (v.4) and an expansion of the earlier prophecy concerning the Lord's messenger (vv.5–6; cf. 3:1). Since the earlier oracles expose specific violations of the Law (cf. 1:7–14; 2:10–11; 3:8–9), the general charge to remember the Law of Moses (v.4) is quite appropriate at this point. Attention is then drawn to Elijah's coming, for it would be the next event in God's program as outlined previously in the book. His appearance would signal "the Day of the LORD" (v.5), in which the community would be purified through judgment (cf. 3:2–5; 4:1–3) and God's ideal for His covenant people would finally be realized (cf. 3:17–18). Elijah's task would be to effect reconciliation in society so that the land might be spared God's curse (v.6).

Verse 6 presents two major interpretive problems. The first concerns the meaning of the words "He will turn the hearts of the fathers to their children, and the hearts of the children to their fathers." As translated by NIV, the statement refers to the reconciliation of conflicts that had arisen within families in the postexilic community. Such conflicts would be another example of the faithlessness and broken relationships that had permeated society (cf. 2:10). Another possibility is to translate, "He will turn the hearts of the fathers together with (those of) the children, and the hearts of the children together with (those of) the fathers (to me)." In this case the reconciliation is between sinful society (including both younger and older generations) and the Lord.[25] This interpretation would be consistent with the Lord's earlier exhortation to the people to return to Him (cf. 3:7, where "return" translates the same Heb. word rendered "turn" in 4:6).

The second problem in verse 6 involves harmonizing the picture presented here with earlier prophecies in the book (3:1–5; 4:1–3). J. M. P. Smith argued that 4:5–6 differs from these earlier passages in two respects. First, it views society as entirely sinful, while the earlier texts distinguish between the righteous and the wicked. Second, this passage anticipates general societal repentance, so that complete destruction might be averted, while the earlier passages envision the judgment itself purging out the wicked and vindicating the righteous.[26]

---

[25] See Glazier-McDonald, *Malachi*, p. 256.
[26] Smith, "Malachi," p. 82.

B. Glazier-McDonald has demonstrated that the various passages can be harmonized.[27] Verse 6 refers not to society as a whole but to the evildoers mentioned and addressed earlier in the book. This group, not the God-fearers, would be the target of Elijah's ministry. If they responded to his message, then the purifying judgment threatened earlier would be unnecessary. However, if they rejected Elijah, the Lord would carry out this judgment as announced. In this interpretation the "curse" (*ḥerem*) of 4:6 refers to the purifying judgment of 4:1–3, which is the culmination of the "curse" (*mᵉʾērâ*) of 3:9, not to a wholesale, indiscriminate destruction of the nation.

THEOLOGY

Summary

According to Malachi, the Exile had not changed God's covenantal relationship to Israel. Despite Israel's history of sin, God demonstrated His love for His people by preserving them. He demanded that they in turn repent of their sins and obey the Mosaic Law. Though the nation was under God's curse for its transgressions, God promised that repentance and obedience would bring His blessings.

Though some charged God with injustice, the coming Day of the Lord would demonstrate His justice by purging out the evildoers in the covenant community and by vindicating His loyal followers. This group of God-fearers would form the nucleus of a renewed covenant community that, led by a purified Levitical order, would take the lead among the nations in genuine worship.

Analysis

In Malachi God appears as Israel's covenant Lord. He is both master and father (1:6). As father He created the covenant community (2:10) at Sinai (4:4). Time and time again the Lord of the covenant demonstrated His unwavering devotion to His people. Though the nation rebelled against Him from the very beginning (3:7), He remained faithful (3:6). By preserving His people through exile and destroying their archenemy Edom, He

[27] Glazier-McDonald, *Malachi,* pp. 259–61.

once again displayed His elective love toward Jacob and his descendents (1:2–5).

As Israel's faithful and loving covenant Lord, He insisted on their loyalty to His covenant demands (4:4). The covenant required faithfulness to God and to one's fellow Israelites (2:10). However, Malachi's generation had violated the covenant by intermarrying with foreigners (2:11–12), divorcing their wives (2:14–16), and neglecting prescribed tithes and offerings (3:8–9). The priests, with whom God had made a special covenant (2:5, 8), had even sinned by offering defiled sacrifices (1:6–14), misleading the people (2:8), and acting unjustly (2:9).

In accordance with the principles of the covenant, whereby obedience brought divine blessing and disobedience punishment, the Lord had placed the nation and the priests under a curse (2:1–2; 3:9). If the people failed to repent (cf. 2:1–4; 3:7), they would experience even worse consequences (cf. 2:3; 3:1–5; 4:1–3, 6). On the other hand, a proper response to God's admonition would bring a restoration of divine blessings (3:10–12).

One of the major themes of the book is God's justice. Some complained that the prosperity of the wicked (2:17; 3:14–15; cf. 3:7) indicated that God was unconcerned about justice. In response, God argued that the coming Day of the Lord's judgment would reveal His justice to all. This judgment, which is likened to fire, would purify the nation, including the Levitical order (3:2–3; 4:1). Having taken careful note of those who feared Him (3:16), the Lord would separate the righteous from the wicked (3:5, 18). He would compassionately deliver His loyal followers (3:17b) and vindicate them before their enemies (4:2–3). After he destroyed the wicked (3:5; 4:1), He would make the righteous His "treasured possession," the ideal covenant community envisioned by Moses (3:17a). This renewed community would offer acceptable sacrifices to the Lord (3:3–4) as the whole world worshiped the one true God (1:11).

The Lord would send the prophet Elijah prior to this Day of Judgment (3:1; 4:5). His task would be to "prepare the way" for the Lord (3:1) by proclaiming the necessity of repentance as the only way to escape the impending judgment (4:6). According to the New Testament, John the Baptist, who came as a second Elijah (Matt. 11:14; 17:12–13; Luke 1:17), eventually emerged as the Lord's messenger prophesied here (Matt. 11:10; Mark 1:2; Luke 1:76; 7:27).

BIBLIOGRAPHY

Abbreviations used throughout the following sections are:

NICOT   *New International Commentary of the Old Testament*
TOTC   *Tyndale Old Testament Commentaries*
CBSC   *Cambridge Bible for Schools and Colleges*
SBLMS   *Society of Biblical Literature Monograph Services*
OTL   *Old Testament Library*
ICC   *International Critical Commentary*
WBC   *Word Bible Commentary*

Aharoni, Yohanan. *The Land of the Bible.* Rev.ed. Translated by A. F. Rainey. Philadelphia: Westminster Press, 1979.

Aharoni, Yohanan, and Avi-Yonah, Michael. *The Macmillan Bible Atlas.* Rev.ed. New York: Macmillan, 1977.

Allen, Leslie C. *Joel, Obadiah, Jonah, and Micah.* NICOT. Grand Rapids: Eerdmans, 1976.

Andersen, Francis I., and Freedman, David N. *Hosea.* AB. Garden City, N.Y.: Doubleday, 1980.

Archer, Gleason L., Jr. *A Survey of Old Testament Introduction.* Chicago: Moody Press, 1974.

Armerding, Carl E. "Habakkuk." In *The Expositor's Bible Commentary,* edited by Frank E. Gaebelein, vol. 7. Grand Rapids: Zondervan, 1985.

_____. "Nahum." In *The Expositor's Bible Commentary,* edited by Frank E. Gaebelein, vol. 7. Grand Rapids: Zondervan, 1985.

_____. "Obadiah." In *The Expositor's Bible Commentary,* edited by Frank Gaebelein, vol. 7. Grand Rapids: Zondervan, 1985.

Baldwin, Joyce G. *Haggai, Zechariah, Malachi.* TOTC. London: Inter-Varsity Press, 1972.

Ball, Ivan J., Jr. "A Rhetorical Study of Zephaniah." Ph.D. diss., Graduate Theological Union, 1972.

Barker, Kenneth L. "Zechariah." In *The Expositor's Bible Commentary,* edited by Frank E. Gaebelein, vol. 7. Grand Rapids: Zondervan, 1985.

Barstad, Hans M. *The Religious Polemics of Amos.* SVT, 34. Leiden: E. J. Brill, 1984.

BIBLIOGRAPHY

Bergren, Richard V. *The Prophets and the Law*. Monographs of the Hebrew Union College, 4. Cincinnati: Hebrew Union College Press, 1974.

Borowski, Oded. *Agriculture in Iron Age Israel*. Winona Lake, Ind.: Eisenbrauns, 1987.

Bright, John. *A History of Israel*. 3d ed. Philadelphia: Westminster Press, 1981.

Bullinger, E. W. *Figures of Speech Used in the Bible*. 1898. Reprint. Grand Rapids: Baker, 1968.

Bullock, C. Hassell. *An Introduction to the Old Testament Prophetic Books*. Chicago: Moody Press, 1986.

Buren, E. D. van. *Symbols of the Gods in Mesopotamian Art*. Rome: Pontifical Biblical Institute, 1945.

Cathcart, Kevin J. *Nahum in the Light of Northwest Semitic Studies*. Rome: Biblical Institute Press, 1973.

Childs, Brevard S. *Introduction to the Old Testament as Scripture*. Philadelphia: Fortress Press, 1979.

Chisholm, Robert B., Jr. "Wordplay in the Eighth-Century Prophets." *Bibliotheca Sacra* 144 (1987): 44–52.

Collins, John J. *Daniel, with an Introduction to Apocalyptic Literature*. The Forms of the OT Literature, 20. Grand Rapids: Eerdmans, 1984.

Day, John. "New Light on the Mythological Background of the Allusion to Resheph in Habakkuk III 5." *Vetus Testamentum* 29 (1979): 353–55.

Driver, S. R. *Joel and Amos*. 2d ed. CBSC. Cambridge: Cambridge University Press, 1915.

Edgerton, William F., and Wilson, John A. *Historical Records of Ramses III: The Texts in Medinet Habu*. Vols. 1–2. Chicago: University of Chicago Press, 1936.

Fee, Gordon D., and Stuart, Douglas. *How to Read the Bible for All Its Worth*. Grand Rapids: Zondervan, 1982.

Fensham, F. C. "Common Trends in Curses of the Near Eastern Treaties and *kudurru*-Inscriptions Compared with Maledictions of Amos and Isaiah." *Zeitschrift für die alttestamentliche Wissenschaft* 75 (1963): 155–75.

Fohrer, Georg. *Introduction to the Old Testament*. Translated by David E. Green. Nashville: Abingdon, 1968.

France, R. T. *Jesus and the Old Testament*. Paperback ed. Grand Rapids: Baker, 1982.

Freeman, Hobart E. *An Introduction to the Old Testament Prophets*. Chicago: Moody Press, 1968.

Fretheim, Terence E. *The Message of Jonah*. Minneapolis: Augsburg, 1977.

Gibson, J. C. L. *Canaanite Myths and Legends*. 2d ed. Edinburgh: T. & T. Clark, 1978.

_____. *Syrian Semitic Inscriptions*. 3 vols. Edinburgh: T. & T. Clark, 1971–82.

Gitay, Yehoshua. "A Study of Amos's Art of Speech: A Rhetorical Analysis of Amos 3:1–15." *Catholic Biblical Quarterly* 42 (1980): 293–309.

Glazier-McDonald, Beth. *Malachi*. Atlanta: Scholars Press, 1987.

Gottwald, Norman K. *The Hebrew Bible: A Socio-Literary Introduction*. Philadelphia: Fortress Press, 1985.

Grayson, Albert K. *Assyrian Royal Inscriptions*. 2 vols. Wiesbaden: Otto Harrassowitz, 1972–76.

Hanson, Paul D. "Apocalyptic Literature." In *The Hebrew Bible and Its Modern Interpreters*, edited by Douglas A. Knight and Gene M. Tucker, pp. 465–88. Philadelphia: Fortress Press; Chico, Calif.: Scholars Press, 1985.

_____. *The Dawn of Apocalyptic*. Rev.ed. Philadelphia: Fortress Press, 1979.

Harper, William R. *Amos and Hosea*. ICC. Edinburgh: T. & T. Clark, 1905.

Harrison, R. K. *Introduction to the Old Testament*. Grand Rapids: Eerdmans, 1969.

Hilber, John W. "A Biblical Theology of Zephaniah." Th.M. thesis, Dallas Theological Seminary, 1984.

Huffmon, Herbert B. "The Treaty Background of Hebrew $Y\bar{A}DA'$." *Bulletin of the American Schools of Oriental Research* 181 (1966): 31–37.

Kapelrud, Arvid S. *Joel Studies*. Uppsala: A. B. Lundequistska Bokhandeln, 1948.

Kautzsch, E., ed. *Gesenius' Hebrew Grammar*. Translated by A. E. Cowley. 2d Eng. ed. Oxford: Clarendon Press, 1910.

BIBLIOGRAPHY

Keil, Carl F. *The Twelve Minor Prophets.* Translated by James Martin. 2 vols. Grand Rapids: Eerdmans, 1949.

King, Philip J. *Amos, Hosea, Micah: An Archaeological Commentary.* Philadelphia: Westminster Press, 1988.

Koch, Klaus. *The Prophets.* Translated by Margaret Kohl. 2 vols. Philadelphia: Fortress Press, 1983.

Landes, George M. "The Kerygma of the Book of Jonah." *Interpretation* 21 (1967): 3–31.

Laney, J. Carl. *Zechariah.* Chicago: Moody Press, 1984.

Lichtheim, Miriam. *Ancient Egyptian Literature.* 3 vols. Berkeley: University of California Press, 1975–80.

Limburg, James. "Sevenfold Structures in the Book of Amos." *Journal of Biblical Literature* 106 (1987): 217–22.

Lipinski, E. "Recherches sur le Livre de Zacharie." *Vetus Testamentum* 20 (1970): 25–55.

Longenecker, Richard N. *Biblical Exegesis in the Apostolic Period.* Grand Rapids: Eerdmans, 1975.

Luckenbill, Daniel D. *Ancient Records of Assyria and Babylonia.* 2 vols. Chicago: University of Chicago Press, 1926–27.

McCarter, P. Kyle, Jr. *Textual Criticism.* Philadelphia: Fortress Press, 1986.

McComiskey, Thomas E. "Amos." In *The Expositor's Bible Commentary,* edited by Frank E. Gaebelein, vol. 7. Grand Rapids: Zondervan, 1985.

_____. "The Hymnic Elements of the Prophecy of Amos: A Study of Form-Critical Methodology." In *A Tribute to Gleason Archer,* edited by Walter C. Kaiser, Jr., and Ronald F. Youngblood, pp. 105–28. Chicago: Moody Press, 1986.

_____. "Micah." In *The Expositor's Bible Commentary,* edited by Frank E. Gaebelein, vol. 7. Grand Rapids: Zondervan, 1985.

Mays, James L. *Hosea.* OTL. Philadelphia: Westminster Press, 1969.

Meyers, Carol L., and Meyers, Eric M. *Haggai, Zechariah 1–8.* AB. Garden City, N.Y.: Doubleday, 1987.

Miller, Patrick D., Jr. *Sin and Judgment in the Prophets.* SBLMS, 27. Chico, Calif.: Scholars Press, 1982.

Mitchell, H. G. "A Critical and Exegetical Commentary on Haggai and Zechariah." In *A Critical and Exegetical Commentary on Haggai,*

Zechariah, Malachi, and Jonah. New York: Charles Scribner's Sons, 1912.

Patterson, Richard D. "Joel." In *The Expositor's Bible Commentary,* edited by Frank E. Gaebelein, vol. 7. Grand Rapids: Zondervan, 1985.

Paul, Shalom M. "Amos 3:3–8: The Irresistible Sequence of Cause and Effect." *Hebrew Annual Review* 7 (1983): 203–20.

————. "Fishing Imagery in Amos 4:2." *Journal of Biblical Literature* 97 (1978): 183–90.

————. "A Literary Reinvestigation of the Authenticity of the Oracles Against the Nations of Amos." In *De la Tôrah au Messie,* edited by J. Dore, P. Grelot, and M. Carrez, pp. 189–204. Paris: Descleé, 1981.

Perowne, T. T. *Haggai and Zechariah.* CBSC. Cambridge: Cambridge University Press, 1897.

Petersen, David L. *Haggai and Zechariah 1–8.* OTL. Philadelphia: Westminster Press, 1984.

Pitard, Wayne T. *Ancient Damascus.* Winona Lake, Ind.: Eisenbrauns, 1987.

Pritchard, James, ed. *Ancient Near Eastern Texts Relating to the Old Testament.* 3d ed. Princeton: Princeton University Press, 1969.

Rad, Gerhard von. *The Message of the Prophets.* Translated by D. M. G. Stalker. New York: Harper & Row, 1968.

Rendtorff, Rolf. *The Old Testament: An Introduction.* Translated by John Bowden. Philadelphia: Fortress Press, 1986.

Roux, Georges. *Ancient Iraq.* Baltimore: Penguin Books, 1964.

Schoville, Keith N. "A Note on the Oracles of Amos Against Gaza, Tyre, and Edom." *Supplements to Vetus Testamentum* 26 (1974): 55–63.

Smith, George A. *The Book of the Twelve Prophets.* Rev.ed. 2 vols. New York: Harper & Brothers, n.d.

Smith, J. M. P. "A Critical and Exegetical Commentary on the Book of Malachi." ICC. In *A Critical and Exegetical Commentary on Haggai, Zechariah, Malachi, and Jonah.* New York: Charles Scribner's Sons, 1912.

Smith, Ralph L. *Micah–Malachi.* WBC. Waco: Word Books, 1984.

Spalinger, A. "Assurbanipal and Egypt: A Source Study." *Journal of the American Oriental Society* 94 (1974): 316–28.

BIBLIOGRAPHY

Stuart, Douglas. *Hosea–Jonah.* WBC. Waco: Word Books, 1987.

Thiele, Edwin R. *The Mysterious Numbers of the Hebrew Kings.* Rev.ed. Grand Rapids: Zondervan, 1983.

Ulrich, Eugene C., Jr. *The Qumran Text of Samuel and Josephus.* Missoula, Mont.: Scholars Press, 1978.

Verhoef, Pieter A. *Haggai and Malachi.* NICOT. Grand Rapids: Eerdmans, 1987.

Weinfeld, Moshe. " 'Rider of the Clouds' and 'Gatherer of the Clouds.' " *Journal of the Ancient Near Eastern Society of Columbia University* 5 (1973): 421–26.

White, John B. "Universalization of History in Deutero-Isaiah." In *Scripture in Context,* edited by C. D. Evans, W. W. Hallo, and J. B. White, pp. 179–95. Pittsburgh: Pickwick Press, 1980.

Whiting, John D. "Jerusalem's Locust Plague." *National Geographic Magazine* 28 (December 1915): 511–50.

Williams, Ronald J. *Hebrew Syntax: An Outline.* 2d ed. Toronto: University of Toronto Press, 1976.

Wolf, Herbert. *Haggai and Malachi.* Chicago: Moody Press, 1976.

Wolff, Hans W. *Hosea.* Hermeneia Translated by Gary Stansell. Philadelphia: Fortress Press, 1974.

_____. *Joel and Amos.* Hermeneia. Translated by Waldemar Janzen, S. Dean McBride, Jr., and Charles Muenchow. Philadelphia: Fortress Press, 1977.

_____. *Obadiah and Jonah.* Translated by Margaret Kohl. Minneapolis: Augsburg, 1986.

Young, Edward J. *An Introduction to the Old Testament.* Rev.ed. Grand Rapids: Eerdmans, 1960.

FOR FURTHER READING

GENERAL STUDIES AND INTRODUCTIONS

Archer, Gleason L., Jr. *A Survey of Old Testament Introduction.* Rev.ed. Chicago: Moody, 1974.

Bullock, C. Hassell. *An Introduction to the Old Testament Prophetic Books.* Chicago: Moody, 1986.

Childs, Brevard S. *An Introduction to the Old Testament as Scripture.* Philadelphia: Fortress, 1979.

Freeman, Hobart E. *An Introduction to the Old Testament Prophets.* Chicago: Moody, 1968.

Harrison, Roland K. *Introduction to the Old Testament.* Grand Rapids: Eerdmans, 1969.

Koch, Klaus. *The Prophets.* 2 vols. Translated by M. Kohl. Philadelphia: Fortress, 1983–84.

Rad, Gerhard von. *The Message of the Prophets.* Translated by D. M. G. Stalker. New York: Harper & Row, 1968.

Rendtorff, Rolf. *The Old Testament: An Introduction.* Translated by J. Bowden. Philadelphia: Fortress, 1986.

HOSEA

Achtemeier, Elizabeth. "The Theological Message of Hosea: Its Preaching Values." *Review and Expositor* 72 (1975): 473–85.

Andersen, Francis I., and Freedman, David N. *Hosea.* AB. Garden City, N.Y.: Doubleday, 1980.

Brueggemann, Walter. *Tradition for Crisis: A Study in Hosea.* Richmond: John Knox, 1968.

Fensham, F. Charles. "The Covenant-Idea in the Book of Hosea." *Die Ou Testamentiese Werkgemeenskap in Suid-Afrika* 7/8 (1964–65): 35–49.

Harper, William R. *A Critical and Exegetical Commentary on Amos and Hosea.* ICC. Edinburgh: T. & T. Clark, 1905.

Kidner, Derek. *Love to the Loveless: The Message of Hosea.* The Bible Speaks Today. Downers Grove, Ill.: InterVarsity, 1981.

King, Philip J. *Amos, Hosea, Micah—An Archaeological Commentary.* Philadelphia: Westminster, 1988.

Labuschagne, Charles J. "The Similes in the Book of Hosea." *Die Ou Testamentiese Werkgemeenskap in Suid-Afrika* 7/8 (1964–65): 64–76.

Lundbom, Jack R. "Poetic Structure and Prophetic Rhetoric in Hosea." *Vetus Testamentum* 29 (1979): 300–308.

Mays, James L. *Hosea*. Old Testament Library. Philadelphia: Westminster, 1969.

Miller, Patrick D., Jr. *Sin and Judgment in the Prophets*. Chico, Calif.: Scholars Press, 1982.

Stuart, Douglas. *Hosea–Jonah*. Word Biblical Commentary. Waco: Word Books, 1987.

Wolff, Hans W. *Hosea*. Hermeneia. Translated by G. Stansell. Philadelphia: Fortress, 1974.

Wyrtzen, David B. "A Biblical Theology of Hosea." Th.D. dissertation. Dallas Theological Seminary, 1980.

————. "The Theological Center of the Book of Hosea." *Bibliotheca Sacra* 141 (1984): 315–29.

JOEL

Ahlstrom, G. W. *Joel and the Temple Cult of Jerusalem*. Leiden: Brill, 1971.

Allen, Leslie C. *Joel, Obadiah, Jonah and Micah*. NICOT. Grand Rapids: Eerdmans, 1976.

Driver, Samuel R. *The Books of Joel and Amos*. CBSC. Cambridge: Cambridge University, 1901.

Kapelrud, Arvid S. *Joel Studies*. Uppsala: A. B. Lundequist, 1948.

Myers, Jacob. "Some Considerations Bearing on the Date of Joel." *Zeitschrift für die alttestamentliche Wissenschaft* 74 (1962): 177–95.

Patterson, Richard D. "Joel." In *The Expositor's Bible Commentary*, vol. 7. Edited by F. E. Gaebelein. Grand Rapids: Zondervan, 1985.

Prinsloo, Willem S. *The Theology of the Book of Joel*. Berlin: de Gruyter, 1985.

Stuart, Douglas. (See under Hosea.)

Thompson, John A. "The Date of Joel." In *A Light Unto My Path: Old Testament Studies in Honor of Jacob M. Myers*. Edited by H. N. Bream, R. D. Heim, and C. A. Moore. Philadelphia: Temple University, 1974 (pp. 453–64).

Wolff, Hans W. *Joel and Amos.* Hermeneia. Translated by W. Janzen, S. D. McBride, and C. A. Muenchow. Philadelphia: Fortress, 1977.

AMOS

Barstad, Hans. *The Religious Polemics of Amos.* Leiden: Brill, 1984.

Barton, John. *Amos's Oracles Against the Nations.* Cambridge: Cambridge University, 1980.

Cripps, Richard S. *A Critical and Exegetical Commentary on the Book of Amos.* 2d ed. London: SPCK, 1955.

Hammershaimb, Erling. *The Book of Amos: A Commentary.* Translated by J. Sturdy. New York: Schocken, 1970.

Harper, William R. (See under Hosea.)

Hayes, John H. *Amos.* Nashville: Abingdon, 1988.

King, Philip J. (See under Hosea.)

Limburg, James. "Sevenfold Structures in the Book of Amos." *Journal of Biblical Literature* 106 (1987): 217–22.

Mays, James L. *Amos.* Old Testament Library. Philadelphia: Westminster, 1969.

McComiskey, Thomas E. "Amos." In *The Expositor's Bible Commentary,* vol. 7. Edited by F. E. Gaebelein. Grand Rapids: Zondervan, 1985.

—————. "The Hymnic Elements of the Prophecy of Amos: A Study of Form-Critical Methodology." In *A Tribute to Gleason Archer.* Edited by W. C. Kaiser, Jr., and R. F. Youngblood. Chicago: Moody, 1986 (pp. 105–28).

Miller, Patrick D., Jr. (See under Hosea.)

Motyer, J. A. *The Day of the Lion: The Message of Amos.* The Bible Speaks Today. Leicester: Inter-Varsity, 1974.

Paul, Shalom M. "A Literary Reinvestigation of the Authenticity of the Oracles Against the Nations of Amos." In *De la Tôrah au Messie.* Edited by J. Dore, P. Grelot, and M. Carrez. Paris: Deslcée, 1981 (pp. 189–204).

Seilhamer, Frank H. "The Role of Covenant in the Mission and Message of Amos." In *A Light Unto My Path: Old Testament Studies in Honor of Jacob M. Myers.* Edited by H. N. Bream, R. D. Heim, and C. A. Moore. Philadelphia: Temple University, 1974 (pp. 435–51).

Smith, Gary V. *Amos: A Commentary.* Grand Rapids: Zondervan, 1989.

Soggin, J. A. *The Prophet Amos: A Translation and Commentary.* Translated by J. Bowden. London: SCM, 1987.

Stuart, Douglas. (See under Hosea.)

Waard, Jan de, and Smalley, William A. *A Translator's Handbook on the Book of Amos.* Stuttgart: United Bible Societies, 1979.

Wolff, Hans. W. (See under Joel.)

OBADIAH

Allen, Leslie C. (See under Joel.)

Amerding, Carl E. "Obadiah." In *The Expositor's Bible Commentary,* vol. 7. Edited by F. E. Gaebelein. Grand Rapids: Zondervan, 1985.

Stuart, Douglas. (See under Hosea.)

Watts, John D. W. *Obadiah: A Critical Exegetical Commentary.* Grand Rapids: Eerdmans, 1969.

Wolff, Hans W. *Obadiah and Jonah.* Translated by M. Kohl. Minneapolis: Augsburg, 1986.

JONAH

Ackerman, James S. "Satire and Symbolism in the Song of Jonah." In *Traditions in Transformation.* Edited by B. Halpern and J. D. Levenson. Winona Lake, Ind.: Eisenbrauns, 1981 (pp. 213–46).

Alexander, T. E. "Jonah and Genre." *Tyndale Bulletin* 36 (1985): 35–59.

Allen, Leslie C. (See under Joel.)

Fretheim, Terence E. *The Message of Jonah: A Theological Commentary.* Minneapolis: Augsburg, 1977.

Halpern, Baruch, and Friedman, R. E. "Composition and Paronomasia in the Book of Johan." *Hebrew Annual Review* 4 (1980): 79–92.

Holbert, J. "Deliverance Belongs to Yahweh!: Satire in the Book of Jonah." *Journal for the Study of the Old Testament* 21 (1981): 59–81.

Landes, George M. "The Kerygma of the Book of Jonah." *Interpretation* 21 (1967): 3–31.

Magonet, Jonathan. *Form and Meaning: Studies in Literary Techniques in the Book of Jonah.* 2d ed. Sheffield: Almond, 1983.

Stek, John H. "The Message of the Book of Jonah." *Calvin Theological Journal* 4 (1969): 23–50.

Stuart, Douglas. (See under Hosea.)

Walsh, Jerome T. "Jonah 2, 3–10: A Rhetorical Critical Study." *Biblica* 63 (1982): 219–29.

Wolff, Hans W. (See under Obadiah.)

MICAH

Allen, Leslie C. (See under Joel.)

Hagstrom, David G. *The Coherence of the Book of Micah: A Literary Analysis*. Atlanta: Scholars Press, 1988.

Hillers, Delbert R. *Micah*. Hermeneia. Philadelphia: Fortress, 1984.

King, Philip J. (See under Hosea.)

Mays, James L. *Micah*. Old Testament Library. Philadelphia: Westminster, 1976.

McComiskey, Thomas E. "Micah." In *The Expositor's Bible Commentary*, vol. 7. Edited by F. E. Gaebelein. Grand Rapids: Zondervan, 1985.

Miller, Patrick D., Jr. (See under Hosea.)

Smith, Ralph L. *Micah-Malachi*. Word Biblical Commentary. Waco: Word Books, 1984.

Willis, John T. "The Structure of Micah 3–5 and the Function of Micah 5:9–14 in the Book." *Zeitschrift für die alttestamentliche Wissenschaft* 81 (1969): 191–214.

_____. "The Structure of the Book of Micah." *Svensk Exegetisk Arsbok* 34 (1969): 5–42.

_____. "The Structure, Setting and Interrelationships of the Pericopes in the Book of Micah." Ph.D. dissertation, Vanderbilt Divinity School, 1966.

NAHUM

Achtemeier, Elizabeth. *Nahum–Malachi*. Interpretation. Atlanta: John Knox, 1986.

Amerding, Carl E. "Nahum." In *The Expositor's Bible Commentary*, vol. 7. Edited by F. E. Gaebelein. Grand Rapids: Zondervan, 1985.

Cathcart, Kevin J. *Nahum in the Light of Northwest Semitic*. Rome: Biblical Institute, 1973.

————. "Treaty Curses and the Book of Nahum." *Catholic Biblical Quarterly* 35 (1973): 179–87.

Johnston, Gordon H. "The Book of Nahum: An Exegetical, Rhetorical, and Theological Study." Th.M. thesis, Dallas Theological Semilnary, 1985.

Maier, Walter A. *The Book of Nahum*. St. Louis: Concordia, 1959.

Smith, Ralph L. (See under Micah.)

HABAKKUK

Achtemeier, Elizabeth. (See under Nahum.)

Albright, William F. "The Psalm of Habakkuk." In *Studies in Old Testament Prophecy*. Edited by H. H. Rowley. Edinburgh: T. & T. Clark, 1950 (pp. 1–18).

Armerding, Carl E. "Habakkuk." In *The Expositor's Bible Commentary,* vol. 7. Edited by F. E. Gaebelein. Grand Rapids: Zondervan, 1985.

Eaton, John H. "The Origin and Meaning of Habakkuk 3." *Zeitschrift für die alttestamentliche Wissenschaft* 76 (1964): 144–70.

Gowan, Donald. *The Triumph of Faith in Habakkuk*. Atlanta: John Knox, 1976.

Hiebert, Theodore. "God of My Victory: An Ancient Hymn of Triumph in Habakkuk 3." Ph.D. dissertation, Harvard University, 1984.

Margulis, B. "The Psalm of Habakkuk: A Reconstruction and Interpretation." *Zeitschrift für die alttestamentliche Wissenschaft* 82 (1970): 409–41.

Patterson, Richard D. "The Psalm of Habakkuk." *Grace Theological Journal* 8 (1987): 163–94.

Smith, Ralph L. (See under Micah.)

Szeles, Maria E. *Wrath and Marcy: A Commentary on the Books of Habakkuk and Zephaniah*. ITC. Grand Rapids: Eerdmans, 1987.

Walker, H. H., and Lund, N. W. "The Literary Structure of Habakkuk." *Journal of Biblical Literature* 53 (1934): 355–70.

ZEPHANIAH

Achtemeier, Elizabeth. (See under Nahum.)

Ball, Ivan J., Jr. "A Rhetorical Study of Zephaniah." Th.D. dissertation, Graduate Theological Union, 1972.

————. "The Rhetorical Shape of Zephaniah." In *Perspectives on Language and Text*. Edited by E. W. Conrad and E. G. Newing. Winona Lake, Ind.: Eisenbrauns, 1987 (pp. 155–65).

DeRoche, Michael. "Zephaniah I 2–3: The 'Sweeping' of Creation." *Vetus Testamentum* 30 (1980): 104–9.

Hilber, John W. "A Biblical Theology of Zephaniah." Th.M. thesis, Dallas Theological Seminary, 1984.

House, Paul R. *Zephaniah: A Prophetic Drama*. Sheffield: Almond, 1988.

Kapelrud, Arvid S. *The Message of the Prophet Zephaniah*. Oslo: Universitesforlaget, 1975.

Smith, Ralph L. (See under Micah.)

Szeles, Maria E. (See under Habakkuk.)

Walker, Larry L. "Zephaniah." In *The Expositor's Bible Commentary*, vol. 7. Edited by F. E. Gaebelein. Grand Rapids: Zondervan, 1985.

HAGGAI

Achtemeier, Elizabeth. (See under Nahum.)

Alden, Robert L. "Haggai." In *The Expositor's Bible Commentary*, vol. 7. Edited by F. E. Gaebelein. Grand Rapids: Zondervan, 1985.

Baldwin, Joyce G. *Haggai, Zechariah, Malachi*. TOTC. London: Inter-Varsity, 1972.

Meyers, Carol L. and Eric M. *Haggai, Zechariah 1–8*. AB. Garden City, N.Y.: Doubleday, 1987.

Mitchell, Hinckley G. "A Critical Commentary on Haggai and Zechariah." In *A Critical and Exegetical Commentary on Haggai, Zechariah, Malachi and Jonah*. ICC. New York: Charles Scribner's Sons, 1912.

Petersen, David L. *Haggai and Zechariah 1–8*. Old Testament Library. Philadelphia: Westminster, 1984.

Smith, Ralph L. (See under Micah.)

Verhoef, Pieter A. *Haggai and Malachi*. NICOT. Grand Rapids: Eerdmans, 1987.

Wolf, Herbert. *Haggai/Malachi: Rededication and Renewal*. Chicago: Moody, 1976.

Wolff, Hans W. *Haggai*. Translated by M. Kohl. Minneapolis: Augusburg, 1988.

ZECHARIAH

Achtemeier, Elizabeth. (See under Nahum.)

Baldwin, Joyce G. (See under Haggai.)

Barker, Kenneth L. "Zechariah." In *The Expositor's Bible Commentary*, vol. 7. Edited by F. E. Gaebelein. Grand Rapids: Zondervan, 1985.

Halpern, Baruch. "The Ritual Background of Zechariah's Temple Song." *Catholic Biblical Quarterly* 40 (1978): 167–90.

Hanson, Paul D. *The Dawn of Apocalyptic*. Rev.ed. Philadelphia: Fortress, 1979.

Laney, Carl. *Zechariah*. Chicago: Moody, 1984.

Mason, Rex A. "The Relation of Zech. 9–14 to Proto-Zechariah." *Zeitschrift für die alttestamentliche Wissenschaft* 88 (1976): 227–39.

Meyers, Carol L. alnd Eric M. (See under Haggai.)

Mitchell, Hinckley G. (See under Haggai.)

Petersen, David L. (See under Haggai.)

Radday, Yehuda, and Wickmann, Dieter. "The Unity of Zechariah Examined in the Light of Statistical Linguistics." *Zeitschrift für die alttestamentliche Wissenschaft* 87 (1975): 30–55.

Smith, Ralph L. (See under Micah.)

MALACHI

Achtemeier, Elizabeth. (See under Nahum.)

Alden, Robert L. "Malachi." In *Expositor's Bible Commentary*, vol. 7. Edited by F. E. Gaebelein. Grand Rapids: Zondervan, 1985.

Baldwin, Joyce G. (See under Haggai.)

Fischer, James A. "Notes on the Literary Form and Message of Malachi." *Catholic Biblical Quarterly* 34 (1972): 315–20.

Glazier-MacDonald, Beth. *Malachi.* Atlanta: Scholars Press, 1987.

Kaiser, Walter C. *Malachi: God's Unchanging Love.* Grand Rapids: Baker, 1984.

McKenzie, Steven L., and Wallace, Howard N. "Covenant Themes in Malachi." *Catholic Biblical Quarterly* 45 (1984): 549–63.

Smith, J. M. Powis. "A Critical and Exegetical Commentary on Malachi." In *A Critical and Exegetical Commentary on Haggai, Zechariah, Malachi and Jonah.* ICC. New York: Charles Scribner's Sons, 1912.

Smith, Ralph L. (See under Micah.)

Verhoef, Pieter A. (See under Haggai.)

Wolf, Herbert. (See under Haggai.)

GENERAL INDEX

Abraham, 18, 105–8, 117, 146, 159, 162, 163
Acrostic poem, 165
Adadnirari II, 80
Adam, town of, 35
Adultery, Israel's spiritual, 29, 31, 82
Ahaz, 21, 32, 131
Ahaziah, 24
Alexander, 64
Amaziah, 70, 97–101
Ammon, 74, 80, 208
Amos, 9, 10, 69–108; call of, to prophetic ministry, 73; and Day of the Lord, 92, 93; and Israel's repentance, 89–93; and judgment, 77–83, 88, 106; judgment speeches of, 73–76, 85–96, 101, 102; his visions of judgment, 96–104; his visions of restoration, 104, 105
Angel of the Lord, 238
Angry warrior, 168
Antiochus III, 64
Armerding, Carl, 165
Asherah, 31, 151
Ashurbanipal, 11
Assyria, attack of, on Palestine, 150; demise of, 167, 168, 173–79; invasion of Israel by, 10, 32, 38, 41, 42, 46
Autumn rains, 62

Baal, 23–31, 37, 40, 45, 135, 169, 170, 204
Babel, 212
Babylon, as invaders, 11, 132, 133, 183, 186, 188–92, 197; judgment of, 188–97
Baldwin, 226
Beersheba, 89
Beth Aven, 31
Bethel, 88
Bethlehem, 148, 162
Blast of breath, 169
Branch, the, 245, 254, 274
Brother Israel, 114

Cain and Abel, 40

Calf idols, 37, 41, 46
Call to Repentance, 14, 93, 234, 237
Canaan, 82, 117, 194
Carousing of wealthy class, 74, 94
Chaldeans, 183, 186
Chiasmus, 12
Children of unfaithfulness, 23
Christ Jesus, in the temple, 224; the Good Shepherd, 267, 269, 274; the Messiah, 29, 119, 254; prophecy of birth of, 148, 149, 171, 227, 245, 261, 262
City of troops, 146
City of truth, 257
Collins, J., 233
Corruption, 157
Covenantal life, 155
Cows of Bashan, 87
Crimes, of Israel, 75
Crown of Joshua, 253, 274
Cup of judgment, 115

Daniel, 233
Darius, 219
David, 19, 23, 25, 29, 148, 149, 162, 163, 227, 268
Davidic ruler, 29, 50, 104, 107, 146, 148, 149
Day of the Lord, 53–66, 92, 112–17, 202–10, 215, 216, 290
Day of reckoning, 64
Day of Restoration, 25, 43, 47, 48, 104, 219, 262
Deborah, 194
Decalogue, 249, 250
Desired of all nations, 223
Destruction of God's enemies, 171–73
Destructive firebolt, 195
Devouring vulture, 196
Dishonest and unjust, the 101
Divine: blessing, 145, 258; judgment, 106; lawsuit, 153, 154; opposition, 175; wrath, 103, 135
Doxologies, 70
Drunken carousing, 74, 94

309

SCRIPTURE INDEX

SCRIPTURE INDEX